Stephen Clarke lives in Paris where he divides his time between writing and not writing.

His first novel, *A Year in the Merde*, originally became a word-of-mouth hit in Paris in 2004. Since then it has been published all over the world, and earned Stephen a nomination for the British Book Award for Best Newcomer. The follow-up, *Merde Actually*, went to number one in the Bookseller chart. In 2006, he published his guide to understanding the French, *Talk to the Snail*, which he divided into ten 'commandments' or chapters that include 'Thou Shalt Not Work', 'Thou Shalt Not Love Thy Neighbour' and 'Thou Shalt Not Be Served'.

His next novel, *Merde Happens*, was shortlisted for the Melissa Nathan Award for Comedy Romance, but didn't win, perhaps because it isn't really a comedy romance.

You can find out more about Stephen Clarke and his books on www.stephenclarkewriter.com

Also by Stephen Clarke

A Year in the Merde
Merde Actually
Merde Happens
Talk to the Snail: Ten Commandments for
Understanding the French

Dial M for Merde

Stephen Clarke

BANTAM PRESS

LONDON · TORONTO · SYDNEY · AUCKLAND · JOHANNESBURG

TRANSWORLD PUBLISHERS
61–63 Uxbridge Road, London W5 5SA
A Random House Group Company
www.rbooks.co.uk

First published in Great Britain
in 2008 by Bantam Press
an imprint of Transworld Publishers

A CIP catalogue record for this book
is available from the British Library.

ISBN 9780593056301

Addresses for Random House Group Ltd companies outside the UK
can be found at: www.randomhouse.co.uk
The Random House Group Ltd Reg. No. 954009

The Random House Group Ltd supports The Forest Stewardship
Council (FSC), the leading international forest-certification organization.
All our titles that are printed on Greenpeace-approved FSC-certified
paper carry the FSC logo.
Our paper procurement policy can be found at
www.rbooks.co.uk/environment

Typeset in 11/14pt Janson by
Falcon Oast Graphic Art Ltd.
Printed in the UK by CPI Mackays, Chatham, ME5 8TD

2 4 6 8 10 9 7 5 3 1

Faust: 'Give me a week and I could seduce even an innocent young creature like her.'
Mephistopheles: 'You're starting to talk like a Frenchman.'

Johann Wolfgang von Goethe, *Faust* (1808)

For legal reasons, I am obliged to stress that this novel *in no way* implies that the current President of France receives sexual favours from his female staff. That would be an outrageous – and totally unbelievable – allegation.

Stephen Clarke, Paris, 2008

To the crew of the good ship Esperanza.

Contents

The Pitch

'Do you want to come to the South of France with me?'

Before the girl had finished her question, my mind was lit up by a shimmering horizon of olive-green hills, with ochre villas crouching amongst the—

No, I told myself, skip the landscape stuff. I cut to a snap-shot of a glossy white yacht, a bottle of rosé chilling on ice, and this girl stretched temptingly along a lounger, her skin soaking up the muted September sun.

I opened my eyes, aware that she was speaking again.

And what she said didn't just bring me back down to Earth – it pitched me headfirst into the Mediterranean.

ALL THAT GLITTERS IS NOT PLATINUM

Paris

1

'Bonjour.'

'Bonjour.' The young woman with metal-rimmed glasses smiled.

Good start, I thought. I'd just got back to Paris after several months in America, where my French had faded away like a winter suntan. It felt good to be topping it up again.

'Je m'appelle West. Paul West.' I slid my credit card across the counter.

'You can speak English with me. Many foreign visitors come to our bank.'

Ah, the new generation of French workers, I thought. While their parents are moaning that their language is being killed off by English, the kids are merrily going global.

'Merci.' I told her she was very kind but I really needed

to speak French. 'J'ai travaillé en Amérique,' I explained, 'et mon français, er . . .' How did you say 'faded'? And what the hell was 'winter suntan'?

'Mon français est blanc comme l'après-ski?' I hazarded.

The woman was looking confused, so I gave up on the improvisation and returned to the speech I'd prepared earlier. I informed her that I had transferred 'beaucoup de dollars' from California, and wanted to consult my 'solde', or balance. I was especially proud of myself for remembering 'solde', because I knew that the term 'balance' existed in French and had come perilously close to using it, in which case the bank clerk would have thought that I was anxious to consult my bathroom scales.

'Vous êtes à cette agence?' she asked. Was I with this branch? The answer was no, but I decided to play the English fool. It sometimes wins you favours in France.

'I am now,' I told her.

'Hm.' It hadn't worked. She pushed my card back across the counter and adopted a stern pout. 'If you are not a client of this branch, you must use the machines.' She pointed at the four screens in the entrance lobby behind me.

'Oui, mais . . .' I did my best to mime that two of them were out of order, two were being used, and that she was clearly not doing anything very urgent.

'Vous voulez une petite formation?' she asked.

'Pardon?'

'You want me to show you how to use the machines?' she translated.

'Non, merci.' I told her I would try my best to put my card in the slot and choose 'solde' on the screen.

'Très bien,' she said, and went off to shuffle some papers around on a printer. I had been dismissed.

It only took ten minutes for the guy using the 'general banking operations' machine to call up a list of every cheque he'd written since 1990 and order five new credit cards.

At last, I was able to print out my balance, and then spent several seconds reeling in shock at the weak state of the dollar compared to the euro. My cargo of cash had taken a cruel beating during its transatlantic voyage. About a third of it had gone overboard. I was in such deep mourning that I didn't hear the machine beeping at me until it was too late.

'La machine!' I called out to the bank clerk, who was now staring out of the window. She tore her attention away from a passing bus. 'La machine, er, ma carte . . .' I made a slurping noise to get my point across.

'You have your passport?' she asked in English. She'd obviously given up trying to deal with my French.

'Why?'

'You must prove your identity before I can open the machine and get the card for you.'

'But you know who I am. I showed you my card a few minutes ago.'

She shrugged. 'I must see your passport.'

Normally this wouldn't have been a problem, because I almost always carry my passport with me in case I get deported from somewhere at short notice. But I'd come straight from the airport, dumped my luggage at my new apartment and nipped out to see whether I was solvent in euros. My passport was currently nestling in the small front pocket of my shoulder bag, along with my boarding-card stub, a tube of mints and a Los Angeles gym membership card.

'I don't have it on me,' I confessed.

'You must bring it here.'

'But the bank's closing in five minutes, isn't it? Will you wait for me?'

Her answering smile was as angelically innocent as her words were merciless. 'We open at eight forty-five in the morning,' she said.

My phone began vibrating in my trouser pocket. The number wasn't showing on the screen, so I took the call, irrationally hoping that it would be someone from the British Embassy offering to 'copter in a duplicate passport within the next four minutes.

'I'm staring at your underpants,' a female voice informed me.

'My underpants?' I looked down to check that my zip was securely fastened. 'So what colour are they?' I challenged.

'Black,' came the answer.

'Oh yeah?' Trouble was, like any sane man with more important things to think about, I had no idea what colour my underwear was that day.

'And why is there a six-pack of condoms in your pocket?'

'Condoms? I don't have any condoms.' My pockets were empty of everything except my keys and enough cash to buy a baguette. There wasn't even a credit card any more.

I turned away from the bank woman, who was now looking at me as if she might not open up tomorrow morning after all.

'Yes, a packet of French condoms,' the caller went on. 'It says, "For the intense stimulation of both partners." You want to know how they say that in Belgium? "Extra genoot voor beide partners." I must remember that in case I ever feel like fucking a Belgian.'

At last the penny dropped. It was Elodie, an old French friend of mine, whose conversation was almost always about money or sex, or – when she was describing her last 'house-sitting' job in New York – both.

She explained that she wasn't spying on me from outside the bank. She was inspecting a collection of my underwear and other private belongings that had recently been relocated to her apartment by my ex-girlfriend Alexa. There wasn't much, she said, but I might like to pick it up because it was getting embarrassing explaining to people why there was a bag of male clothing in the corner of her bedroom.

'You've seen Alexa?' I asked. 'How is she?'

Elodie tutted. 'Forget Alexa,' she said. 'I adore her, but haven't you noticed the "ex" in the middle of her name? You must forget your exes. That's why they're called exes. If you were meant to think about them all the time, they would be called nows.'

'But I'm one of your exes,' I objected, 'and you're calling me.'

'No, no, Paul, you were never really a boyfriend. We just had sex for sociological reasons. We were sharing an apartment, you were single, I was taking lots of drugs . . .'

'Gee, thanks,' I said.

'Are you free now?' Elodie asked. 'Do you want to meet up?'

'Yes, there's nothing useful I can do till tomorrow morning. I can't even buy myself dinner.' I looked at the bank woman, who was now standing by the glass exit door. She met my stare with shameless indifference. She even held up a set of keys to show that she was about to throw me penniless into the street.

'Let's meet at the Vélib station in the rue des Ecoles,' Elodie said. 'We'll go for a ride.'

'The what station?' I asked.

'Vélib. You know, the rental bikes.'

'Oh yes, I read about them. But don't you need a subscription to hire one?'

'No, all you need is your credit card.'

2

A dozen impatient Parisians were huddled around what looked like an eight-foot-tall TV remote control planted in the pavement. Spread along the street in front of this tower was a row of identical bicycles. They all wore grey body armour on their handlebars and frame, and had a silver basket over their front wheel.

Elodie was huffing down the neck of the man in front of her.

Her blonde hair was longer than when I'd last seen her, and her ponytail was tighter. She'd relegated her time in America to the past, it seemed, and was now dressed in a loose grey skirt and tight white blouse, a glistening black handbag in the crook of her arm. A classic Parisian mademoiselle.

No, that wasn't right. She'd lost the mademoiselle's air of trying to evolve an identity. She'd become a fully formed French 'dame'. Yes, that was it – she looked like her mum. Scary, I thought, only twenty-six and she'd already adopted the look she'd have for the rest of her life.

Now she was using all her fully evolved Parisian guile to avoid wasting her time in the queue to rent a bike.

If I got the gist right, she was giving orders about how to log on to the Vélib system to a harassed man, who was sweating and gritting his teeth and rapidly losing any desire to ride a bike ever again.

'Press the green button. The green button with a V on it. Here.' Elodie leaned forward and jabbed a long, pink-varnished fingernail at the little keypad. 'No, don't put your credit card in yet. Did it tell you to put your credit card in? No. Push the red button. Red! Honestly, now you've crashed it. Let me try.'

With a swivel of her hips, Elodie slid in front of the little screen and the poor man was a mere spectactor. This new bike-sharing scheme had been publicized as an almost hippie-style communal operation, but the Parisians had instantly turned it into a Darwinian test of your powers of self-assertion.

'Bonjour, Paul.' Elodie offered me her cheeks to kiss, and gave me her usual top-to-toe examination, as if she could tell how often, and with whom, I'd been having sex recently. 'You're looking good,' she said. 'Very Californian.'

'Madame?' A guy behind Elodie, an office worker in a suit who was probably in a hurry to cycle home, was starting his own Darwinian campaign.

'Oui, oui, I can't go faster than the machine, can I?' Elodie snapped. She jabbed the green button and put her credit card in the slot. 'I don't believe it,' she said to me, in French so that the guy behind her would understand. 'The system has been up for I don't know how long, and there are still idiots who don't know how to use it.'

'Oui,' I agreed. My French was too Californian to say any more.

'Even if it's hypocritical of me to complain,' she went on in English, 'because I am going to marry one of them.'

'You're what?'

She giggled at my amazement, the happy gurgle of a girl who's just sprung a massive surprise on a guy.

'I'll explain later. Now can you go and get the bike from

stand number twelve? Just press the button and pull the handle thingy.'

Elodie rented a second bike for herself, and we were away.

I didn't know where we were going, and I didn't much care, because I spent the first few minutes praying that I wasn't about to die.

Following a chic Parisian girl around on a bicycle is a mixture of intense pleasure and abject terror. Although it is a joy to admire the way her artistically sculpted derrière bounces and flexes on the saddle, this joy is tempered somewhat by the realization that she has been programmed since birth to ignore red lights and to freewheel down one-way streets the wrong way, even when the density of the traffic makes it obvious to a non-Parisian that death is the only possible outcome.

'Yes, I'm getting married,' she shouted over her shoulder as an oncoming van beeped furiously at her and looked certain to bring her engagement to a bloody end.

'Is he American?' I asked, shutting my eyes and praying as the van whisked past, a millimetre from my ear. 'That plantation owner we met in Louisiana?'

'Oh no! A French girl cannot possibly marry an American from anywhere except New York or California. It would be too cruel. No, my fiancé is—' She shot across a busy junction, and the last word was drowned out by a screech of taxi brakes.

'He's what?' I asked when I had pedalled gingerly through the traffic jam and caught up with her again.

'He's French. I met him at a Vélib stand. He didn't know how to get a bike, and I helped him hire one – with a *platinum* credit card.' She turned around to stress the key word and almost killed a young guy trying to cross the road, who'd dared to assume that she might stop at the red light.

I pulled up and took the full force of the pedestrian's tirade against undisciplined bike riders. He was carrying a motorbike helmet, and ranted at me about 'Vélibeurs' being amateurs and giving two-wheelers a bad name. All I could do was nod and shrug, while Elodie giggled at me from the far side of the crossroads.

'You should be grateful to Valéry,' she said, pedalling away as soon as I drew level with her.

'Who?'

'Valéry, my fiancé.'

'He's called Valéry?' These poor French guys stuck with girls' names, I thought. It's no wonder they have to prove their virility by trying to shag every female they meet.

'It's a very traditional man's name,' Elodie said, swivelling in the saddle to glower at me, and swerving into the path of an oncoming bus. 'A president's name,' she shouted above the hoot of panic from the bus driver.

'Why should I be grateful to Valéry?' I asked when she was back on track.

'It was his credit card that hired your bike for you.'

'He gave you his platinum card?'

'Yes, of course,' she said, bumping up on to the pavement to avoid a red light, and narrowly missing an old man who had chosen a bad time to totter out of a boulangerie. 'He has lots of cards,' she added, above the man's yelp of terror.

'I don't want to insult your future husband, but is he crazy?' I asked once we'd reached the safety of an empty side street.

'No, he's just very, very kind. He's a total *chou-chou*. He's lived his whole life in the cocoon of his family, and he works for a private bank, so he thinks that everyone in the world is rich and civilized. And I have no intention of – how do you say? – disabusing him.'

'Doing what?'

'Telling him he's wrong. Well, not yet anyway.' Her laughter filled the narrow street, and a young guy smoking at his apartment window waved down to her. Like many Parisian men, he probably thought that if a girl laughed within twenty yards of him, she wanted to sleep with him.

'But Elodie, even *you* can't be that cynical about marriage, surely?'

'No? You know, the best marriages end in death.'

'What?'

'Bad marriages end in divorce, good ones in death. What's to be positive about?'

I must have looked shocked. Even tough-girl, business-school Elodie didn't come out with statements like that very often.

'It's OK, Paul, I'm only joking. I love him. It's just that I don't really care about getting married. Well, not yet, anyway.'

'So why are you marrying him?'

'Aha, c'est ma surprise! Now come, you must teach me to dance.'

3

It took us a few goes to find a Vélib stand where we could return our bikes. The touristy areas down by the Seine were favourite dropping-off points and were all full, so we ended up parking them near the gare d'Austerlitz.

As we walked towards the river, Elodie told me some

more about this instant courtship of hers. She'd met the guy just weeks before and they were already engaged.

'He's called Valéry de Bonnepoire,' she said proudly.

'He sounds like a medieval princess. Er, prince,' I corrected myself.

'I suppose he is, a little. Except that he takes more cocaine. All the really chic men in Paris do, you know. And Valéry is très, très chic. He comes from a grande famille.'

'Lots of brothers and sisters?' I asked.

'No, you imbecile. Well yes, he has five or six brothers or sisters or something, but no. A grande famille is one of the noble Catholic families of France. They have chateaux and horses and stuff. The private bank he works for is *their* private bank.'

'So you're not marrying him for his money, then?'

'Quelle idée!'

Pausing only to yell at a Vélibeur who failed to stop at a red light to let us cross the road, Elodie led me down to the river bank, where a group of firemen were unravelling hoses and testing for leaks. Several of the young, muscular guys stopped work to admire Elodie as she clip-clopped past on her low heels.

'Vous allez danser?' one of them asked.

'Yes, but not with you,' she answered, grinning, and took my arm.

'Dance?' I said nervously. Above the noise from the street, I could hear amplified music. Not very good music, either. A warbling voice and someone trying to drown a saxophonist.

'Yes. I never learned to waltz,' Elodie told me, 'and you can be sure that the wedding party will begin with a waltz. You must help me to learn.'

'There are waltz classes down by the river?' I asked.

'I hope so, yes.'

The river bank here was wide, and people were sitting on lawns, benches and in small amphitheatres, chatting, picnicking or drinking wine they'd brought along. The setting sun was glinting off the churning wake of a river police speedboat, its crew of four out for an evening joyride. Flashbulbs were popping at them from the top deck of a glass-sided bateau mouche that was speeding its cargo of tourists back towards Notre Dame.

'Up here,' Elodie said, climbing a set of concrete steps towards the source of the warbling. I finally identified what sort of music it was, and the blood clotted in my veins.

On a flat area overlooking the river, fifty or so people were doing the typically French dance that they call 'le rock'. Couples, ranging in age from eighteen to fifty, were pirouetting, holding hands, pulling each other in and out, jiving to a soundtrack of old-school rock 'n' roll, with a French crooner doing an impression of Elvis with a chronic sinus problem. I'd been outside France long enough to forget their lasting passion for this kind of music, which had caused me so much suffering when I'd lived here. The last time had been at an outdoor dance a lot like this one, when I'd been forced to grab my ex-girlfriend's drunk dad and do 'le rock' with him to deter his attempt to molest an old lady in Breton folk costume. The memory still made me sweat.

The music was pounding out of a stack of speakers clustered around a sculpture that looked like a giant TV aerial. A guy in a 'Vive le rock' T-shirt was crouching by the speakers checking cables.

'Come, we will ask him,' Elodie said, pulling me in a precarious zig-zag between the dancing couples. She bent down and shouted her question into the guy's ear. He grimaced to show that he hadn't understood. She shouted again, and his grimace turned into a look of complete bafflement. He shook his head and laughed.

'Idiot!' Elodie flounced away.

'What did you ask him?' I said when we were far enough away to hear each other.

'To play a waltz, of course. They can't listen to this stuff non-stop, can they?'

'I think they can,' I said. 'They're French.'

Further along the river bank, a small audience of picknickers and passers-by were watching two couples swaying expertly to salsa.

'This is no good.' Elodie sighed and turned on her heel.

'Why the rush to get married?' I asked. 'You're not—?'

'Don't be an idiot, Paul. If there's one thing I control in this world, it is my biology.'

'But you've only known the guy, what . . . ?'

'Almost two months. Yes, it has been – what do you call it? – a whirlpool romance.'

It sounded as though at least one of them had been sucked under like a rowing boat.

'Who asked whom?' I said.

She looked offended. 'Valéry asked me, of course.'

'So it was eternal love at first sight?'

'Yes. I don't really care about getting married, but Valéry . . .' She stopped herself and shook her head. She'd obviously been about to reveal something significant, but for once in her life, discretion won the day, and she smiled enigmatically. 'All you need to know is that we're getting married and I have to learn the waltz.'

'And when is the wedding?'

'Two weeks.' Before I could even laugh, she went on. 'You must be there.'

'Well, thanks, I'd be delighted—'
'At such short notice, I'll never find another caterer.'

It turned out that Elodie had already discussed the matter with her father, Jean-Marie Martin, the co-owner of my English tea room in the office district near the Champs-Elysées. The last time I'd seen father and daughter together, Elodie had been furiously lobbing fruit at Jean-Marie's expensive suit, but family harmony had obviously been restored, because Papa had promised to do everything he could to help with the wedding. Or rather, everything *I* could. The tea room was managed by Elodie's brother, Benoit, and the two men of the Martin family had apparently decided that as I was due back from California, I was the ideal candidate for the task of ordering several tons of luxury food for the party, thereby eliminating the need for a costly catering service.

'Ah, this looks promising.' Elodie gave me no time to recover my breath as she dragged me towards another of the little riverside amphitheatres, where a small amplifier was broadcasting weird accordion/orchestra music with no discernible rhythm at all. Half a dozen couples, their cheeks pressed together, were shuffling around, deep in concentration.

'Perfect,' Elodie declared.
'But is it a waltz?' It was impossible to tell.
'Who cares?'

We climbed down the steps into the amphitheatre and Elodie gripped my waist, waiting for me to take the lead. But I have never learned to waltz, and was afraid that the only place I'd lead her was into the river.

'Paul!' Elodie was impatient. There was no escape. I took a few tentative steps, and we both recited '*one* two three, *one* two three', trying to ignore the fact that our counting in no way matched whatever rhythm the music was trying to achieve. I found that I got into the dance surprisingly quickly, doing two steps and then having a quick rest on three while I decided where to go next.

'*One* two left, *one* two right, *one* two over there,' I told her. '*One* two watch out, *one* two oops, *one* two excusez-moi, Madame,' and so on.

Elodie relaxed and began to enjoy herself. 'What about you, Paul? No marriage in two weeks for you?' she asked.

'*One* two no,' I answered.

'You must have had some fun out in California, though. You were famous, right?'

'*One* two kind of,' I admitted.

I'd spent the last few months having my legs photographed. By a freak accident, I (and my knees) had become known for wearing a kilt, and we'd done several photo campaigns and TV ads selling, amongst other things, jogging shoes, socks and – thanks to computer wizardry, I must stress – depilatory cream.

I'd achieved that level of fame where you spend a lot of time travelling in taxis you don't have to pay for, where you get into nightclubs without waiting, and the people there think everything you say is fascinating and are quite keen to sleep with you. The Californian girls I met, though, were thinking about their careers even in mid-orgasm, and weren't looking for a lasting relationship with anyone less important than an assistant director.

'*One* two, there was, one girl – oops.' We hammered into a couple who until then had had their cheeks and upper bodies welded together. Now they were separated at the hip and staring furiously at us.

'Mais qu'est-ce que vous foutez?' the man demanded, an old

guy in a black suit and slim tie. What the hell were we up to?

'Je ne sais pas,' I told him honestly.

'What is zees one two, one two?' his partner demanded, a woman with hair dyed as black as wet tarmac.

'We are doing a waltz,' Elodie told her.

'Ici, c'est le tong-go,' the guy said. The tango.

'And what about them? Are they doing the tong-go?' Elodie pointed at a couple who were simply swaying and snogging.

'At least zey do not say ze one two, one two. C'est pas le tong-go, ça.' The woman's painted-on eyebrows shivered indignantly.

'This is a public park. We have the right to count as loud as we want. Just watch!' Elodie held out her arms defiantly, waiting for me to lead her in another of our imitation waltzes, but I took her hand and led her away.

'Come on,' I told her. 'If you lend me some money I'll buy you a drink.'

4

'So who is this Californian girl who is so important that she makes you forget how to count up to three?' Elodie asked.

We had taken another Vélib and ridden to a crowded café terrace at Odéon. Elodie had ordered two glasses of champagne to celebrate our reunion, and the bubbles were reminding me how good it felt to be back in Paris.

'She's not Californian, she's English. We met once in Las Vegas, and then again at Venice Beach, just after you had that fruit fight with your dad.'

'And who is she?' Elodie wasn't going to let the memory of the family dispute distract her from the prospect of gossip to be had.

'An ocean ecologist.'

'A hippy? Does she shave her legs?'

'Yes.'

'And her—?'

'None of your business, Elodie.'

'What's her name?'

'Gloria, but her surname's Monday, so people call her M.'

'M?'

'Yes, like James Bond's boss.'

'I hope she is younger and more beautiful than James Bond's boss.'

I smiled, remembering how I'd last seen M – her body golden in the dawn light of a hotel-room window, her warm, Mediterranean-blue eyes expressing all the fun we'd had since we'd met on the beach about twelve hours earlier, her hair still ruffled from the night as she kissed me goodbye and told me to call her as soon as I got back to Europe.

'And what happened?' Elodie ploughed on.

'We spent one night together before she had to come back to London. That was three or four months ago, before the summer.'

'Do you have her phone number?'

'Yes.'

'So call her now. Why wait?'

I hesitated. There are a million reasons not to call someone you once had a fling with while you were both a very long way from everyday life.

'Do it now,' Elodie insisted.

'No.'

'Look, there's an empty call box. Go over there for some privacy if you want.'

'I'll call her later.'

'Do it now. Now!' This was typical Elodie. Her time at business school had turned her from bullish into a bulldozer.

I sighed and reached for my phone. With her in this mood, resistance was useless.

'M? It's Paul. Paul from Venice Beach?'

I said it as a question, casually, as if two cosmopolitan people like us might forget a night of sex in California.

'Paul. You're back in Europe?' Her voice was as warm as I remembered it. She sounded pleased to hear from me.

'Yeah, in Paris.' No need to say it was my first day back. I didn't want to look desperate. 'You in London?'

'Yes.'

'What are you up to?' I asked.

'Oh, the usual, you know. The ocean isn't getting any healthier. Things need to be cleaned up.' She laughed, as if this was a private joke. 'I'm coming to France for work, as it happens.'

'Yeah? Maybe we could hook up?'

'Sure. I have to go to the south coast. Collioure, down by the Spanish border. Do you want to come with me?' Which was the trigger for my aforementioned fantasies about chilled rosé, a yacht and a sunbathing girl.

'Great,' I said.

'Oh,' she said, as if she was surprised I'd accepted. 'I can't pay you.'

'Pay me? What on earth do you want me to do for you?'

'Ah, sorry, I thought . . .' Her voice trailed off in embarrassment.

'I'm not looking for a job,' I told her. 'So I wouldn't expect anything in return for helping you out. Well . . .'

She laughed, and we were both teleported back to that hot night in Los Angeles. The pleasure was clearly mutual.

'Alors?' Elodie had finished her glass of champagne while I'd been phoning, and her eyes were bright with alcohol and expectation.

'Does Valéry love you very, very much?' I asked.

'Yes, he's crazy for me. Why?' She looked apprehensive.

'Well, do you reckon he'd mind if we went back to your place right now?'

'What?' Elodie blushed, an event that probably happens less frequently than the creation of a planet hosting intelligent carbon-based life forms.

'I'm sorry, but I just can't wait,' I told her.

'Paul,' she whispered, 'this passion is very un-English of you.'

'I know. Do you think Valéry would understand if we went online straight away and used his platinum card to book me a plane ticket?'

M's the Word

Collioure

1

Collioure is since always the inspiration of artistes who was inspired by her celebratted tour and the colourful life of the fisher's boat's activities thanks to the anchovies, and the sun. Here is the reason for the painters to be mounting their easel in Collioure since one century or plus already.

THE WEBSITE had obviously been translated by a French person who got the job because they once managed to understand the ingredients on an imported ketchup label. But after a couple of glasses of honey-coloured rosé, it started to make sense, and I was able to deduce two things about the town where M had invited me to join her.

One, judging by the photos, it had a church belltower shaped like a giant willy.

And two, it was where the painters Matisse and Derain invented Fauvism.

Fauve was translated as 'big cat', but French artists have always taken themselves very seriously, so Matisse and co. were probably thinking more along the lines of a lion or tiger than a large tabby. The paintings on the website were impressionistic landscapes of primary-coloured blobs. The painters had clearly decided that they were doing something very wild – throwing away their black paint and capturing Collioure's colours in their most primeval form.

The site said that in the summer of 1905, Matisse and Derain produced 242 paintings there. By my reckoning, that had to make Collioure one of the most frequently painted locations in all of French art, on a par with the Moulin Rouge, Monet's lily pond and Madame Renoir's thighs.

'And then they slit them along the belly and harvest the eggs,' M was saying. 'They get up to twenty-five kilos of caviar from one adult fish. Though hardly any of the poor creatures reach full adulthood these days.'

'Yuk,' was my only comment. Unscientific, perhaps, but then a PowerPoint presentation on caviar production is not how I usually choose to spend the morning after a romantic reunion with a girl I haven't seen for three months.

The reunion itself had been very romantic. I'd strolled into the arrivals lounge at Perpignan airport to be greeted by the smiling babe that all the guys had been checking out. I guessed they were praying that she was there to meet her ageing grandma, and then in I walked, shattering a dozen Frenchmen's fantasies. A moment for any Englishman to relish.

M was every bit as hot as when I'd last seen her – her long, blonde hair was ruffled as if it had just dried out in the sea breeze, her amber tan was highlighted by a floaty white dress that she'd gathered on her hips with a leather belt, and to cap it all, there was her brilliant smile, aimed straight at me.

We kissed, on the lips but chastely, and hugged American style – cheek to cheek and zero pelvic thrust. Suddenly both of us seemed self-conscious. This was natural enough, I reasoned, because we didn't have any kind of status. We'd spent one night together, but we hadn't been exchanging breathless promises by text and email ever since. It was all very tentative.

We chatted in the taxi about what we'd been up to since LA, and seemed to be making a conscious effort to keep our hands to ourselves. Even so, it felt as though we were sizing each other up like two dancers at a nightclub, enjoying the sensation of being so physically near to someone that we intended to get even closer to as soon as possible.

And sure enough, as soon as we got into the entrance lobby of her hotel, we both decided that the time for coyness was over, and took up right where we'd left off in California, showing the surprised receptionist just how entangled two bodies can get without actually making love.

We went up to M's room, kissing all the way, stumbling and fumbling with stairs, keys and door handles. I was glad of the tango practice I'd got in Paris. We dived straight under the duvet, and hardly an intelligible sentence was spoken till the next morning, when I woke up to find myself alone in bed.

The French windows were open, warm sunlight was shafting in from the courtyard, and the only sounds were the chatter of starlings, the soft sloshing of a pool filter and the distant hubbub of a waking town.

M was out on the terrace, wrapped in a dawn-yellow bathrobe, dividing her attention between a croissant and her small unfolded laptop.

'Bonjour,' I called out.

'Sorry if I abandoned you,' she said. 'But this is a working trip for me, remember.'

I forgave her when she let her bathrobe fall to the floor and came back to bed, bringing me not only her warm, perfumed body but also a cup of coffee. The ideal woman.

Except that she'd also brought her laptop, and proceeded to show me precisely what kind of work she was doing, which mainly involved disembowelled fish.

'It's like the rhino, really,' she said. 'Sturgeon are born unlucky. Sadly for them, their bodies are worth a fortune to us predatorial humans.'

'A bit like supermodels.'

'Yes, but we prefer our supermodels alive,' she said.

'Some of them aren't far off starvation. Unlike you, you're more than alive . . .' Invigorated by a dose of fresh coffee, I tried to divert her attention from her screen to her erogenous zones.

M, however, had a scientist's ability to shut out everything in the universe that didn't relate to her specialist subject. She planted a quick kiss on my forehead and then carried on with her fish show.

'For a while, exports from the Caspian Sea were banned by the UN, but they're legal again now, which has just about condemned the beluga sturgeon to extinction. Sad when you consider it's been around, almost unchanged, since prehistoric times.'

She clicked open a photo of a baby sturgeon, only just big enough to fill the hand that was holding it. It was a scaly-backed, dinosaur-looking creature, a cross between a shark, a crocodile and a leech.

'Cute,' I said.

'Millions of young sturgeon are introduced into the

Caspian every year, but only about 3 per cent survive till sexual maturity, and they tend to be caught pretty well immediately after that. So you're right – they are like models. As soon as they hit adolescence it's all over.'

I looked up at the frown crinkling M's forehead and had to suppress a laugh. Not that I was indifferent to the tragic story of yet another of our planet's species biting the dust because of human shortsightedness. No, it had suddenly struck me that this was like the start of a James Bond movie, with 007 getting briefed on the ins and outs of the bullion trade or diamond smuggling. I, though, was getting the lecture on sturgeon and caviar from a nude Bond girl instead of a pipe-smoking boffin. Who says 007 gets all the action?

'Which is why I'm down here,' M concluded. 'Beluga caviar is such a valuable commodity that it's a prime target for counterfeiting. A clever dealer can make as much from fake Iranian caviar as from heroin. And fish eggs are totally legal until you put them in a tin with a fake label, so there's infinitely less risk. Sturgeon are farmed legally in the south of France, but we suspect that the fake caviar is coming from fish being captured in the wild and then matured in secret offshore pens. These were spotted last year.' She invited me to examine an aerial photo of faint shadows darkening the seabed.

I nodded, although it could just as well have been a fleet of nuclear submarines or a family of lobsters out for an afternoon stroll.

'Who spotted them?' I asked, punctuating my question with a squeeze of her bare inner thigh.

'My institute in the UK. But the photo leaked out, and the fish pen had gone by the time the French government reacted. I'm down here to pinpoint the sources of all the counterfeit caviar that gets sold along the Riviera, and be a bit more discreet about my findings.'

'Great,' I said. 'Are we going to hire boats and spotter planes and go out looking for them?'

'No, not on this trip anyway,' she said. 'I want to have a snoop around, but officially I'm just going to try and convince the French oceanography institutes to help fund an aerial survey of the coastline. They say that it should be left up to the police. But we're afraid that if the French police get involved, there'll be another leak and it'll all be a waste of time. Or they'll just destroy all the illegal sturgeon. We want to save them, maybe even set them free from their illegal farms. If the environmental impact isn't too heavy,' she went on, apparently unaware of the impact of several male fingers that were now softly caressing the smooth, hot flesh of her stomach. 'Because when sturgeon are left in peace, the population recovers remarkably quickly. In Florida, for example, the Gulf of Mexico sturgeon has got so common, and so big, that several boaters have been seriously injured in accidental encounters.'

M clicked on a window and started up an amateur film. A guy in a canoe was holding his paddle aloft weightlifter-style, clowning around for his friend with the camera. He slapped the water a few times, and I could hear him yelling for the gators to come and get their asses kicked. Then suddenly, the tranquil river erupted, and a giant fish soared out of the water, the scaly ribs running down its flank practically slicing the nose off the guy's canoe. As soon as the cameraman stopped lurching about, we saw the look of shock on the canoeist's face turn to horror as he realized that he was going to get dumped into the water with the prehistoric monster, plus any gators that had decided to take up his challenge. The macho man of a moment ago had been transformed into a shrieking hysteric, frantically scrabbling to get free of the canoe and almost weeping with panic.

'That's amazing,' I said. 'Can we watch it again?' I leaned over to scroll back.

M's hand leapt out as fast as the sturgeon and clamped down on my wrist. 'Please don't,' she hissed.

It was a reflex, the kind you often come up against when you're in bed with someone for the first time. We all have taboos about what other people can't touch. It's easy to go too far in the heat of the moment. But this was the first time I'd gone too far with a computer.

'Sorry,' I said.

She relaxed her grip and smiled apologetically. 'No, *I'm* sorry. Scientist, laptop, sensitive files, you understand.'

'Yes,' I said, though I didn't.

'Now,' she said, putting the laptop on the floor and rolling on top of me, 'why don't we forget about fish and get down to some prehistoric action of our own?'

2

Our hotel, I discovered, was an elegant Spanish-style mansion, and our room looked out over a courtyard with a splashing fountain. I'd had no time to take in all the details the previous night. I'd been distracted by the rush to reach the bedroom.

We strolled through the empty garden, sniffing at plants, and I stopped to examine a plaque on the bare brick wall. I was trying to piece together a translation when M leaned forward and helped me.

'Le sage est celui qui s'étonne de tout,' she read, fluently. 'A wise man is amazed by everything.'

'Like leaping sturgeon,' I said. 'Or the fact that you speak such good French. How come?'

'I took a course at uni,' she said. 'And you'd be surprised how many oceanographers are French, so I get a lot of practice. Now come on, let's go and find the giant willy.'

We walked down a cobbled lane, in the cool shadow of the castle mound, and emerged beside a tiny harbour. The sun had climbed up out of the Med and was lighting a scene that Matisse might not have found unfamiliar. The beach was a curve of fine grey pebbles running between the castle and the famous phallic church tower.

'People pretend to like Collioure because of the art,' M said, 'but what they really enjoy is staring at an erection.'

'It's suntanned and circumcized,' I said. 'Perhaps it was originally built by the Moors.'

'Or the Romans. An erect willy was a good-luck charm for them. They used to carve them over their doorways to ward off evil spirits and attract prosperity.'

We agreed that Collioure must have been a very prosperous place indeed.

The castle, which loomed up to our right, had small slitty windows and sheer stone walls, and looked like a cross between a Spanish villa and a Scottish fortress. It was built on a rocky hill, and its walls tumbled more than a hundred feet straight down into the water.

The promenade behind the beach was taken up by four café terraces. They formed a small village of bamboo arm-chairs and coffee tables, differentiated by the colours of the cushions and parasols – blue, red, yellow and white. There were hardly any customers, though, just a few solo newspaper readers and a group of six or seven women in sunglasses. I noticed them because you don't often see a large female gang in France, except at a department-store sale or a nurses' protest march. These women were in their early twenties, wearing short skirts and bikini tops. Judging by their snow-white skin, they had very recently arrived from somewhere much less sunny. They were dozing peacefully in their wicker armchairs as if they'd been there all night.

Matisse would probably not have recognized the silence that reigned in Collioure this morning, I thought. A century ago, fishermen would have been unloading their catch, and women would have been yelling out prices, heckled by flocks of seagulls. Now, half a dozen old fishing boats swayed emptily by the jetty, lined up like an outdoor museum display.

'Can't you ask the fishermen if they've seen any sturgeon pens?' I asked M.

'Tricky,' she said. 'Some of them might be on a back-hander from the caviar guys.'

We stretched out on the beach, and I let the pebbles give my back a warm massage.

M sighed. 'Shame I have to work,' she said, reaching into her bag and pulling out what looked like a small sandwich-maker. She unfolded it, and seemed about to toast her phone.

'What's that?' I asked.

'It's a solar-powered phone-charger. Haven't you ever seen one before?'

I had to confess I hadn't.

'I never charge up my phone or iPod with anything else. You should get one. Every little helps when it comes to reducing our carbon footprint.'

'I do my bit,' I said. 'I've been using the Vélibs in Paris. And I've cut down on fizzy drinks.'

M turned to stare at me. 'Are you serious?' she asked. There was a sudden edge to her voice.

'Yes,' I assured her. 'When I was in California, there was this guy campaigning against the billions of carbon-dioxide bubbles released when we pop open a can of soda or a bottle of fizzy water.'

M shook her head in disbelief. 'Loonies. There's infinitely more damage done by Californians importing French mineral water so they'll have chic kidneys. I only drink tap water these days.'

Wow, I thought, she must be the only woman ever to say that last sentence on French soil – she is one serious environmentalist.

M plugged her phone into the charger. 'I'm waiting for an important call,' she said. 'I might have to go and meet someone.'

'No problem,' I said. 'I think I'll see if there are any giant sturgeon out there. Coming?' I nodded towards the glinting sea.

'No, thanks. I dipped my little toe in yesterday. Freezing. You're on your own.'

I grabbed my snorkel and strode manfully in up to my knees, at which point I was paralysed by a massive electric shock zinging up from my toes to my testicles. But when a guy's being watched by a beautiful girl, he doesn't let a little groin agony put him off, and I waded out over the slippery pebbles until my lower body was totally numb. A quick rinse of my mask, a puff through the snorkel and I dived forward into a different world.

Whole schools of edible-sized fish were parading back and forward just a few feet from the beach. They were practically tame. They swam towards me to stare goggle-eyed at the new giant in town, and only darted out of reach if I actually tried to touch them. Occasionally they plunged down as a group and started chomping at something on the seabed. I could hear their jaws snapping open and shut.

I thought I recognized one or two of the larger species from past dinners – mullet and sea bream – but there were others that I'd never seen before. Fat silver-green torpedoes with gold stripes running along their backs, and flatter, bream-shaped fish with a black spot at the base of their tails. And then down amongst the rocks, in about ten feet of water, I saw a flash of crimson that stood out against the background of silver, green and blue. I dived, and the crimson turned to vivid white – it was the tentacle of an octopus turning over to reveal the suckers. Before I ran out of breath, I just had time to peer into a staring eye, and watch the octopus's soft flesh rippling as it pulled small stones on top of itself to improve its cover.

I was as crimson as the octopus when I got out of the sea and hobbled over the stones to grab my beach towel. Only when I'd rubbed off every drop of water did I start to fade to my usual colour.

'No sturgeon that I could see,' I said. I stretched out in the sun beside M, and described the fish I'd seen. 'What are they?' I asked.

She shrugged.

'You don't know?'

'No.'

'But you're an oceanographer.'

'What are you trying to say, Paul?' Her large, dark sunglasses stared challengingly at me.

'Nothing, I'm just doing what the sign said at the hotel

– being amazed by everything. I assumed you'd know.'

'Look, I'm a marine ecologist, not a fish catalogue. I know a lot about endangered species, but I doubt that the ones you saw are endangered, otherwise they wouldn't be swimming merrily about near a fishing harbour. Fish may be stupid but they're not idiots.'

Despite the joke, the hard edge had come back into her voice, just like when I'd tried to use her laptop. There were so many touchy subjects with her. It struck me how little we knew about each other, no matter how intimate we'd become physically.

'Sorry,' I said. 'I'm not trying to say you don't know your job. I expect you get that a lot, being a female scientist. I know how you feel – I'm an Englishman working in the French food business.'

This softened her mood, and she was just about to lick some droplets of seawater from my chin when her phone buzzed.

'Excuse me.' She jumped to her feet and walked away along the empty beach to take the call. She was holding the phone in one hand and the charger in the other, pointing it up at the sun as if she was listening to someone out in space. A bizarre sight.

Less bizarre, though, than the group of about twenty identically dressed men who had come into view, trooping silently along the jetty. They were wearing short-sleeved vests and wetsuit bottoms, and each man was carrying a belt of lead weights and long, pear-shaped flippers. Every piece of their kit was black. The local undertakers' diving club, perhaps?

When they got to the end of the jetty, they helped each other on with their wetsuit tops, and then swam out into the bay in pairs. I watched them gather around a buoy and begin diving down one by one. Each of them came back up clutching a rock, which he held aloft as proof that he'd reached the seabed. It was evidently some kind of exercise.

As soon as they'd all completed their dives, they set out towards the shore, where M was still pacing up and down, alternately talking and listening earnestly. She must have been on the phone for a full half-hour, I thought. The sun had risen high in the sky and warmed away all the after-effects of my chilly swim, and the café terraces had filled with mid-morning coffee drinkers.

M appeared beside me and apologized for taking so long.

'I've got to go to Banyuls,' she said. 'There's a marine research institute there. They've been looking into unusual offshore activity.'

'Exactly what I've been watching.' I nodded towards the divers.

'Soldiers,' she said. 'There's a commando training centre in the castle. They go out on night dives and climb cliffs and stuff.'

'Surely they'd notice if there were any sturgeon in the neighbourhood,' I said. 'Why don't you ask them?'

'I couldn't. A foreign scientist trying to get secrets out of the French military? They'd never let me in the country again.'

'Maybe I could talk to them,' I suggested. 'I want to help with your investigation.'

M laughed. 'So you're going to wander over and casually inquire whether any of their canoes have been savaged by prehistoric fish?'

'I may be a man, but I am capable of some subtlety, you know.'

'Oh, I know.' She gave me a lascivious grin that a commando would have been proud of.

I was just about to suggest that she might enjoy a little more subtlety back at the hotel before she left for Banyuls when there was a barrage of whistling and whooping from the café terrace. The snoozing women had woken up and were giving the commandos a hard time as they wandered past in their diving gear.

Judging by the shouts of 'Wahay', 'Get 'em off' and 'Is that a snorkel in your pocket or are you just pleased to see me?' I guessed that the women were English. After raping and pillaging their way through Dublin, Prague and Cracow, it seemed that hen parties were coming south in search of prey.

Poor French soldiers, I thought. Nothing in their training could possibly prepare them for an English hen party.

I found the commando training centre with no difficulty at all. It was completely open to the public.

It was little more than an alcove at the base of the castle wall, a damp platform the size of a tennis court containing a rack of canoes and various bits of diving equipment. There was a ladder down to sea level, where three inflatable dinghies were moored, their massive outboards on open display for anyone to steal or sabotage. Of the commandos themselves, there was no sign at all, unless they were camouflaged as lumps of seaweed.

The only security measure I could see was a metal gate painted with the unit's name: 'CNEC, 1er Choc'. I presumed that the second part of the name meant something like 'First Shock Battalion' and was in no way related to the common French abbreviation for chocolate. Though the whole scene did smack of chocolate soldiers. Surely these guys couldn't be serious commandos?

'The soldiers, do they often swim?' I asked a French guy who was filming the inflatables. A fellow spy, perhaps.

'Oh yes, every morning,' he said. 'Beautiful motors, no? Wah!' Not a spy, then, but an outboard fetishist.

Resolving to try my luck with the commandos the following morning, I strolled around the foot of the castle wall. M had left for Banyuls, so I was on my own for lunch, and I'd spotted an open-air restaurant that was catching the midday sun.

The meal would have delighted the strictest ecologist. The anchovies had been marinated a kilometre or so away, the waiter told me. The rosé was Appellation Contrôlée Collioure, so I could probably have spotted the vineyards just by turning round and looking inland. And my main course – whole grilled sea bream – looked so like the fish I'd swum with that morning that I felt a pang of guilt. Apart from the rice and the coffee, the item on the table that had travelled furthest might well have been the glass of tap water, which had probably been piped down from the Pyrenees. Practically everything else – braised courgettes and tomatoes included – could have been produced within a few miles of the restaurant. Vive la France, I thought. I hoped the other G8 members would remember things like that when they were handing out their carbon dioxide credits.

I was bathing in a rosé-tinted haze of self-satisfaction when I noticed that the people around me were gasping and swearing at something.

'Merde!'

'Putain!'

I followed their gaze and joined in myself.

'Holy shit!'

On top of the castle wall, a dizzying hundred-foot drop

to the concrete path below, a woman was walking along the battlements.

'On va la ramasser à la petite cuillère, celle-là,' the waiter said, meaning that if she fell, they'd need a spoon to scrape up her remains.

Like everyone else, I held my breath as the woman swivelled and walked back towards us again. She was filming with a small handheld camera, and seemed to be talking to someone inside the castle. She was going to trip and fall, I knew it. She would scream and then splat sickeningly on the ground, no doubt ending up a lot like my sea bream after I'd finished forking it open. I wanted to shut my eyes, but like everyone else I was riveted.

She had black hair hanging loose down to her shoulders, what looked like a trim figure, and an air of complete self-confidence. She had to be a model, I decided, and had been ordered to risk her life to make an ad for shampoo or digital cameras. She was pacing back and forward, not even looking where she was treading, and calmly filming the beach.

I stared up at her and mouthed a silent message at her camera lens. 'Get down,' I told her. 'Descendez, s'il vous plaît.'

Suddenly she lowered the camera from her eye and stared down towards me, as if she'd understood. I was too startled to react, but several other people started gesturing at her, urging her to get down.

At last she jumped back into the castle, out of view, and my fellow lunchers gave a sigh of relief and started an animated discussion about why the castle wardens didn't stop visitors climbing up and risking their lives. But then, as I'd seen, security didn't seem to be the castle's biggest priority.

3

Back at the hotel, I looked up some of my new underwater friends on the internet. The fish with the black spot near its tail was an 'oblade'. In English, a saddled sea bream. The yellow-striped one was a 'sarpa sarpa', and its flesh apparently had hallucinogenic properties. The Romans used to consume it as a recreational drug. And there was a case of one man eating the fish at a restaurant and suffering thirty-six hours of LSD-like visions. Perhaps that was what I'd had at lunch, I thought. I'd hallucinated the girl on the wall.

I surfed around for news stories on the Med, hoping to find something about sturgeon. It was vital, I'd decided, to gather some useful info for M's investigation. It might relax her a little.

She was totally at ease in bed, but as soon as the sex was over, she seemed to become tense and overreact to innocent remarks. It had to be stress-related. If I could help her get ahead with her work, it would reduce her stress levels and make things easier between us. At the moment, we were vacillating between extreme closeness in bed and cold distance out of it. It was all a bit disorienting.

There were plenty of weird things going on beyond Collioure's harbour wall, I discovered. Sardines with herpes, a great white shark attacking a small cargo ship, a cow found floating thirty kilometres off Marseille, and a new species of toxic seaweed that was killing off sea urchins. Not that I could see much wrong with zapping a few of those spiny bastards.

The Med was in turmoil, it seemed. The perfect place to hide some sturgeon. And they had to be very well hidden, because there were no French news stories about

them on the internet. Either they'd been keeping themselves to themselves, or France's caviar pirates were much
better than its commandos at keeping their activities
secret.

'Paul, you haven't forgotten me, have you?'

Elodie woke me up from the depths of a siesta. She was
phoning to remind me that I was meant to be overseeing
the catering arrangements for her wedding.

'No, of course I haven't forgotten you,' I told her, as soon
as I'd remembered where and who I was. 'I'm going to
sketch out some menu ideas. If I email them to you, maybe
your brother and your dad can look after the actual
ordering?'

'No. You know Papa – he will buy illegal meat from
Belgium or China. And Benoit will get the numbers wrong
and order one bottle of wine and five hundred roast pigs.'

I began to defend her younger brother, who had been
managing my tea room very efficiently for the best part of
a year, but Elodie wouldn't listen. I was going to have to
deal with things myself.

'We must satisfy Valéry's bitch grand-mère,' she told me.

'His what?'

'Didn't I tell you? His grandmother is against the
wedding. I don't come from a grande famille, you see, so
I'm not *classe* enough for her. She told Valéry that I am not
– how do you say? – not "digne de porter son voile"?'

'Not fit to carry her sail? She's a sailor?'

'No, imbecile. Her *voile*, the thing the woman wears on
her face for a wedding.'

'Her veil.'

'Yes. In these families, the bride wears the veil of a grandmother or an important female ancestor. And the bitch

grand-mère has told Valéry that I am not worthy to wear her veil. And she has never even met me, the grosse vache.'

'Whereas if she could just hear you talk about her, she'd fall in love with you,' I teased.

'This is serious, Paul. The bitch grand-mère doesn't want Valéry to marry me, so he has organized the wedding himself. He is paying a fortune to have the reception in a chateau near Avignon. But he is starting to weaken. He wants to be independent, but he is from a grande famille. For them, being independent means not going to your parents' house for lunch one Sunday. Which is why you must help.'

'OK. How?'

'I want to silence the old vache with the opulence of my banquet. I want the best of everything. So you must put together a fantastic menu. Don't worry about the cost. Anything you want.'

'OK.' I smiled to myself, wondering how her dad would react if he could hear her spending his money.

'The problem is that the bitch grand-mère wants to meet you first, to make sure you are the right person to be order-ing food for her family.'

'What?'

'You don't know these grandes familles, Paul. They have a family conference every time one of them wants to buy socks. They are terrified that someone might buy red nylon.'

I laughed. 'No worries there – I'm a strictly sweat-free, cotton-socks type of guy.'

'Please, Paul!' Elodie gave a little screech, and I felt guilty for not taking her seriously. Things were obviously getting very panicky. 'You must go and meet the old bitch,' she ordered. 'Valéry will come to see you. He will brief you.

You have to learn more about the vache. She is causing some serious merde.'

'What merde?'

'You'll see. Valéry will phone you to arrange a meeting, OK?'

'OK,' I agreed.

'Thank you. Oh, and one thing you can do. Once, when I was in Collioure with my family, we bought some superb anchois marinés. You know, anchovies hand-fished by Catalans and all that shit. You must get, oh, ten kilos.'

'But you just said I should wait until—'

'Paul!' I could hear her teeth gritting from a thousand kilometres away. 'You are definitely going to convince the bitch grand-mère that you are the right person, OK? Otherwise I will kill you. So you can start ordering food now. There is no time to waste.'

'Fine. I'll buy them for you.'

'You will? Oh Paul, you are a hero.'

Wow, I thought, if only all women could be made so deliriously happy with the promise of a few pickled fish.

4

After my second snorkelling trip of the day, I got back to the hotel to find M's clothes strewn across the bed. Steam was billowing out of the bathroom, and I could hear the roar of a full-open tap.

'Honey, I'm home,' I called out.

'Come into the bathroom if you are who I think you are,' she replied, and the tap clunked off.

She was lying full-length in the tub, only her face, breasts and knees above the surface of the soapy water.

'Come on in, the water's lovely,' she said.

'So is what's in it.'

I threw my own clothes on the bed, and we spent a few awkward seconds deciding how I could slot into the bath with her. It wasn't exactly a jacuzzi. Finally, I got in behind her, and sat with her head on my chest and a breast in each hand.

'Good day?' I asked.

'Oh, lots of talk,' she said. 'The Banyuls people think I'm nuts, asking about sturgeon instead of their local species.'

'You look tense,' I said. 'Perhaps it would help if I rubbed some of that ginger and honey bath gel over you?'

'You could give it a try.'

Now I may be speaking only for myself here, but there aren't many more pleasant things to do with your hands than massage scented bath gel over the body of a beautiful woman, especially one who lets you know how good it feels, with words and miscellaneous other sounds. It felt pretty good for me, too. My hands gliding over her hips, down on to her stomach and then up to cup her breasts. Perfectly shaped breasts, too, heavy but firm. It didn't take long before both of us felt the urgent need for her to slide backwards and sit astride me. Soon her rocking hips were causing tides of water to wash over the side of the bath and on to the floor.

It was only now that I noticed something strange about her body. Watching her in the mirror, I saw that her breasts were exactly the same colour as the rest of her. She was golden brown all over. She really was a Bond girl, a less glittery version of Jill Masterson in *Goldfinger*, the woman who asphyxiates because Oddjob covers her in gold paint. Unlike Jill, though, M had left a gap in her all-over colour scheme. Thanks to her bikini thong, she'd kept a tiny triangle of pale skin at the base of her spine. This I could see very clearly, because it was bouncing up and down right in front of me. Thank God for that, I thought, she's not going to asphyxiate. At which point her breathless gasps cut off, and she sank back lifeless on top of me. It's what the French call orgasm, isn't it? La petite mort.

When we left for dinner, two almost identical guys were sitting side by side at a table in the hotel courtyard, reading newspapers by the light of a lamp hanging in the tree overhead. They were both wearing cardigans to protect themselves against the early autumn chill. Their woollies, like their hair and their shirts, were white. If it hadn't been for the black newsprint in their hands, they would have been invisible against the pale stone of the courtyard floor and the white of the garden furniture.

I wished them 'Bonsoir' and they nodded in reply.

M, in a boisterous post-lovemaking mood, wasn't satisfied with this, and repeated a loud, accusatory 'Bonsoir!'

The men answered 'Monsieur, Madame,' and smiled as they watched M walk past.

Yes, I thought, she was looking good enough to turn gay men straight. She gripped my hand and I felt a surge of happiness. I was experiencing that irreplaceable thrill you get when you go to bed with someone and then find that you want to do so again. And again. And again.

I'd reserved a table at a restaurant in the old town. It was a tiny, dark place in a narrow street that had caught my eye because its menu was so short. In touristy areas, restaurant menus can seem too eager to please, offering everything that a hungry visitor could possibly want to eat. And you can be pretty sure that most of it will come out of the freezer. At this place, though, the handwritten menu told us what chef was making today, and that all of it was fresh.

We ordered a bottle of Collioure rosé and clinked glasses, looking each other in the eye as you must.

'To our reunion,' I said. 'What do they say in French – *retrouvailles*? Finding each other again.'

'We certainly found the right spot in the bath,' M whispered. 'And you found a great little restaurant,' she added, looking around at the dark red and black décor. 'Very intimate.'

She was right. In the candlelight it was so intimate that you could only just see the person sitting opposite you. I did see, though, that we weren't the only people there. Half of the restaurant's ten or so tables were occupied, mostly by middle-aged couples. The only lone diner was a woman in a corner, apparently reading a book. She was sitting in deep shade against the dark background of the wall. It was so gloomy that she had to be reading with infra-red glasses.

'Exactly my kind of place,' M said. 'Clever of you to know.'

'It was a lucky guess,' I said. 'I hardly know anything about you.' It had occurred to me that when we'd come down from Perpignan in the taxi, I'd done all the talking. She'd answered all my questions with questions of her own.

'You know me a lot more intimately than most men,' she said.

'No, but seriously. I mean, I don't know what films you like, what music. Who are your heroes, for example?'

'Heroes?' She looked surprised by the question.

'Or heroines, of course.'

'No, I have a hero,' she said. 'Peter Willcox.'

'Who?'

'Exactly.' She tutted. 'Not your fault. No one's heard of him. He's an environmentalist. He's spent most of his life trying to protect the oceans against nuclear testing and whaling. He never gives up, never lets the politicians get him down, even though he's taken some very hard knocks. He's a real hero. And half the people who've actually heard of him are trying to stop him.' She paused and took a sip of wine.

'And he inspired you to go into marine ecology?' I asked.

'Yes.' She looked uncomfortable. 'But just for tonight, can't we give work a miss?' she said. 'I want to relax, have a good time. OK?'

'Sure,' I agreed. 'Let's get shallow. If you stay too long in the deep end, you only get tired and sink. And you're never far from the serious end of the pool, are you? There's always heavy stuff going on just beneath the surface.'

'You're probably right.' M looked down into her glass, staring almost sadly through the transparent wine. 'It goes with the job.'

'But you devote time to shallow stuff, as well. Your suntan, for instance.' I told her that I'd noticed her all-over colour. 'I thought that as a scientist, you'd have been more concerned about skin cancer.'

'As a scientist, I know that it's essential to tan very gradually and put on lots of sunblock. But yes, I travel a lot, and I like to spend siesta time stretched out in the sun. Where's the harm in that?'

'No harm at all,' I said. Seemed I'd hit a nerve yet again. 'You look fantastic.'

'Thanks.' She smiled, and stroked my hand as if to apologize for the way she'd reacted.

I refilled our glasses and we drank to M's beautiful body. As I let the cold wine wash over my taste buds, I couldn't help sneaking a glance towards the table where the lone woman was eating. Not very gallant when you're sitting opposite your lover, but there is something intriguing about a young woman eating dinner on her own. She had just finished her salad, and as she reached forward to pick up her glass, for a moment her face was lit in the glow from her candle. She raised a hand to flick her black hair off her cheek, and suddenly I knew why I'd felt the urge to stare at her. It was the girl who'd been parading around up on the castle wall. Our eyes met, and I was certain that there was a flash of recognition before she retreated to the shadows again. Which was weird. Had she really seen me mouthing warnings at her?

'You OK?' M asked.

'Yes, great. Hungry, though,' I said. It would have been too complicated to explain.

5

Next morning, I went out to buy some fruit to supplement our room-service breakfast. If there's one thing France has taught me, it's to seize every opportunity to eat seasonal fruit. Balls to year-round strawberries – in September, you binge on figs and Muscat grapes.

The two white ghosts were sitting out in the courtyard, side by side, drinking coffee. They met my 'Bonjour' with curt nods.

When I got back with my bags of fruit, M was up and dressed. The breakfast had been delivered and she'd poured us each a cup of coffee. Hers was almost empty. She was just getting off the phone.

'Can you pass me a pen?' She flicked her fingers towards

the CNEC, 1er Choc. I had nothing against
my days snorkelling, but those Lycra shorts
killers.

ly, the commando had also helped me in my
tigation, because on the way to the base he'd
ast exactly the shop I needed for Elodie's

back down towards the harbour and found it
as a typically French 'produits régionaux' store.
display was a tangle of fishing nets that
ny pots of hand-harvested salt, a jar of honey in
f Collioure's belltower, a glass bull filled with
d, yes, small tubs of local anchovies. No caviar,
cal or foreign.
's tweeness was offset by its location. It was in
illage's steep, labyrinthine alleys, on the ground
ustard-yellow house. The façade was framed by
e that provided shade and refreshment to
ppers. I helped myself to a few purple
were hanging, juicy and tempting, just within

shelves were stacked solid with boxes, bags,
les of all shapes and sizes. Ribbons and animal
nded, and the whole place smelt of distilled
avender, olive oil and sunscreen.
urists were jostling carefully between the
ing and smelling things, trying to work out
eir presents for the folks back home could be
g cheap. But at four euros a toffee lollipop,
lots of grandchildren were going to be
of pocket.
my way to a shelf where there was an almost

the bedside table. I picked up the nearest ballpoint. 'No, not that one, the other one,' she said. I handed the second pen to her, and she scribbled something on a corner of newspaper that she tore off and folded up. 'Sorry,' she said. 'The other pen's black. I never write with a black pen.'

'Why not?' I asked.

'Oh, long story. I can't stand anything black. Black clothes, black cars.' I'd noticed that none of her clothes, even her underwear, was darker than chocolate brown. She was a Fauve at heart.

'Well, I hope you don't mind black grapes and black figs,' I said, sliding the bags of fruit towards her.

'They're purple, not black,' she said, nipping off a small bunch of grapes. 'Oh, I have to go back to Banyuls, by the way. I'll probably be gone all day.'

'Again?' I knew she'd come down here to work, but I couldn't help showing my disappointment. I'd thought we could take a boat out, explore the coast, do things together.

'Yes, again,' she said defensively.

'Shall I come with you? We can meet up for lunch or something.'

'Better not. I can't let anyone know I'm mixing business with pleasure – they'd stop my subsidies. Anyway, it'll take ages. You don't know what it's like when us scientists get going. Lunch would be deathly boring unless you want to listen to them rabbiting on about the infestation rate of toxic algae in the northern Mediterranean.'

'Ah,' I said, 'well as it happens, I was reading on the web about that, and—'

She interrupted me with a kiss. 'What are your plans for today?'

I had a think. I didn't fancy lying on the beach all day. 'I have to get some stuff for Elodie's wedding,' I said. Which would take me about ten minutes. 'Why don't I see if I can get chatting to those commandos?'

'What?' M looked almost scared of the idea.

'They spend half their lives underwater,' I said. 'I could hang around and—'

'Please, Paul,' she interrupted me. 'Let me do things my way. No improvised interrogations, OK?'

'OK.'

'Promise?'

'Promise. M's the word.'

We sealed the deal with a kiss and she went trotting down the stairs.

Normally, I'm not the kind of guy who stops in his tracks when he sees an athletic young man with tight buns. But these were extraordinary times, and when I arrived in the village centre and saw the commando striding past in his black vest and shorts, I began to follow the muscular, nylon-clad buttocks.

I knew that I'd just promised M that I wouldn't interrogate the soldiers, but surely a little discreet trailing would do no harm? This guy was heading away from the castle, looking very purposeful. What was it that the plaque in the hotel garden had said – a wise man is astonished by everything? Well, this soldier's buttocks were clenching and unclenching with astonishing speed, showing far more military efficiency than anything else I'd seen the French army do. It was only natural to try and find out why.

He marched up a steep lane of pastel-painted houses, his black shadow flitting through a palette of Mediterranean colours. The houses were dormant in the afternoon sun, their blue and green shutters closed to the outside world.

The commando paused at
out of his shorts pocket, and I
vegetation, which turned out
hanging from a terraced ga
twenty yards or so up the hil
whether he had noticed the
ently trapped in a shrub.

The voice began to fade –
engrossed in his conversatio
honeysuckle, sneezed some
and followed.

Soon, the street petered
were drenched in the he
commando bounded up the
between two parked cars
the top of the stairway to
back.

Around the next corner
saying 'Défense d'entrer'.
spies included – that this
Choc. But apart from the
the base didn't look very
simple, unguarded barrier
beside it was an old canoe
be used as a flower bed.
shock gardening troops?
from the sea bed were fo
unbelievably French an
would love to have a cha
them out of her investig

If only I could think
with them.

One thing was for su

up to joi
spending
looked lik

Unwitting
own inves
led me p
anchovies.

I heade
again. It w
Its windov
ensnared ti
the shape
red wine a
I noticed, l

The sho
one of the
floor of a m
a leafy vir
window-sh
grapes that
reach.

Inside, th
tins and bot
shapes abou
Provence –

Elderly
displays, po
how small th
before looki
people with
seriously out

I squeezed

inexhaustibly imaginative selection of things to do with fish – squid paté, swordfish rillettes, mackerel fillets, crab flesh, monkfish livers and whole white anchovies in Banyuls vinegar. I looked at the price tag and calculated that buying Elodie's ten kilos here would probably cost more than the boat that had fished them.

I went up the counter, where the shop-owner was holding the world's smallest jar of honey – the product of a single, world-famous bee to judge by the price ticket.

'Bonjour,' I said, adding a quick 'excusez-moi'.

She ignored me, and I had time to admire her dexterity as she twisted wrapping paper around the honeypot and stuck a little gold label on top.

'J'ai juste une petite question,' I said as she looked for a paper bag that wouldn't dwarf the honey.

Again she ignored me completely. I stood patiently and waited for her to grant me an audience.

I had to admit that it was fascinating to get a close-up view of a type of French woman I'd never seen in Paris. A late middle-aged Parisienne would not have plaited her hair in auburn schoolgirl pigtails, or worn a skin-tight sleeveless vest with a desert warfare camouflage pattern. The cleavage was way too uncovered, as well. A Parisienne of any age is proud of a well-proportioned chest, but she usually covers up her boobs as soon they stop looking like the creamy-smooth orbs in moisturizer adverts. I admired this woman's self-confidence. She had strawberry-red lips and eyelashes like dreadlocks, but she didn't look at all tarty, or what people insultingly call mutton dressed as lamb. She was simply a woman who didn't see why she should stop flaunting her sexiness just because she was over twenty-five. Go for it girl, I thought.

'Oui?' she said when she had finally handed the

thimble-sized package to her customer and taken a credit card in exchange.

'Your anchovies, are they from Collioure?' I asked.

'Oui,' she answered, though she was more interested in watching her customer type his pin number.

'Is it possible to visit the factory?'

Now I had her full attention.

'The factory? No, it's closed to the public,' she said. 'This is the only place you can buy them.'

'Ah.' I may not be that experienced with women, especially those from the Mediterranean basin, but I can usually tell if a lady is fibbing. When she's telling me an unpleasant truth, she's either apologetic or (like the Paris bank worker who'd deprived me of my credit card) triumphant. The fibbers always sound too offhand and unemotional. I knew that this lady was lying.

'What size jar would you like?' she asked.

'I'll go and look,' I said, and returned to the fish product section. The anchovies had been labelled with the shop's golden logo, but by lifting up a sticker I was able to see the name of the producer. 'Conserves Franchois,' it said, one of those puns that the French are so fond of. The English equivalent would be to call them 'Preserved Frenchovies'.

Peeling the label further up, I saw that there was an address for the factory, too, a street that I could easily find on my town map. I rubbed the gold sticker back into place as best I could with my thumbnail, and strode out the door.

Straight into a black T-shirt.

'Merde,' was my first thought, closely followed by, 'The shop has a security guard, and he saw me damaging the goods.'

I changed my assessment of the situation, though, when I saw that the guy blocking my way had bare legs. No one has a bare-legged security guard. And he had skintight Lycra shorts on. He was a commando. Correction – *the* commando. The guy I'd followed.

I went back to my original assessment of 'merde'.

'Toi,' he said. 'You were following me.'

'Moi?' I said.

'Oui, toi. I followed you back here.'

Oh merde, I thought yet again. So much for my spying skills. The commando saw my discomfort and laughed. He had a friendly face, in a brutal kind of way. His head was shaven, and his jaw was massive, with a dimpled chin that made him look like one of the French rugby players they photograph for calendars.

'Why were you following me?' he demanded, flexing his biceps through his T-shirt as though the wrong answer might earn me a pair of punches.

'I am interested in the commandos,' I said. 'My grand-father was in Normandy.' This was true, though granddad hadn't been there on D-Day, only for a day-trip with my gran to watch the tall ships in Le Havre.

'But that doesn't explain why you were following me.' There was a cruel glint in his eye. 'You're English, aren't you?'

'Yes,' I said, as if this might be enough explanation.

He didn't have time to pursue his line of questioning, because three old ladies brandishing cameras came out of the shop and swarmed around him, asking if he was one of the courageous young men that they saw every day at the harbour, and begging for a photo. His attention was distracted long enough by the bobbing white heads clustered around his midriff for me to edge past him and start walking downhill.

'Hey, you!' he shouted, but when I looked back he was

still entangled in the gaggle of old ladies, and unable to move without swatting them away. 'I know why you were following me,' I heard him call out.

I didn't stop to check whether he'd guessed right.

'I do this all day.' The woman was dressed in a white overall, with a hairnet holding her black curls in place. Her fingers were bare, and she hardly looked at them as they pulled the little anchovies to pieces, stripping away their skeletons and laying the bare fillets side by side on a sheet of gauze. 'It helps me think,' she said.

I didn't like to imagine what ripping the skeletons out of several thousand fish a day made the woman think about, so I asked why she was putting them all to bed like that.

The anchovies had just spent a month soaking in salt, she told me, and were now getting ready to hibernate in a barrel.

I had made good my escape from the commando, and taken refuge in the anchovy warehouse, where things were going very well. When I'd mentioned to the assistant in the factory shop that I wanted to place a large order, I'd been ushered straight through to a preparation area and invited to take my time tasting the full selection of products available. It was all very appetizing. I forked up a long, white anchovy fillet in vinegar that was almost sweet. All that was missing was a glass of rosé to wash it down.

'It must be hard,' I said, 'your fingers, the little fish.' My French wasn't up to expressing it more eloquently.

'No, you get used to it. It's like knitting.'

'Ah yes.' I nodded, imagining a jumper made of anchovies. It would have been only slightly less wearable than the patterns my aunt used to inflict on me at Christmas. 'You never do any big fish?' I asked.

'Big fish? We do sardines sometimes, they're bigger.'

'No, even bigger fish.'

'There used to be tuna around here, but they've all gone.'

'No, not tuna. Other fish.' I tried to look casual. 'Salmon, for example . . .'

'No.'

'Sturgeon?'

'What?' I still hadn't mastered the pronunciation of 'esturgeon'. I made it sound too like 'detergent'.

'Ay-stoor-djo?' I tried again, and this time she understood.

'No, we never do them,' she said. 'The company only prepares anchovies and sardines. We sell other fish, but they're imported. From Brittany and places like that.' She was apologetic. I could see that she was telling the truth. 'Why do you want sturgeon?' she asked.

'I want to buy different fish,' I explained. 'It's for the wedding of a friend. Ten kilos of the white anchovies, and maybe some other fish, too.'

'Ten kilos of anchovies? I'm not sure they will like that. Why don't you get them a vase or a lamp?'

'No, it's not a present. I'm the caterer.'

Probably for the first time in hours, she stopped pulling fish to bits. She held her hands up in the air, closed her eyes and enjoyed a long, shoulder-shaking fit of the giggles. I could only assume that her days of sitting here alone with the anchovies were so dull that the thrill of meeting a caterer had been too much for her nervous system.

'I'm sorry,' she finally said, and her fingers got back to work. 'But you said that you are the *traître*. You mean the *traiteur*. You see the difference?'

I managed a short laugh of my own. I'd mispronounced caterer and called myself 'the traitor'.

Proof yet again that I definitely wasn't cut out for espionage.

6

It was just after seven in the evening.

I was walking down from the hotel to the harbourfront. At the foot of the castle walls, a group of men were drinking pastis and playing pétanque, the game invented by Frenchmen so that they don't have to help with the cooking.

Floodlights were throwing a sheet of white light over the battlements, and I thought about the girl I'd seen walking up there. I wondered if it really had been her at the restaurant. After our eyes met, she hadn't looked at me again, and I had made an effort not to stare at her. But now I half hoped to see her again.

I was on my way down to the row of cafés near the beach, Collioure's favourite evening drinking spot. If she was sitting alone, I would go over and ask her – why had she been risking her life at the top of the wall?

I couldn't see her, so I chose an empty seat on the front line overlooking the beach, swivelled my neck like a crazed owl until I managed to attract the attention of one of the fast-moving waiters, and ordered myself a glass of red Banyuls. Carbon footprint practically zero on that wine, I congratulated myself. It could almost have been delivered on foot.

The sun had gone down behind the town, but it was still high enough to glare bright gold in the windows of the houses on the headland opposite me.

Yellow street lights wound left out of sight, following the coast road south to Spain. Banyuls was two or three bays further down. M was due back from there at around eight. I was to meet her at the café. On the phone, she'd sounded tense, as if the talks with her fellow scientists had gone badly again.

I felt my pocket vibrating. I'd received a couple of text messages.

The first was from Elodie: **'Val coming 2 Collioure 2 find u and talk. He will call. Give him kiss from me.'**

OK to all of that, I thought, except perhaps kissing her fiancé.

The second message had been sent from a long international number starting with a plus sign.

'Being on place in person maybe its easy for you to get money from strange affairs.'

I recognized the unique style of non-verbal communication. Or rather verbal non-communication. This had to be from my friend Jake, the American who'd gone to Louisiana to try and help the Cajuns learn French again. Meanwhile, it seemed that they'd been helping him to un-learn English.

I called him back and asked him to explain what the hell he was talking about.

'Hey, Paul, it is my lunch pause,' he said. His English, which had been polluted by ten years in France, had now had an extra layer of Frenchness grafted on. He had a Cajun twang, and said 'lonsh pose'. Soon only a handful of Bayou swamp-dwellers would be able to understand him. And me, of course.

After some careful questioning, I managed to ascertain what he had been trying to say. As I was in France, he had meant, I was in an ideal position to ask for funding from the French Foreign Affairs department.

'Funding for what?' I asked.

'For posy,' he said.

This was one word that I had no trouble understanding. Ever since I'd first met him, he'd been going on about 'posy', his twisted pronunciation of the French word for poetry. He'd been writing a series of odes to having sex with women of all the different nationalities living in Paris. My least favourite had been the one which started something like 'I once asked a girl from Kirkuk . . .'

More recently, he'd been translating Baudelaire into what he loosely defined as 'English', as part of his mission to deprive Americans of their blissful ignorance of French poetry.

'Now I am creating a site web to put on ligne the posy of my élèves,' he said.

'Your pupils?'

'Yeah. And for all Cajuns. After that, I want to make a Cajun festival of posy. And we need some fon.'

'Some fun?'

'No, *fon*. You know, money, man. Euros, dollars. And the posy is in Frinsh, so I was thinking, maybe the francais government will pay something. They have a Francophonie minister, non? They support the Frinsh language in the world. You are in Paris, maybe you can make the demand?'

Listening to him was such hard work that I felt like paying for the festival myself just to stop him talking about it.

'I'd be happy to pass on a letter,' I said. 'Via Jean-Marie, maybe. You know, Elodie's dad. He's in politics, he has friends in the right places. I'm not in Paris right now, though. I'm down south.' I explained about meeting up with M.

'That Anglaise? But you sautéed her already, man. Why you want to sautée her again?' He wasn't suggesting that I'd sliced and fried her. He was using the French word 'sauter', to jump.

'Some of us are in it for more than a tick in the atlas,' I said. 'We're looking for something a bit more romantic. You know, a lifetime of love and sexual compatibility, stuff like that.'

'With an Anglaise? No, man. The Anglaise I had, she was interested only in beer and, how do you say, pipes?'

'Blowjobs,' I said. 'You think English girls are only interested in beer and blowjobs?'

'I'll send you the poem, man, you read it and learn.'

I hung up on him. A lot of our phone calls ended that way, and it never really bothered him.

'That's awful.' A shocked woman was staring at me from under a straggly, copper-red fringe. 'Beer and blowjobs?' she said incredulously.

'I'm sorry,' I said, pointing to my phone. 'It's this friend of—'

'It's total bollocks,' she interrupted me. 'When we're in France, it's *wine* and blowjobs.'

The redhead, it turned out, was from the hen party. They were a bunch of friends from 'sexy Sussex', she told me. 'You know what it means in French? Soo-sex?' She didn't wait for a reply. 'Suck dick.' She giggled.

'Is one of you getting married?' I asked, hoping to change the subject.

'No, we're just down here on the piss and the pull,' she slurred. 'We're getting some guys together for a little beach party. And you were on your own, so we figured you might like to come along.'

'That's very flattering,' I said, 'but no thanks.'

'You scared or what?'

'Frankly, yes,' I wanted to answer. I'd noticed that two of her buddies were watching our conversation from the promenade. Both were holding supermarket bags full of wine bottles, and their evenly divided loads seemed to be the only things keeping them standing upright. All of the girls were dressed as though the airline had lost their luggage and they were having to economize on clothes. They were in bikini tops and either tight trousers or mini-skirts. They were tattooed Amazons on the hunt for male flesh.

'I'm waiting for my girlfriend,' I said.

'Bollocks,' my new friend said. 'Girls!' She shouted over her shoulder, and the two wine-bearers clinked unsteadily over to join us. 'He won't come,' the first girl told her chums.

They dropped their shopping bags and tried to lift me out of my seat.

'No, honestly, my girlfriend will be here any minute.' I pulled my arms free. 'You'll only make her jealous.'

'She can come as well,' the redhead said. 'There'll be loads of blokes. Look.'

I turned to see four more girls staggering along the promenade, arm in arm with a bunch of guys. I recognized the commandos, even though they'd changed out of their shorts and into a different kind of uniform – clean jeans and short-sleeved shirts that showed off their biceps.

The redhead beckoned her pals and their male escorts over, and my table was suddenly surrounded by loud drunks, including at least five soldiers.

'Hey, c'est l'Anglais!' It was the commando with the dimpled chin, waving a beer bottle in my face.

'Bonsoir,' I said, as you must.

'You know this tourist?' another commando asked, a guy with a bulbous broken nose.

'Oui.' The dimple-chinned guy told his mates how I'd followed him up the hill to the base. He didn't look too annoyed, though. They were all laughing about it.

'What's your name?' the guy with the broken nose asked me.

'Paul West,' I told him. No reason to lie.

'Ça n'existe pas,' he said.

'Yes it does exist,' I protested.

'Paul North yes, Paul South yes, but West? No.'

There were loud groans, and the other soldiers laughed and slapped him on the back.

I groaned the loudest of all. Spoken with a French accent, my name sounded like 'West Pole'. I had spent most of the two or so years I'd been in France pouring scorn on the French love of bad puns. And now I was one.

'What are they laughing at?' the redhead asked me.

'Me,' I said.

'They know you?'

'We've met,' I said, and suddenly realized that I'd have to go to the beach party after all. These guys were drunk enough to draw me a map of every secret base in France, never mind discuss what fish they'd bumped into while diving.

And M couldn't possibly object. This wasn't going to be an interrogation – it was going to be a drunken chat that the soldiers wouldn't even remember in the morning.

'OK,' I said. 'Where's the party, then?'

My question was greeted with a victory whoop, and the broken-nosed soldier leaned in and breathed at me that they were taking the Anglaises to a little beach just around the headland, a very *tranquil* beach, he sniggered meaningfully.

'I'll just call my girlfriend and let her know where I'm going,' I said, and walked away a few yards to make the call, while the others gathered up all the bottles and had a bit of a snog and a grope to pass the time.

M was on voicemail, so I left a message telling her what I was doing. Then, feeling the need to let as many people as possible know where I was disappearing to, I tried Elodie. She was on voicemail, too, and I gave her the same information. If they had to send out search parties, there were now two women who could testify to my last known whereabouts.

'Let's go,' I said, returning to the group and offering myself up for sacrifice.

'Yeah!' The redhead flashed her boobs in celebration.

We wound our noisy, cheering way along the promenade and past the church tower, to a dark path that led around the base of the cliffs. Most of the guys and girls were pairing off, trying each other's mouths for size. Male and female hands were getting busy, drawing shocked looks from families on a sedate evening stroll.

I tried to divert the broken-nosed guy's attention from the nearest bikini top by asking him about his diving exploits.

In between attempts to bite through a bikini strap, he said that they often went diving in completely uninhabited coves and bays along the coast. He had a strong southern accent, I noticed. He pronounced all this syllables very clearly, and said 'kota' for 'côte' and 'baza' for 'base'. But he soon lost interest in shoptalk and started telling the girl that he was going to give her 'a bang'.

'A bang?' she echoed. 'Hey girls, François here says we're going to get a bang.'

There were renewed shouts of 'wahay' and more jokes about snorkels, and I wondered whether coming along had been such a good idea after all. We had now arrived on a section of beach that was practically invisible from the main part of the village, and unlit by the street lamps. I didn't think it would be very long before clothes were being shed and Anglo-French friendships sealed with much more than a kiss.

'You going to give me a bang?' the redhead asked me.

'He means a bath,' I said, feeling like a party-pooper. 'It's the way he pronounces *bain*.'

'Oh. Well, it'll do for starters,' she said. 'Fancy a skinny dip?'

'Let's have a drink first, shall we?' I grabbed a bottle from a shopping bag and went over to one of the soldiers who had produced a corkscrew. It was the dimple-chinned guy.

'Do you often come to the beach at night?' I asked him in careful French. 'To swim or dive, I mean.'

'Uh?' The sound of small waves breaking on the pebbles had drowned out part of my question, so I repeated it. 'Oh, oui,' he answered. 'Day, night, anytime. But not usually with girls, uh?'

He was having a bit of trouble aiming his corkscrew so I took it off him and got to work on my own bottle.

'It is frightening, no, swimming at night?' I asked. 'The big fish?'

'Oh, pff,' he replied, sniffing at danger. 'These Anglaises are more frightening, no? Are all English girls like this? Can't they at least *pretend* they're not easy? I prefer Spanish girls. They are more Catholic, they resist. You have to—'

'Sharks?' I asked quickly, before he could tell me how to break down Spanish resistance. 'You see sharks?'

'Uh? No, not here. In Martinique sometimes. In Djibouti, yes. But I'm not scared of them.' He gripped my shoulder as if to protect me from marauding sea life.

'Djibouti, that is near Iran, no?' Before he could correct my wildly inaccurate geography, I got in with my key question. 'Did you see *esturgeon* in Djibouti? Or here?'

'*Esturgeon?* What do they look like?'

'Just like those girls,' I wanted to say, 'white bellies and big floppy gills.' Behind the commando's back, several of the girls were stripping off, aided by helpful soldiers. The girls were squealing and egging each other on, and a couple of them were starting to tug at the guys' belts. I only had a few minutes before all conversation would be at an end, I calculated, and did my best to describe the sturgeon I'd seen in M's photos. 'You know,' I told the guy, 'the fish that give caviar. I have heard that they live here, too, near Collioure.'

'Near Collioure?'

The first couple was now down on a makeshift mattress of discarded clothes and getting into some serious entente cordiale, but the guy with the dimpled chin was gazing deep into my eyes as if he might see a picture of a sturgeon, or even a tin of caviar, engraved there.

'Yes, near Collioure,' I said, trying not to whimper as his massaging thumb began to drill into my collar bone. 'Have you seen any?'

'Paul!' An urgent female cry cut through the breaking waves. I hoped it was M, come to get mad at me for joining in at a beach orgy. Anything to escape from here.

But suddenly my other shoulder was getting punished, and this time it was the redhead who'd come to claim her pound of flesh.

'You're missing out on the party,' she said, tugging hard at my shirt.

'Fous le camp, grognasse,' the commando hissed at her.

'What did he say to me?' she demanded.

I didn't like to translate that it was 'Go fuck the camp, silly whining woman.'

'Casse-toi, pauvre conne,' he said, tugging at the other half of my shirt. 'Can't you see we're talking?'

'You what?' She looked to me for help.

I kept silent, although I'd worked out that it was something like 'Bugger off, you poor vagina.' She seemed to have got the gist, though, because a bare female arm shot across my line of vision and just missed the commando's chin.

This violence was clearly more his kind of thing. He laughed and pushed her back. Her grasp of the basic skill of standing up must have been weakened by alcohol and the slippery pebbles, because she fell backwards, taking one sleeve of my shirt with her. Before I could complain, she was upright again, and trying to kick the commando, using my body as a shield from retaliation.

The soldier, who still had his hand clamped to my collar-bone, chortled at her drunkenly swinging feet until one of them connected with his ankle, at which point he swore and leapt backwards, a large portion of my shirt still clutched between his fingers.

'Merde!' I'd had enough of all this violent possessiveness. 'Look, I'm not into boxing threesomes. So just give me those bits of my shirt back and I'll say goodnight.'

'Er, excuse me.'

I felt a timid tap on my bare right shoulder, and swivelled to find a young guy grinning at me.

'And you can fuck off, too,' I told him.

Deciding to leave my shirt to its two new co-owners, I made for the lights of the village, swigging on bad red wine and trying my best to steer a path through the maze of writhing limbs without stepping on anything vital.

I had got temporarily stranded between a large rock and a particularly active couple when a shadow appeared a few yards in front of me and started to shout in French, 'Police, nobody move!'

A large group of similar shadows emerged from the gloom and began rushing towards us.

The French are not an obedient nation, even when they're in the services, and the commandos were on their feet in an instant and sprinting away, chased by dark-uniformed men with fluorescent 'gendarmerie' banners on the back of their jackets.

I was a sitting – or standing – duck. A man in a blue pullover appeared in front of me and ordered the naked girl at my feet to stand up.

'I can't find me knickers,' she told him.

'You don't understand,' I said, scanning the pebbles for her clothes. I saw some likely-looking panties and handed them to her. 'I wasn't – I didn't want to . . .'

My stuttered protests were ignored by the cop, who grabbed my arm and stood waiting for the girl to wiggle into the knickers.

'They're not mine,' she complained. 'They're about ten sizes too small.'

'I am not with one of these drunken women,' I protested, but the cop was watching the chases going on along the shoreline. Two canny soldiers had swum out to sea and were breast-stroking to freedom. A couple of others had been caught in the shallows and were writhing like fish trying to jump out of the net. Closer by, the young blond guy who had tapped me on the shoulder was also in the grip of a stony-faced cop. He was much too long-haired and thin, I now saw, to be a soldier. I was horrified to hear him telling his arresting officer that he wanted to talk to me.

'Non, go fuck the camp,' I shouted at him. 'I don't know him, honestly,' I told my cop. 'He just came and . . .' I searched desperately for a safe way of saying that he'd accosted me. But my loss for words suggested something totally different to the gendarme, who raised one sceptical eyebrow.

You're wrong, I wanted to tell him, I'm not a public shagger of drunken females, or a soldier groupie, even though I have nothing against either.

Just then, the dimple-chinned commando ran past, chortling and using my shirt-sleeve as a kind of whip to ward off the gendarme who was chasing him. My arresting officer eyed the whip, then my bare shoulder.

'Oui,' I said, 'he tore it off. Not that . . . I mean, we weren't . . .'

The cop's sceptical eyebrow was raised once again. Oh bollocks to it, I thought. It's not a crime to be involved in a public bisexual SM orgy, is it?

7

There was one consolation. At least I had most of my clothes on.

Having been escorted from the beach, I spent the next twenty or so very uncomfortable minutes in the police van rubbing shoulders with, on one side, my arresting officer, and on the other, the woman who'd been lying at my feet on the beach. She had clearly not been able to find any clothing to add to the knickers belonging to her much thinner friend. Her only conversation during the trip to the police station was to ask whether I'd got any cigarettes, so it seemed that at least she'd had enough fun to warrant a post-coital smoke.

Her own arresting officer, sitting opposite, told her to shut up and warned us all to do the same or incur an increased fine.

The blond civilian guy was at the far end of my own bench. He kept leaning forward and making faces at me, but I ignored him.

A few seats down from me, the commando with the dimpled chin was looking impatient, but didn't seem too worried by his fate. He turned to grin at me.

'You know, I think I have seen a sturgeon,' he said.

I gave him an 'Oh yeah?' look.

'Really,' he went on. 'A couple of months ago. We were doing some beach landing exercises.'

'Shut up,' the policeman opposite me ordered.

'Tranquille, mon ami,' the commando told him. 'We're only chatting to pass the time.' A little staring-down contest ensued, the commando apparently warning the gendarme telepathically not to get too uppity with guys who spend their days learning how to hurt people.

The policeman looked away, and the commando took up his story again. 'It wasn't near here in Collioure,' he said. 'Where was it? Where did we do that beach landing?' He nudged one of his naked colleagues, who was engrossed in making lewd faces at an undressed English girl.

'The Camargue,' the guy grunted, and went back to his tongue aerobics.

'Ah oui,' Dimpled Chin said. 'You know Saintes Maries de la Mer?'

'No,' I told him, making a mental note of all this for M. If it was true, then it was prime information.

'The sea wasn't too clear,' he went on, 'but I'm sure that's what it was. Long brute, half-catfish, half-shark.'

'That's it,' I said. 'Did you see just one?'

'Yes, only one. But why are you so interested in them, anyway?'

Good question. What could I say to allay his suspicions?

'Photography,' I blurted out. 'My girlfriend, she takes photos of fish.'

Any further conversation was ruled out when the van lurched into movement, its engine rattling like a tumble dryer full of spanners, causing the seats to vibrate so much that one of the English girls said she was going to buy one for her bedroom.

We drove along the promenade, away from the phallic church. The van edged its way through the crowds of curious tourists, who took photos and filmed the semi-nudity through the windows as we passed by. A couple of the girls stood up to flash their boobs at the cameras. To them it was all part of the party.

We were unloaded in a brightly lit car park, then herded across chilly tarmac into the entrance hall of the gendarmerie. Here, we were greeted with a shocked silence. Two cops at the coffee machine stopped feeding in coins and gaped. An old lady who had come to register some kind of complaint broke off in mid-sentence and clung on to the edge of the reception desk for support.

The officer on duty barked an order at the arriving gendarmes, and we were shoved into a corridor with five or six doors leading off it and a long bench running along one wall.

'Sit down and shut up,' a gendarme told us. Two of the soldiers and four of the women were completely naked, and perched gingerly on the edge of the seat. The blond guy was still gesturing at me. Now he was giving me the thumbs-up. Bloody hell, I thought, didn't he think we were in enough trouble already?

I tried to get talking to my sturgeon informant again, but we weren't allowed to hang around for a chat.

'You, in there. You, in there.' An officer strode down the bench, assigning interview rooms. 'You, you, you, you, you and you, don't sit on the chairs until someone brings paper towels.'

I went and sat in a tiny cubicle just big enough for two chairs and a desk. It was a modern plastic-and-steel space, the only decoration a large, labelled diagram giving the French names for every part of a door, a doorframe and a lock. This was presumably so that burglary victims could describe exactly how their house had been broken into. I thought it would probably be just as useful to have a similar diagram of the human body. If you were grabbed by a visiting hen party, you'd be able to give a precise medical description of your attackers. 'I noticed that one of the girls had a very pronounced ventral cyclops, and a tattoo that ran right down to her rectal fibula . . .'

I was still smiling at this idea when a painful thought hit me. The computer on the desk was almost certainly going to reveal that the French police and I had had dealings before. There was the little matter of a car crash after which the guilty party had not only left the scene of the accident but also blamed it on me. And, worse, there was the fine for refusing to translate the menu of my English tea room into French on the grounds that 'sandwich' was already English, and if you didn't know what a 'cup of tea' was, then you were too stupid to drink one anyway. This disdain for the French language would tie in all too neatly, I thought, with my apparent lack of respect for public decency. They'd put me down as an amoral outlaw and lock me up with lots of men, who would see the arrival of a half-naked young Englishman on the cell block as a gift from the gods.

Despite the cold, I started to sweat.

My arresting officer came in and shut the door behind him. He booted up the computer with brisk little gestures. He was very thin and clean-cut, his hair shaved to exactly one black millimetre all over, his uniform neatly pressed, even though he'd just been out on a mission. All the tags and buttons were in place, and the leather of his belt shone as if he'd painted it with nail varnish.

He asked for my name, address, age and whatnot, and then got down to the interrogation itself. I could hear voices murmuring along the corridor. We were all getting the same treatment.

'Now tell me what happened,' he said, not at all accusingly. He had an open, almost gentle face. I found it hard to believe that he'd be good at the truncheoning and shooting parts of his job. Or interrogation, for that matter. 'Give me the whole truth, and it'll be OK,' he told me. 'No need to be ashamed.'

'Well, I was having a drink on the beach . . .'

'OK.' The gendarme made a sign for me to stop while he typed the beginning of my statement.

'I was having a drink on the beach, talking to a soldier,

and then suddenly the Anglaises and the other soldiers began to . . .' The next bit involved a delicate choice of verb, but the gendarme nodded and told me that he was typing that I'd seen certain men and women disrobing. So far so tame.

'And when I, er, saw this, what you said, there were suddenly maybe eight or ten people, er, you know, on the sand.'

The policeman nodded again. 'So they were engaging in heterosexual relations in public?'

'Oui,' I confirmed, and he typed out this sentence that could never have come from my limited linguistic repertoire.

'And?' The policeman was looking hopeful.

'And then the police arrived,' I said.

'Yes, but you were not a participant,' he said.

'Yes, please say, you know, I do not do these things on the beach with drunken women.' I left it to my interpreter to express this in decent French.

'Exactly.' He typed a long sentence.

'I have done other things,' I said, referring to the two misdemeanours he was going to find out about when he hooked me up to his database, 'but I don't do that.'

'No.' He typed some more, and then lifted his fingers from the keyboard with a sigh of satisfaction. 'Now, I'll read this back to you, and you can sign it.'

He began to read, and I began to lose consciousness.

Apparently, I'd been chatting on the beach with my boyfriend, engaging in some manly horseplay that had resulted in my torn shirt, when we were shocked to find heterosexual relations being conducted nearby. We naturally found this repulsive, and had been in the act of leaving the scene to alert the authorities when the police arrived and arrested everyone present. As a morally upright homo-sexual, it was unthinkable that I could have been involved in, or approve of, the indecent acts that I'd been forced to witness on the beach today.

'No, no,' I pleaded. 'I am – how do you say? – happy for gays to be gay. But I am not.'

'Listen, mon ami,' the gendarme whispered. 'If you want to escape this charge of indecency, tell the truth and you will be OK. I guarantee it. You know, we're much more interested in discouraging these gangs of Anglaises than . . . anything else.'

'But . . . Oh, merde.' I'd do anything to get out of here, I thought. What did a little fib about my sexual preferences matter? Besides, how could they prove anything? They weren't going to get me to shag a guy on oath. I hoped. 'OK,' I said.

He printed out the statement and I signed.

'Wait here a moment.' The gendarme stood up, my false confession in his clean white hand. 'Would you like a coffee?'

'Yes, please.' With brandy and morphine, I wanted to add.

He left me sitting there, shivering.

A minute or two later, there was a commotion in the corridor and my door burst open. In strode a short, stocky man with close-cropped grey hair and a battered leather jacket. He didn't look pleased.

'What's this merde?' He slammed my statement down on the desk. 'You're here with your girlfriend. Why did you lie?'

Oh shit, so it had been a game of good cop, bad cop, and I'd fallen right into the trap.

'If you know I'm heterosexual, why do you tell me I'm

gay?' I asked, a question that was confusing enough to stop the bad cop in his tracks and make him frown.

'Why are you here in Collioure?' he demanded, plonking down on the seat opposite me. 'Answer!' He was calling me 'tu', as if I was a child or a poodle, and he bawled this at maximum volume. I jumped.

'I'm just—'

'We know who you are! We know why you're here! You're the Englishman come to fuck the merde in France!' A rough translation.

'No, I—'

'Shut your mouth!'

I did so, but this only enraged him more.

'Your girlfriend, what is she doing?' he shouted.

Oh shit, I thought, they'd found out about her attempts to prove that the French authorities weren't doing enough to clamp down on caviar piracy and save the sturgeon.

'She's trying to help France,' I said.

'Help France?' He looked as though he was about to have a convulsion.

'Yes, the . . .' Dammit, how did you pronounce the word for sturgeon? The commando had said it only minutes ago. What a time for my French to let me down. It had to be the stress. 'The big fish.'

'The big fish?' He suddenly looked serious. 'You know where the big fish is?'

'No, not exactly. But maybe here on the coast.'

'He's not French, is he?' It sounded as if the cop was talking about a man, but of course the word for fish, *poisson*, is masculine in French, so they refer to it as 'he'.

'I think now he lives in France, in the Camargue, maybe.

But originally, he was from Iran. Or Russia, no?'

'Iran or Russia? Putain!' The cop sank back in his chair and gazed into space.

The door burst open again, and a new official face appeared, looking just as angry as the leather-jacketed cop had done. This guy, though, was a uniformed gendarme with lots of braids and tags that seemed to suggest authority.

'You,' he growled. 'What the hell are you doing here?' To my surprise, he was saying this to the cop, not me, and calling him 'tu' into the bargain.

'What?' The leather-jacketed cop looked as though he couldn't believe anyone would dare to talk to him like this.

'This is my station, and I'm ordering you to get out. Now!' The braided guy didn't back down.

'You know who this is?' Leather Jacket was pointing at me.

'Yes, and he's my prisoner.' It sounded as if I'd just been auctioned off on eBay. I didn't like to think what for.

'Ecoute, mon vieux.' Leather Jacket stood up and appealed to the other guy's sense of solidarity. 'Let's talk. You – don't move.' He seemed to think I might go wandering off in search of a new shirt.

They went outside for a confab, and the solidarity came to a swift end. Voices were raised, threats exchanged and one of them was forced to back down, yelling all the while that it wasn't the end of the matter. I wondered who had won, and where it was all leading. All I'd done was go for a drink on the beach, and now I seemed to be at the centre of a tug-of-war between two rival police departments, one specializing in sexual orientation and the other in the nationality of endangered fish.

The door opened, and Leather Jacket walked in, looking rabid.

'You and me, we haven't finished,' he snarled, pointing a pistol-like finger in my face. And then, to my surprise, he left, slamming the door behind him.

Almost immediately, the braided officer walked in. Time for another interrogation about who I liked to shag, and where, I thought, but all he did was rip up my confession and ask me to follow him.

'Please excuse us for the inconvenience, Monsieur West,' he said, politely calling me 'vous' and leading me along the empty corridor like the maître d' at a posh restaurant. 'A car is waiting outside for you.'

'Thank you,' I said, wondering why I was suddenly so innocent.

'Your friend is there already.'

'Really?' So M had pulled some strings? I wondered how she'd managed that.

'Yes.' The officer opened the door and there, sitting in the back of a police car, beaming a huge smile of welcome and relief, was the blond civilian guy from the beach, the one who'd tried to pick me up.

8

'I'm so happy that at last we have an opportunity to talk in person together.' His English was slow and formal, but I didn't mind. I would have forgiven him anything.

'Yes, and thanks for getting me out of there. It was scary.'

'All your problems are finished now.' He put a hand on my knee and laughed.

His looks, like his laugh, were boyish. He was very

fresh-faced, and the tiny wrinkles at the corner of his blue eyes seemed out of place, like theatrical make-up on a teenager. He had floppy blond hair that had probably been cut exactly the same way since Hugh Grant made it fashionable in the 1990s. He could have put on a school uniform and enrolled in the sixth form at Eton.

'I hope the gendarme will not be sad that we don't invite him when we have a drink together,' he said.

'I don't think there'll be enough for anyone else to drink,' I said. 'The way I'm feeling, I could empty half the bar, and I'm sure you're feeling the same way, too.'

'I am.'

No, I wasn't eloping with my new lover. The young guy had told me his name as soon as we had enough time to exchange a full sentence. It was Valéry. He'd come to Collioure to brief me about his family, hadn't been able to reach me on the phone, and had been told by Elodie to try the small beach I'd told her about in my voicemail message.

And once he'd convinced the cops that his uncle's brother-in-law was the region's Préfet de Police, he'd been given the use of a telephone and the loan of a gendarmerie driver, and here we were.

'It's one of the two advantages of a grande famille,' he told me as we cruised back towards the old town. 'The first is that you don't need to *do* anything. You *are* everything. You have the family name, so you will never be a nobody, even if you are a total imbecile. Like at least one of my uncles,' he added softly, in case the driver understood English. 'And the second is, there is always someone with your name, or who is part of your family, to save you from the little sufferings of life, like being poor or arrested.'

Suddenly I knew why Elodie wanted in. This was a club worth belonging to.

Valéry wasn't arrogant, I realized. He was just being realistic. His family was rich, and always would be as long as France's economy didn't collapse entirely. And no matter how much the French complain, their economy has to be amongst the most stable in the world. It would take a nuclear holocaust that wiped out all of the country's vineyards, mineral water springs, car plants, oil refineries, art collections and picturesque chateaux to make a dent in its fundamental stability. And given that France is on suspiciously good terms with all the planet's rogue powers, that probably isn't going to happen soon.

'But there is a disadvantage to the grande famille, too,' Valéry said. 'We are not free. To us, a marriage is not just two lovers who promise that they will pay their rent together until they divorce.' He was speaking insistently, keen to get across the full import of what he was saying. 'It is the – how do you say? – the initiation of someone into the family. It is like accepting an immigrant into your home. Except if you marry a cousin, of course, and I don't want to marry a cousin. I have fucked most of the ones it is legal to fuck, and it felt like fucking my sister, so no thanks.' The driver looked up into his mirror. He didn't need a degree in English to get the drift of that bit of the conversation. 'This is why Bonne Maman is so nervous.'

'Bonne Maman?' I asked.

'Yes.' Valéry laughed. 'Bonne Maman is the jargon in our milieu for the grandmother.'

'So Bonne Maman is who Elodie calls grand-mère?'

'The bitch grand-mère, yes,' he said. 'It is not a secret. And Elodie is right. She is the reason why you must be very, very diplomatic. She is the reason for our merde.'

'She wants to stop the wedding, right?'

'Ah, she wants to. This is why I am organizing it myself, and not in one of the family houses. But she can't legally stop me. It is the twenty-first century, after all. So she is doing even worse. She is making a sort of campaign in the family to say that this is a wrong marriage. She wants them to – you know – boycotter la cérémonie. This is too bad. I love Elodie, but if all my family is against the marriage, it is very difficult for me. I am at the bank, I am *de la famille*, you understand?'

'Sure,' I said, though I couldn't remember when I'd last asked my family's advice or permission to do anything.

'Bonne Maman is making propaganda against Elodie and me with la famille. So you must come to our home, meet my parents and everybody. Elodie is coming, too. We must show them that you and Elodie's father are good people, and that you can organize a fantastic reception, and then Bonne Maman cannot oppose so easily.'

'She's even objecting to the food?' I asked.

'Oh yes, when my cousin Bénédicte married last year, there was a terrible incident with the traiteur.'

'The caterer? What did he do?' Valéry made it sound as if he'd shagged the bride on top of the petits fours.

'Bonne Maman will give you the details, I am sure,' he said, unable to broach the painful subject. 'When can you come to Saint Tropez?'

'Saint Tropez?'

'Yes, to my parents' country home. If possible, you must come this weekend. Things are urgent.'

'Great.' A weekend at a posh house near Saint Tropez – what kind of idiot would say no to that?

'Oof. Merci.' Valéry sighed with gratitude. 'Now, I am

very sorry but I have no time for a drink. I must return to Saint Tropez. It is like a diplomatic war.'

We pulled up at the train station.

'This is au revoir,' Valéry said. 'Lucky they didn't take my coke or I would be forced to call the Préfet again. You want some?' He started fishing around in his blazer pocket, practically under the nose of the driver, who was watching him in the mirror.

'No, thanks,' I said. 'I'm going to hit the rose. Sure you can't join me?'

'No, I must go.'

We shook hands, and I thanked him again for rescuing me from the police. He got out of the police car and ordered the driver to take me to my hotel as if the guy was his personal chauffeur. He and Elodie were an excellent match, I decided. They both had the self-assertiveness skills of a herd of water buffalo.

All things considered, I was in a sprightly mood as I wandered through the hotel garden. The two whitewashed guys watched me pass with more than their usual interest, and answered my bright 'Bonsoir'.

It wasn't till I opened the door of the hotel room and saw the look of seething fury on M's face that I realized not everyone in the world was feeling as jolly as I was.

9

I've always found it very difficult to have an argument with a beautiful woman. She's trying to bawl me out, and I just can't stop myself admiring her face, or other picturesque parts of her.

M's bawling-out style, though, demanded attention. She

was staring me straight in the eyes, defying me to look anywhere else, while shouting at a volume that would have had
heavy-metal fans reaching for the ear muffs.

I was, it seemed, a 'bloody idiot' to get myself arrested
like that, especially after she'd 'bloody well begged me' not
to go anywhere near the soldiers.

How did she know I'd been arrested, I asked, to which
she replied that it was 'pretty bloody obvious' considering
the number of 'flics' (the slang word for policemen) crawl-
ing all over the village, and the way we'd been paraded
through the crowds in our panoramic-windowed van. I was
also, she went on, 'totally fucking nuts' to hang around
while the drunken shaggers were shagging right under my
nose, and I was obviously 'doing my level best to screw
things up' for her at every opportunity by attracting the
attention of 'any dickhead in a uniform' who came within a
hundred yards of me.

While she paused for breath, I told her that apart from
getting arrested, the evening had actually been a minor
success. A sturgeon had been located.

'What? Where?' She seemed sceptical.

I told her.

'The Camargue?' She thought about this. 'Logical,' she
eventually concluded. 'Lots of brackish lakes. And there's
the river, the Petit Rhône. The sturgeon might make for
that. But how do you know all this? Who told you?' she
demanded.

'One of the commandos,' I confessed.

Which only unleashed another volley of verbal torpedoes.
I'd *promised* not to go chasing after them. How could she trust
me ever again if I broke a simple promise like that?

'Sorry,' I said, 'but they hijacked me, not vice versa. And
I did get a result.'

'But at what cost?' She refused to be placated. 'You have no idea what you're cocking up here, Paul. God! I don't even know why I waited for you. I should have buggered off.'

I didn't know what to say. When someone tells you that they ought to have dumped you, you can't help feeling somewhat dumped.

'Well, why did you stay?' I eventually asked.

'I don't know.' She groaned and flopped back on to the bed. 'You weren't supposed to attract the attention of the authorities,' she said.

'Hang on, what are you saying exactly?' I asked. 'You invited me along on this trip because you thought you'd be less noticeable if you were in a couple? I was some kind of male camouflage while you got on with your investigation?'

'No, of course not. I thought it'd be fun, the two of us. After LA and all that.' She sighed. 'But you have to admit it's a bit of a pain if the guy you invite along starts getting the police and the army all excited while you're trying to keep a low profile and ask a few discreet questions. What if you'd been charged and sent to court?'

'I wasn't charged, though,' I said. 'And I did find out where there might be some sturgeon. Which is the whole point of your trip, right? I was only trying to help.'

'True,' she conceded, edging a few millimetres towards forgiving me at last. She sighed and went to gaze out of the window. 'We're going to have to leave Collioure, though,' she said. 'I know where we can hide out.'

'Hide out?'

'Yes, I need to keep you away from hen parties and men in uniform. I know an island with no police, no commandos. I'm pretty sure they haven't even got a postman.'

I didn't like to spoil her change of mood by saying it

wasn't the uniforms that worried me. Judging by my various interrogations back at the gendarmerie, it was the plain-clothes guy, the cop in the leather jacket, we had to worry about.

LIVING IN THE PASTIS

Bandol

1

THE FRENCH COMEDIAN Fernandel said that a glass of pastis is like a breast. One isn't enough, and three are too many.

Another similarity between breasts and pastis is that French men love to play with them both. Give a French guy a glass of the aniseed alcohol and a carafe of water and he regresses to when he was a baby filling cups in the bathtub. It's all because of pastis's fascinating ability to change colour when you add water, not just diluting the shade but turning the liquid from transparent amber to milky gold.

Not surprisingly, Paul Ricard, the guy who patented the drink, made a packet, and used the proceeds very wisely (in my humble opinion), buying two islands off the Côte d'Azur – Embiez, which is big enough to contain twenty-odd acres of vineyards, and the tiny Bendor, his personal hotel island a couple of hundred yards off the resort of Bandol.

And it was to the smaller of these that M and I were now headed, to 'hide out' as she put it. I just wish I'd remembered what a Parisian barman once told me – that pastis has made its way not only into Provençal hearts and livers, but also into their language. When they say 'Quel pastis!' they mean that something is a total mess, a situation as mixed-up and cloudy as the drink of the same name.

I was about to get myself into a right pastis.

We were on a train rattling out of Collioure, and the morning sun was already high over the rooftops.

'What did you tell the police?' M said, for at least the fifth time, like a cop who keeps hoping you'll change your story and contradict yourself.

I repeated the key points of the previous night's various interviews.

'And how exactly did you ask the commando guy about sturgeon?' she said.

'I simply asked if he'd seen any while they were out diving.'

'Straight out, just like that?'

'You think I should have started with sardines and worked my way up?'

It was meant to be a joke, but she didn't laugh. Instead, she began to explain some paranoid theory about the police being after me rather than the drunken exhibitionists.

I didn't want to tell her that she was taking it all a bit too seriously. So what if the police knew she was investigating sturgeon farms? We were only talking about a few fish, after all, not nuclear submarines. They'd let me go, hadn't they? And no one had tried to arrest her.

'Look,' I told her, 'they came to get us because a gang bang on the beach doesn't fit in with the town's arty image, that's all. Someone saw naked buttocks and called the cops.'

She gave a faint smile, her first of the day. 'Yeah, you're probably right.'

'So what will you do about the sturgeon sighting?' I asked.

'I've reported it. We'll try to find out where the soldiers do their exercises along that bit of the coast.'

Personally, I would have been making plans to hire a microlight aircraft and do some zig-zagging over the sea at Saintes Maries, but M's dynamism seemed to be dulled by her worries this morning.

As soon as we had trundled through a pitch-dark tunnel, I opened that day's *Midi Libre*. I'd bought a copy in case my beach party had made the news. In French local papers, nothing is too minor to warrant a write-up.

To my relief, there were no puns on 'Sussex' in the headlines, but the previous day had been pretty eventful in the region. I read out a few titbits to try and lighten M's mood.

In Céret, in the Pyrenees, two wild boars had burst into a school classroom. An adult sow and a piglet had scattered desks and terrified children for ten minutes before bursting out again, running into the street and knocking an Englishman off his bike. The boars had escaped unhurt, but the Englishman had suffered a dislocated shoulder.

'The reporter seems to think that was a good result,' I said. 'Local wildlife two, Brits nil.'

M disagreed. She thought the writer had just been reassuring the hunters up in the mountains that their targets hadn't been damaged.

I soldiered on, informing her that windy conditions were predicted all along the coast. I read out the forecast. Down near Collioure, I told her, the sea was going to be 'agitée' – rough. But further northeast, where we were going, it wouldn't be as bad, merely 'ridée', or wrinkly.

'Like me,' she said.

'You're not wrinkly.'

'Yes, I am. And my boobs are drooping.'

'No, they're not. They're perfect. Especially when they're agités.'

She grunted a short laugh, and went back to staring at her phone. She was watching it, hoping to catch it the second it rang.

'I'd never realized oceanography could be so stressful,' I said. 'I thought you floated around in coral reefs and cavorted with dolphins.'

She seemed to force herself to snap out of her gloom.

'Sorry,' she said. 'I'm forgetting. We're on a train in the South of France, it's gloriously sunny, and we both know we're going to shag each other's brains out the second we get to our hotel.'

I indulged in a few seconds of pleasant daydreaming before my phone buzzed, distracting me from the thought of what was to come. It was Elodie, who was in too much of a hurry to bother with pleasantries like 'hello'.

'Did you call my father about getting money for your mad friend Jake?'

'Yes,' I confessed.

'Well, don't bother Papa with things like that. He has enough to think about. And please try not to get Valéry arrested any more, OK? I need him to be at the wedding. Have you arranged to come and see the bitch grand-mère?'

'Yes.'

'And have you prepared those menus?'

'No, not yet,' I said, feeling as though I was back in the gendarmerie again.

'What? Don't you know how urgent this is?' Elodie sounded almost hysterical. 'Haven't you got any ideas at all?

Apart from the anchovies, that is, and they were my idea.'

'Yes, of course I have *ideas*,' I lied. 'I just haven't put them on paper yet.'

'What ideas?'

Oh merde, I thought, staring out of the window for inspiration. Railway tracks marinated in olive oil? Telegraph poles à la vinaigrette? Deep-fried fig trees?

Yes, the curly branches of the tree had given me an idea. 'Local food,' I said. 'Everything local.'

'And?' Elodie wanted more details.

'A local, seasonal banquet. I've ordered your anchovies, I'll buy other local stuff, like figs, olive oil, uh, olives . . .' Shit, what else did they produce down here?

'It doesn't sound very chic,' Elodie said. 'What about champagne and foie gras and a giant exotic fruit salad, with mangoes and passion fruit and—'

'But think about your carbon footprint, Elodie.' Encouraged by a thumbs-up from M, I was warming to my theme.

'My what?'

I tried to translate it for her. 'Your pied de charbon?'

'Coal foot? What is that, a miners' disease?'

'Haven't you heard of food miles? The ecological impact of importing goods from far away?'

Elodie gave one of her trademark shrieks of despair. 'I have less than two weeks, Paul. The mangoes I want are already on their way to France. Do you want me to take them back on a Vélib?'

'But this is your chance to do something for global warming,' I said. 'Every little helps.'

'Global warming? This is my wedding, Paul. Fuck the planet. Send me some menus.'

*

M took two calls on the train. Each time she went out into the corridor to speak, and when she came back she looked troubled, as if she'd just received bad news. No, not bad news. Difficult news, that I wouldn't be pleased to hear.

Not that there was much danger of my being displeased by hearing anything. When I asked her if everything was OK, she shrugged and said 'the usual'.

We changed on to a TGV at Narbonne, and she made a call from the platform while we waited for the train to leave. When she came to sit down, she looked more preoccupied than ever. This time, I knew better than to ask why.

Soon our TGV was rolling smoothly along the shore of an immense lake. M brightened up and said that it might be a good place to hide a few sturgeon pens. The brackish water was perfect for them. And it wasn't far from the Camargue.

Several fishermen were at work on the lake, standing up in one-man boats. I watched them, waiting for a giant fish to torpedo one of the punts, but everything looked serenely peaceful.

The train picked up speed and we skimmed between the sea and a series of smaller, marshy lakes. It was here that I had a hallucination.

'Flamingos? Aren't they meant to be down in Africa somewhere?'

This perked M up even more. 'You know that the French call them pink Belgians,' she said.

'What?'

'*Flamands roses*. Flamand means Flemish. They're pink Belgians.'

'Really?'

'No, it's a joke.' She squeezed my knee as if this might

wake my brain up. '*Flamant* with a "t" at the end is flamingo. The word for Flemish ends in a "d". You see?'

'Yes, typical French joke. It has a kind of medieval originality about it.'

'Now who's being grumpy?' She grabbed me round the neck and kissed me fiercely on the cheek. I'd had less painful things done to me by osteopaths, but I didn't mind. The clouds, it seemed, were dispersing.

'I think I'm going to give up this job,' she said. 'It's doing my head in.' She rubbed her temples to illustrate where the damage was being done. 'Sorry if I've been down. It's just that none of these French guys will take me seriously. They pretend they're listening but they just stare at my tits. They promise they're going to help, then call me up and give me a million reasons why they can't. You report a sighting and they don't even answer. So bugger them. I'll just have to get some money together for my own aerial survey. I'll call London about it as soon as we get to Bendor. Then we can relax and enjoy the last of the summer sun.'

It wasn't a good time to remind her that my immediate horizon was darkened by a meeting with Elodie's bitch grand-mère.

The TGV snaked past another gigantic inland sea, which would have looked inviting except for the petrochemical works along its banks, and then hit the sunny but shabby suburbs of Marseille. At the Gare St Charles, we changed trains again, this time on to a double-decker train bound for Toulon.

It wound its way across some tough-looking neighbourhoods in east Marseille, then broke out into countryside again, clattering between mountainsides cloaked in dark-green pines. There were clumps of villas, too, and occasional flashes of deep-blue sea framed by grey cliffs.

'Won't it be good to be just on holiday?' M said wistfully. 'I don't want my work problems to come between us, like they did with your other girlfriends.' I'd told her about Florence, who left me when I hit merde setting up my tea room, and Alexa, who drifted away from me because of all the work-related chaos in America. 'I'm definitely going to tell the French where to stick their research.'

'Won't that mean you'll get sent back to London?' I asked.

'London?' she said, as if she'd temporarily forgotten the name of her home town. 'Oh, maybe.'

There were no taxis in the forecourt of Bandol station, so we strolled down the hill towards the sea. On the water-front, the marina stretched as far as I could see in either direction, the masts like an infestation of spiny sea urchins. At the end of a row of millionaires' cruisers was a small pontoon decorated with photos of rugged coastline, dramatic sunsets and underwater sea life. This was where we were to get the ferry to Bendor. M was reading a timetable posted on the ticket office.

'Seven minutes,' she said. 'Brilliant.' Her smile faded when her phone began buzzing in her bag. She took it out, looked at the screen and gritted her teeth in frustration. 'I'm going to have to take this, sorry.'

She wandered away down the line of flashy yachts, talking in French. She stopped about thirty yards away, at the foot of a wooden gangplank belonging to an old, classy boat – a long, curvaceous vessel with a brass deckrail. You could imagine 1930s film stars lounging there as they drank cocktails and sucked on cigarette holders. It made a change from the bulky ostentation of the fibreglass pimp cruisers.

M seemed to be arguing, cutting at the air with her free hand. But it didn't look as though she was winning the argument.

'Merde!' I heard her clearly above the traffic noise from thirty yards away.

The Bendor ferry, a flat craft big enough for a single car, was backing up to the quayside when M returned, looking grim.

'Did you tell them to get lost?' I asked.

She grunted one of her short-lived laughs. I gathered that meant no.

There were two other passengers for the island – a businessman with a briefcase and laptop, probably on his way to sell the hotel new windows or management software, and a guy accompanying a pile of oyster boxes. That night's entrée du jour, I guessed.

We sat on the open deck, and as we cruised through the marina I asked M which boat she'd choose if she could afford any of them. She picked a large modern vessel that was built for speed. She really was in the mood to escape from something.

Soon we were out in open water. The sea was surprisingly choppy, and waves were boiling around a low lighthouse that had obviously been built to warn ships away from a reef. Just beyond the lighthouse, Bendor began to fill the horizon. An angular, Italian-looking villa was perched on the left-hand corner of the island, a sort of flat-roofed stone chateau on a rocky outcrop. Behind it and above was a canopy of dark conifers, the treeline broken by one or two half-hidden rooftops.

As soon as the ferry pulled into the harbour, I got a glimpse of how rich and powerful Monsieur Ricard must have been. The waterfront was like a set from *The Prisoner*.

It was a kid's drawing of a fishing harbour, brought to life. He'd built a row of doll's house cottages, one of which was decorated with a colourful fresco depicting medieval galleons. Beyond them was a miniature Italian village, and what looked like a Roman temple. Guests arriving on the island must have felt as if they were entering his personal playground.

The main chateau is now the hotel, and I pulled our bags the twenty yards or so to reception. M announced to a young woman in a suit that she'd booked a room in the 'palais', or palace.

'Wow,' I said.

'They call it the palace, but it's the new annexe on the harbour,' M whispered. 'It's quieter there. They have weddings in the main building sometimes.'

'You've been here before, then?' I asked.

'A couple of times,' she said. 'Business. They have conferences here.'

'Double wow,' I said. 'Clever people, the French.' The only conferences I'd been to were in stuffy rooms overlooking English motorways.

M did her thing with the credit card and then announced that she had to go.

'Go?' I asked. 'Where to?'

'I've got a meeting in town.'

'I thought we were hiding out here? You said you were going to tell these guys you'd had enough of sturgeon-hunting.' As usual, I was uncomfortable about trying to monopolize M, but I was beginning to feel a bit like her luggage, something to be deposited at the hotel before she went off to a meeting.

'I know I did. Sorry,' she said, and shrugged. She'd obviously bottled out.

'Tell you what, I'll come over with you,' I said. When I saw the look of panic in her eyes, I added, 'I'll mooch around town and you can call me when you've finished. We'll have a drink and gaze out at our posh new island.'

She softened. 'OK.'

We dumped our bags and made it back to the jetty in time to catch the boat that had brought us over. The oyster guy was still there, I noticed. Perhaps he was just taking his pet shellfish for a ride.

Back on the mainland, we said a fond farewell, and M headed off towards the casino. Weird place to meet oceanographers, I thought.

I wandered up into the small streets behind the harbour-front. This being the Côte d'Azur, there was a row of postcard shops and lavender-soap stores, but the smell of perfume was damped down by a tangy odour that had me homing in like a pig after truffles.

It was a *caviste*, a wine-seller whose shop was a deep, flag-stone-floored cavern. He was filling bottles from a gigantic barrel set into the wall. The red wine was gushing out like blood from a severed artery. The floor seemed to be coated in a film of velvet, and the vinegary smell was strong enough to make me heady. It wasn't the red wine that interested me, though, it was a proud row of golden bottles in the window – ten different sorts of Muscat, the southern aperitif wine that is as heady as port or sherry, but as light as a sorbet. And it was this comparison that gave me my inspiration – Elodie wanted exotic food? She'd get it, homegrown.

Muscat sorbet. The name alone made my mouth water. I'd seen lots of southerners drinking Muscat on ice, and I'd tried it myself. I had expected the taste to be spoilt by diluting it, but somehow the cold wateriness of the ice actually enhanced the flavour of the wine. A sorbet would have the same effect when it melted in your mouth.

In short, there was absolutely no reason why these local ingredients shouldn't be classier and tastier than anything Elodie wanted to jet in from the tropics. I was going to put together a carbon-neutral banquet that would blow the bitch grand-mère's snooty knickers off.

M called me around six and suggested that we meet in one of the big cafés down by the harbour. When I got there, she held out her glass, which contained a rosé barely pinker than honey.

'What is it?' I asked.

'You tell me, Mister food expert,' she challenged me.

'OK.' I duly sloshed the cool liquid round in the glass and gave the rising aromas a professional sniff. 'Yes, it definitely smells like wine,' I said. 'I'm picking up the scent of grape, and the tiniest hint of vine leaf. But to be sure, you've got to *listen* to it.' I held the glass to my ear. 'Yes, the wind fluttering through the vineyards, the sea in the distance – probably a local wine. Unless it's Italian, Spanish, Californian, South African or Australian, of course. Am I getting warm?'

She laughed loudly, and kissed me. 'I'm glad you're here,' she said.

'I'm glad I'm here too, and that you're here. That we're here.' I held out my arms towards the sun. It was still a recognizable ball of fire down here in the south, whereas it had been a faintly glimmering candle in Paris. 'Did everything go the way you wanted this afternoon?'

'No. Well, yes but no, if you know what I mean.'

I had to confess I didn't. 'Sturgeon problems?' I asked.

'Sorry, Paul, I know you got yourself arrested fighting for their cause, but fuck the sturgeon,' she said.

'I think that might be dangerous, after what it did to that guy's canoe.'

'Actually, that's the sturgeon's biggest problem,' she said. 'No one wants to fuck it. The Aquitaine sturgeon is the only European species still going in the wild, and numbers are critically low, so they can't find any sexual partners. That one the commando saw in the Camargue could be just like your hen-party girls – horny and desperate.'

'Not a good idea to go swimming in a sturgeon costume then?' I said.

She guffawed into her glass, and then suddenly frowned.

I looked over at the source of her annoyance. A stocky guy was shamelessly ogling her, lounging way back in his chair, as if M might want to come over and check out what he had in store for her under the table.

I gave him a 'Point it somewhere else, pal' stare and moved round in my seat to block his view of M. 'Has he been bothering you?' I asked her.

'No,' she said. 'It happens to me all the time in France. Forget him.'

I ordered a couple more glasses of the rosé (which turned out to be called Chateau de Lascaux), and begged for some olives to absorb the alcohol.

The wine seemed to hold the key to the secret compartments in M's life, and she began to open up at last. She told me why she'd dumped her last boyfriend.

'He was French,' she said, as though that might be reason enough. 'And he kept telling me that I was the most beautiful woman in the world – no, the *only* woman in the world – and then I saw an email from some tart calling him "mon amour". It was a reply to an email from him telling her she was the most beautiful woman in the world.'

'Wow.' I took all this in, not least the revelation that she was the kind of girl who read her bloke's emails.

'Don't get me wrong. I didn't hack into his account or anything,' she said. 'The daft berk left his laptop open. And when a message pops up with "baise-moi" – "fuck me" – in the subject field, you kind of get curious. You have a peek.'

'It could have been spam.'

'No, he was spam. I deleted him.'

Any possibility of continuing our conversation was ruled out when a guy started singing a French song that had no chorus, just an endless series of verses, all of which seemed to end on the same rhyme. It was like listening to someone suffering from severe hiccups. The singer, a thirty-something with spiky hair and a tight white sweatshirt that had been attacked by a gang of illiterate graffiti artists, was enjoying himself enormously, and a few of the customers were singing along. Even M was nodding her head in time to what only the French could have called music. She had to be very drunk indeed.

Things got even more painful when a female voice joined in. I looked up and caught my breath.

'She's not bad, but I had hoped you preferred blondes,' M said.

'I do,' I told M. 'It's the song – it sent me into shock.'

This wasn't the whole truth. For a second, I'd thought it was the wall-walking, solo-dining girl from Collioure. Which would have been just plain spooky.

I realized almost immediately that I was wrong. This girl had much longer hair, and she was older, too. Late thirties as opposed to late twenties. I didn't know why I'd had the sudden flashback. It had to be wine lag.

I knew I couldn't say anything to M. She'd only ask why I hadn't mentioned the girl before. Which was a question I couldn't really answer myself. So I kept my peace. What is it they say – discretion is the better part of cowardice?

At the end of the song, the duo decided that they had whipped the crowd of twenty or so into enough of a frenzy to try a bit of audience participation. They hummed the first line of a song and invited everyone to guess the song title. If we didn't get it right, the guy with the spiky hair threatened, they wouldn't sing the song. I said a silent prayer that no one would guess.

At first, my wish came true, and the shy audience all looked down at their plates. But this only goaded the duo into humming a whole verse to try and jog our memories. It was a bouncy playground-chant ditty, the type of thing that is inflicted on you if you get into a French taxi driven by a guy who tunes into an oldies station.

'Allez!' the girl implored us all. 'Vous, Monsieur!' She was looking at me.

'Je suis anglais,' I said, shrugging apologetically.

'That's not your fault,' the spiky-haired guy said. 'I blame your parents.'

I joined in the laughter. At least it meant that we were a few seconds further away from hearing the whole song.

'I know!' M suddenly shouted.

'Oui? Madame knows?' The male singer looked delighted, as did the guy who'd been ogling M earlier. He stood up and started to chant for M to sing the song. He was flexing his trousers at us in a horror-movie version of a belly-dance. I tried to stare him down, but he was too drunk or French to care.

M ignored him and called out the song title, a name of such brainwashing banality that I instantly forgot it.

'Oui!' She earned a cheer from the band, who launched into their first verse again.

I looked at her in astonishment. She actually knew this song?

'I know what you *really* do when you meet up with your French scientists,' I said. 'You don't talk about sturgeon. You play Name That Tune, don't you?'

M blushed so red that I thought it might even be true.

2

Next morning, I made a scientific discovery. Reducing the carbon footprint of your wine does not diminish the impact it will make on your head. OK, not exactly Nobel Prize standard, but it was a fact I was not going to forget in a hurry.

M was moving about in the bedroom, and her footsteps on the tiled floor were like earthquakes in my skull. I, meanwhile, was clamped to the mattress by a force field that would have immobilized a herd of kangaroos.

'Coffee on the bedside table,' M bellowed into my ear, though she probably thought it was a whisper.

'What time is it?' I asked. 'Six? Seven?'

It turned out that it was already late morning. M had been up and about for a couple of hours. She'd been to the island's diving school and asked a few subtle questions about what kinds of fish they saw along this part of the coast. She'd even got a peek at their photo album. No signs of sturgeon, though.

'See, you're a much better spy than me,' she said, and then spoilt it all by announcing, 'I have to go to Marseille. I probably won't be back till tomorrow morning.'

'What?' Suddenly I was awake and sober. Marseille was only an hour away. I didn't see why the short trip merited an overnight stay.

'I have a couple of meetings at an institute there, and then I have to have dinner with some people,' M said. 'But if the dinner ends early, I'll come back tonight. The boats run till eleven or so.'

I sat up in bed. 'I don't know why we even came to Bendor,' I said. 'You spend more time on the ferry than on the island.'

'Don't you like it here?' she asked defensively.

'Sure, but I came down south to be with you, not to go on a singles holiday. Why don't we both go to Marseille, get a hotel there? It's a fun place, so everyone tells me.'

'No, we're fine here.'

'*I'm* fine here, you mean. You'd be better off in Marseille. Are you trying to stash me away, or what? Have I become that much of a liability?'

'Oh Paul, I'd prefer to stay out here on the island and relax with you, believe me,' she said. 'But I can't. Sorry.' She turned away, and opened the wardrobe to get her jacket.

So that's that, I thought. End of discussion.

Standing on the quayside, waving goodbye to the ferry, I knew what Parisian housewives felt like. At the beginning of July or August, husbands drive wifey and kids out to Brittany, settle them into their holiday home, and then drive back to Paris on the Sunday night, back to the real world, and often back to their mistresses, with whom they can now have a few uninterrupted nights out. No need to end the date at nine o'clock and head home complaining about a long meeting.

Not that I thought M was going off to meet up with

some other guy. It would have been too absurd. She didn't need the hassle of inviting me down here, and then cheating on me. No, she was just a woman who kept changing her mind, I told myself. Or who said one thing and did another.

And the bare facts were that I was checked in, free of charge, to a luxury hotel on a Mediterranean island. It was sunny, the sea was inches away from my eager toes, and I had almost nothing to do for the rest of the day except relax, swim and eat. My only obligations were a couple of phone calls about the wedding.

Zero stress.

I changed into shorts and flip-flops, grabbed my snorkelling gear and headed out into the sun. By now it was getting on for lunchtime, and the receptionist told me that there was an open-air restaurant at the far end of the island. 'Far end' being a five-minute stroll away.

Instead of going past the row of fake fishermen's cottages and the Roman temple, I turned up an alleyway and found myself on the 'wild' side of the island. There were almost no buildings here, just a well-maintained coastal path that followed the line of the rocky shore. Every twenty yards or so, Monsieur Ricard had built concrete stairways down to tiny gaps in the rocks so that visitors could get in and out of the sea easily. Considerate kind of guy.

I rounded a small headland and came out on the landward coast again, above the restaurant. It consisted of little more than a couple of rows of white plastic tables, set out in the open air. All of them were laid for two, I noticed – it was a place designed for romance. I felt a niggle of resentment at being alone.

Against the low inland cliff was an open grill that had blackened the stone above it. The slightest shower of rain would force the place to close, which seemed to say volumes about the weather down here. Between the tables and the water's edge there was a smooth concrete bathing platform with just enough room for a line of ten or so loungers. Almost all of these were occupied, either by sunbathers or their towels.

There were already a few people eating, presumably the owners of the towels. They reminded me that I hadn't had any breakfast, so I went straight to a table and ordered some grilled seiche (squid) and a half-bottle of rosé.

'Is it OK if I swim before I eat?' I asked.

'Of course,' the waitress said, as if it would have been absurd to do anything else. On a hot day, people probably dived into the sea between courses the way that Parisians smoke a cigarette.

I stripped to the legal minimum, rinsed my snorkel and climbed down a short metal ladder into the clear sea. The water here was a couple of degrees warmer than at Collioure, and I spent a few joyful minutes renewing acquaintance with my old friends the spotted oblade and the hallucinogenic sarpa sarpa. I was even glad to meet up with a few spiny black urchins.

When I got out, my wine was waiting, the cool bottle sweating slightly in the sun. I dried off, pulled on a T-shirt to protect me from the breeze, and poured the rosé slowly, savouring the faint glugging sound against the background of lapping sea. I held up the glass to let the sun highlight the pale pink liquid, sniffed at the combined tanginess of the wine and the sea air, then tipped the whole glassful over my groin.

This was not a tasting technique that I'd learned at the hen party on Collioure beach. No, it was because something had put me off my aim.

It was a vision.

Climbing out of the water up the metal ladder was the weirdest thing I had ever seen. And in the past few days, I had seen some very weird things indeed.

In itself, the apparition wasn't at all shocking. It was, on the whole, pretty easy on the eye, and reminded me more than anything of that key moment in cinema history when Ursula Andress emerged from the Caribbean and made sure that no one would ever forget seeing the first James Bond film.

It was her. This time, it really was her. The dark hair was wet and tied up in a bunch, but it was definitely hers. The eyes, the lips, were hers. The way she walked back to her lounger. It was the smooth, self-assured walk I'd seen on the ramparts of Collioure castle. And she looked at me, catching my eye and glancing away again, exactly as she had in the restaurant.

It was her.

'Sèche?' the waitress said, presumably a suggestion to dry myself off after my accident with the wine.

'Oui, I will do it myself, merci.' I began to dab at my groin with my towel.

'Sèche, Monsieur?' she repeated, holding a plate of squid under my nose.

'Ah, oui, *seiche*, merci,' I blustered.

The mystery girl, whose lounger was only about six feet from my table, was smiling. She must have heard my linguistic mistake.

I poured another glass of wine and made sure it all went in my mouth this time. The bite of the cold liquid at the back of my throat convinced me that I was awake and not dreaming.

This woman, who had been popping up in my consciousness ever since I first saw her, was now a couple of yards away, smiling at me while she rubbed sea water off her tanned body. She wasn't exactly beautiful, but there was something enticing about her. She was smallish and muscular rather than curvaceous, as if she did some kind of intensive sport. Her face was slightly angular, with high cheekbones, and as she dried herself off, there was a fierce determination about her. She looked almost dangerous. And she kept looking at me.

It was as if M had set this up – a honeytrap to see if I was the faithful kind. She announces that she's going away for a day and a night, and half an hour later a woman starts giving me the come-on.

I prayed that a husband, boyfriend or girlfriend would come along and receive the kind of lingering kiss that would tell everyone she's not available.

But no, her lounger was on its own. It seemed she wasn't expecting company.

Maybe her phone would ring and she'd answer it with a string of *chéri*s and *je t'aime*s?

But she didn't seem to have a phone. Her only visible possessions were a towel, sunglasses, sandals and a bikini.

And she was walking towards my table.

'Bonjour,' she said, holding out a suntanned hand. 'Léanne.'

'Bonjour,' I replied, gripping the proffered fingers. 'Paul.'

'Ah, you're English!' I hoped it was the way I said my name, and not my pronunciation of 'Bonjour' that had told her this. 'I love to speak English. I am a tourist guide.' She had a strongish French accent and a husky voice. 'I am sure we have seen ourselves before,' she added.

'Seen each other? Yes, I think so. In Collioure.'

'Collioure, yes!' She looked even more delighted, and

squeezed the hand that she hadn't yet let go of. She had an almost painful grip. 'In the restaurant, no?'

'Yes.'

'You were with your girlfriend. She is not here on Bendor with you?'

'No. Well, yes, she's gone to Marseille. She won't be back till tomorrow.' I wondered why the hell I'd added that.

'She is English too?'

'Yes.'

'Really?' She looked surprised, for some reason.

'Yes. A scientist.'

'A scientist?' Again, she looked as though she didn't believe me. I guessed it was because M didn't look the classic boffin type.

'Yes,' I said, and was struck dumb. I wanted to ask her what she'd been doing up on the castle ramparts, and whether she'd actually seen me through her camera lens, but I knew that prolonging the conversation wasn't a good idea. It felt like a blatant – and highly flattering – chat-up, which was the last thing I needed. I wanted to make things work out with M.

'Is it good?' She was nodding towards my squid, which was cooling on the plate.

'I don't know. I haven't tasted it yet.'

'Try it, please, and tell me if it is good.'

Holy shit, I thought, next she'll be feeding it to me. The image was a pleasant one, but I banished it from my mind and took a businesslike forkful of squid.

'Mm,' I concluded. 'Very good.' I swallowed, and rinsed it down with a sip of wine, thinking now perhaps she'd wish me 'Bon appétit' and go back to her lounger.

'Well, in that case may I join you? I am very hungry, and I have had enough of eating alone.'

It *had* to be M playing a trick. This woman in a bikini was going to sit there opposite me, slurping down squid tentacles? Only a eunuch saint would have been unmoved.

She ordered squid and the same rosé as me, and asked what I was doing on the island. 'Vacation?'

'Yes.' It seemed the simplest answer. 'We're travelling along the coast.'

'Ah. Where are you going next?'

'Saint Tropez. I have some friends with a house there.' I didn't really know why I felt the need to show off, but it came out very naturally.

'Your friends, or friends of your girlfriend?'

'Friends of mine.'

'Ah. And what do you do? In life, I mean?' she asked.

'I'm in catering.'

'Cat-ring?'

'Catering. I'm a *traître*. I mean, a *traiteur*,' I corrected myself. 'For weddings.'

'Ah.' She smiled and nodded, as if this was exactly what she was looking for. With any luck she'd announce that she was getting married next month and still hadn't ordered any food for the reception. It occurred to me that I'd actually be interested in the job, too. Catering for weddings might be fun in France, I decided. It was worth talking to Jean-Marie about adding this as a permanent sideline to our business.

'In London?' she asked.

'No, I'm based in Paris.'

'Ah.' She was less pleased with this piece of information. I didn't know why.

'And where do you work?' I asked.

'Everywhere. I live in Saint Tropez, but I go with groups or families to different parts of the region.'

'And are you here with a group?'

'No. This is purely, you know, *pleasure*.'

She hadn't said the word provocatively, but I winced all the same.

The spell was broken by a crash and a woman's squeal a few tables away. A parasol had been picked up by the wind and blown from one table to the next. I just had time to see it flop to the ground behind the woman who'd screamed. She was an old, deeply suntanned lady, with a chunky gold bracelet on the wrist that she was now holding. She was grimacing in pain.

The woman with her – her daughter, presumably – stood up and started bawling out the guy at the next table whose parasol had done the damage.

'We told you! We told you!' she yelled.

'Told me what?' The guy shrugged. He was small and frizzy, and his tan was even deeper than the old lady's.

'We told you to put down your parasol!'

'And I told you to watch out because my parasol might get blown away.'

They both had strong southern accents, and were pronouncing their syllables so clearly that I understood every word.

'Look at Maman's hand. It's turning blue!' Maman held up the battered wrist to support her daughter's argument.

'You should have moved.' The guy wasn't letting a milligram of guilt get anywhere near his conscience.

'*We* should have moved? Why should *we* move? We're *chez nous*!' The woman was in even more of a fury now.

'And who do you think I am, a Parisian?' The guy shook his head and returned to his meal.

'It is typical of us,' Léanne said. 'Here on the Côte, we think we can do anything, because we are chez nous.

We can break the law, do anything, because it is Parisian law.'

'Maybe someone should give the old dear a bucket of ice cubes,' I suggested.

'You are right.' Léanne made to stand up, but I told her to finish her squid and went to ask the waitress for a 'seau de glaçons', which I delivered to the table myself.

Mother and daughter were melodramatically grateful, and the wrist-dunking ceremony was performed with a full set of sound effects, including the loud clanking of the mother's gold bracelet against the side of the ice bucket.

'Merci, Monsieur, merci,' the daughter repeated, glaring over her shoulder at her mother's attacker, who was giving his full attention to a chocolate mousse.

I returned to my own table, where Léanne was looking thoughtful.

'That was kind,' she said, almost as if it contradicted something she'd believed about me before.

'I ought to be going,' I said. 'I have to make some important phone calls.'

'Oh.' She looked disappointed. 'You don't want coffee, or dessert?'

'No.' This whole situation was getting dangerously cosy.

'Maybe we can have a drink later?' she said.

'A drink?'

'Yes. If your girlfriend is not returning before tomorrow, I suppose you are free?'

'Well . . .'

'Meet me for a drink at six o'clock in the hotel bar? Please?'

'OK.' She'd made it impossible to refuse.

'Excellent. Do not worry, I will pay the bill,' she said.

'Oh no, no, allow me, please.' I pulled out my credit card

from my shorts and sent my hotel key skidding across the table. The room number landed face up, staring Léanne in the eye like a crude invitation.

Bugger this, I said to myself, pull yourself together. I picked up my key, turned towards the cash desk and collided with the old Maman, who'd been limping from the table to her lounger. The ice bucket tipped down the front of her knee-length T-shirt, making her scream even louder than when her wrist had been hit by the flying parasol.

'You must excuse Monsieur, he's not from chez nous,' Léanne called out, laughing.

3

If I'd been daring or drunk enough, I could have jumped off the balcony of my hotel room into the channel that ran between the island and the mainland, a cobalt-blue current that flowed gently with the breeze, from east to west. The town was so close that from the balcony, I could practically read the gold logos on the sunglasses of people driving along the seafront, and yet here it was completely peaceful, the only sound the slap-slap of the water on the rocks below.

In my head, though, things were much less peaceful. I was being buffeted back and forward between meeting Léanne for a drink and just not turning up. Difficult to avoid her, though, on such a small island.

There was nothing ambiguous about the meeting, I tried to convince myself. I didn't fancy her. There was something too tough about her. Unlike M, who had several layers of fragility just below the surface, Léanne seemed to have a diamond-hard inner core. The way she'd breezed up to me and sat there in her bikini. The completely unconcerned way she'd insisted we meet up for a drink. She didn't give a damn if I had a girlfriend. She'd seen the opening and gone for it. It's what they say about French women – they're fearless, conscience-free man-eaters. And now she wanted to tear a chunk of flesh off me.

No, no, I was being too arrogant. Just because a girl invites you out for a drink doesn't mean there's anything more to it. She was amused by the coincidence of meeting up again, and she was travelling alone, so she wanted a bit of company. And she probably doesn't get that many chances to speak English with a genuine Brit. I'd met language groupies like her before. Groupies of any kind, though, were the last thing I needed.

'Bloody hell, M,' I said to a passing seagull, 'why did you have to bugger off to Marseille?'

I needed advice, and as I'd often done before, I yielded to a self-destructive part of my nature and called the one man who was sure to make me feel even more confused.

'Jake? Hi, it's Paul.'

'Pol! Hey, man. How are you going?'

I told him I was in a bit of a pastis, and described my encounter with Léanne.

'Lay-ann? What nationality is that?' His first question about any girl.

'French.'

'Frinsh? Oh mon dieu, Pol, you're so pre-visible.'

'What?'

'I mean, merde. An English girl, then a Frinsh. Can't you fuck a spaniel for a change?'

'A spaniel?'

124

'Yeah, what do you call them? A girl from Spain. Espagnole. Or at least an Italienne.'

I told him that geography had nothing to do with my problem, and tried to describe the whole M–Léanne situation to him.

'It's très simple, man,' he pronounced. 'You fucked the Anglaise, right? So now fuck the Frinsh. It's repetitive, but at least it's a changement.'

As usual, he was driving me over the cliff of despair.

'God, Jake. Don't you ever think beyond your next orgasm? What about emotions? Have you got a girlfriend at the moment?'

'Yeah.'

'What nationality is she?'

'D'accord, man. Touché.' He sounded sheepish. 'She's American.'

'Aha.'

'But she's a Cajun, so at least she's a different group ethnic. And my posy touches her.'

'Kinky.'

'Don't mock yourself of me, Pol. She comprehends my posy. She *reads* it.'

'Wow.' So Jake's new girlfriend was into SM.

'She likes me to write it on her with maple syrup. I dunk my zizi in the syrup and then—'

'Too much information, Jake, thank you.' I had enough sexual complications overloading my brain without Jake inserting himself into my photo album.

'And parling of posy,' he said, 'what about Elodie's pair?'

'Her pair of what?'

'Her dad – her père.'

'Jean-Marie?'

'Yeah. Have you discuted my festival with him? Can

he pass my demand for fon to the Francophony minister?'

'Maybe, I don't know,' I said.

'It's pressing, man, it's urging.'

'OK, I'll try him again. Meanwhile, thanks a million for all the advice.'

'No problem, man, you sérieusement needed it.'

I hung up, and I had to admit that I was feeling better. Just talking to someone who was a billion times more screwed up than me, and didn't even know it, had done me good. It was like having a headache and then seeing someone else get guillotined.

I speed-dialled Elodie's dad.

'Jean-Marie?'

'Pol. Are you with Elodie?'

'No.'

'Ah. Merde. You know where she is?'

'No, don't you?'

'No. We have had a dispute. She does not answer my calls.'

'A dispute about what?'

'This marriage to the cretin aristocrat, of course.'

'Valéry? I've met him. He's a nice guy.'

'Maybe, but his grandmother is a vieille pétasse.'

So Bonne Maman was an old fartbag as well as a bitch and a vache. This posh lady wasn't getting much respect from Elodie's family. I wondered why father and daughter had fallen out. They seemed to be on exactly the same wavelength.

'Aren't you glad she's marrying into a family like that?' I asked. 'It sure beats some of her old boyfriends, like the bimbo model and the old rock-star dwarf.'

'And you, of course, Pol.'

'And me, yes, merci beaucoup. I think she must be in

Saint Tropez. I've got to go there and discuss the catering with the pétasse, as you call her.'

Jean-Marie laughed and loosened up a little. 'Just don't let yourself be snobbed,' he told me. 'They are not better than us, you know. France is a republic, not a monarchy. Don't let the pétasse think she is a queen.'

'She's going to be a client, Jean-Marie, and I always think that clients ought to feel like royalty.'

He growled at me. 'You have spent too long in the USA, mon ami. Here in France, we want all our clients to be terrified of us.'

'OK, Jean-Marie.' It was usually easiest to agree and ignore him. 'Talking of America, have you had any thoughts about my friend Jake's project?'

'What? Oh, yes. You think I have time for idiots who want to encourage those Cajun losers to write poems? Find Elodie and tell her to call me. OK? Au revoir.'

It seemed Jake might have to look for other sources of support. It was sad, but deep down I felt that anything that limited the supply of Jake's poetry, or even poems that he had influenced, was ultimately kinder to the planet.

I put in a call to Elodie, who ranted on about her dad not understanding what was at stake, and then said she had to go because it was 'la crise totale' over at the chateau in Saint Tropez.

'What kind of crisis?' I asked.

'No time to explain. Just come quickly. Bye.'

She hung up, and left me wondering what sort of chaos I'd be walking into when I went over to Saint Tropez. Although it couldn't possibly be more complicated than the merde I was in here on Bendor.

4

Merde was only one of the words that came to mind when I saw Léanne perched on a stool at the hotel bar. She was wearing a backless black dress, and had her hair loose. Her bare legs were crossed, and her smooth, firm calves tapered down to a pair of chic heels. She was in full man-hunting gear.

What's more, it was six o'clock on the dot. No French woman turns up on time for a drink with a man. If she does, she's being way too keen. A French guy will automatically assume she's gagging for sex and probably suggest skipping dinner and going straight upstairs.

Being a Brit, though, and not at all on the prowl, I said good evening and told her she was looking beautiful. A gentleman could do no less.

She hopped off the stool and raised her face so that I could kiss her cheeks.

'You're drinking pastis,' I said.

'Yes, I'm a Susan girl,' she replied.

'A what?'

She laughed, and had another go. 'A sudden girl?'

'Sorry?'

'You know, from the thouse.'

'Ah yes.' It was that old French chestnut, the problem of pronouncing 'southern' and 'south'. They have the same problem with clothes – 'clo-zez'. I gave her a short lesson and we laughed together at her lisping attempts to get the 's' and 'th' in the right place.

'I thought it was mainly a man's drink,' I said when we'd got her lip–tongue coordination more or less sorted out.

'Yes, maybe I drink it because I work in a man's world.'

'I would have thought there'd be more women tourist guides.'

'Oh. No, in the, uh, *south*, there are lots of men guides. What do you drink?'

I opted for a Muscat. We clinked glasses, looking each other in the eyes to ensure that we had ten years of good sexual luck (though not necessarily with each other, of course), and she suggested we move outside to the terrace.

'There's a bit of a wind,' I said. 'I wouldn't want you to catch cold.' Large areas of her ribcage and upper chest were bare.

'I never feel the cold.' She watched me, completely aware of where my eyes were pointing.

We went outside on to a wide terrace that overlooked a small swimming pool and the wrinkly sea. The sun was well on its way to the horizon for its evening dip, and the town opposite us was beginning to sink into shadow. Streetlamps were flickering like candles, as if the breeze could bend rays of light. It was amazingly peaceful. This was the jetski beach disco Côte d'Azur, half an hour from the big city of Marseille? Maybe, but off season there was only dusk and sea breeze.

'Your girlfriend, what is her job exactly?' Léanne asked.

I tried to summarize what M had told me about ocean ecology without revealing anything to do with sturgeon.

'And for what institute does she work?'

I had to confess I didn't know. I told her we hadn't known each other very long.

'An English university, I suppose, or a French one?'

'I didn't ask the name, I'm afraid.' I felt stupid, not even knowing where my girlfriend worked. But then I didn't think I'd actually mentioned the address of my tea room, either. 'She's a freelance, on a kind of mission down here,' I said.

'Ah? What mission?'

'She's working with French scientists at the ocean-ography institutes and aquariums. On some obscure ecological problem. Toxic algae,' I improvised.

'Algae?'

'Yes, seaweed.'

'Ah, *algues*. What is the problem?'

'They suffocate fish, I think. And kill sea urchins.'

'Oocheens?'

'Yes. You call them *oursins*.'

'Ah.' Léanne nodded, apparently satisfied. 'Now tell me about this marriage. Your, uh, cat-ring?'

'Catering, yes.' I gave her a run-through of the main characters in my gastronomic soap opera, starting with Elodie the emergency waltzer, going on to the farting bitch grand-mère, and even following up with a short portrait of Valéry winking at me in the police van.

As she listened, Léanne laughed, and something in her expression changed. It was like when I'd gone to get the iced water for the old lady with the bruised wrist. My story seemed to reveal things about me that didn't quite tally with her preconceptions. I wondered what she'd assumed I'd be like. A typical businessman lothario, maybe, or a millionaire yacht owner, rather than a wholesale buyer of anchovies.

'And how did you meet M?' she asked. Léanne really was interested in her, I thought, which very strange if she was trying to pick me up. Maybe she did just want company.

I told her how we'd bumped into each other by an aquarium in Las Vegas, met again on a pier in LA, and then hooked up as soon as I got back from America.

'So you weren't with her for the summer?' she asked.

'No, I was in California. What about you? Do you have a boyfriend or a husband?' I looked pointedly down at her bare ring finger.

'No,' she said quickly. 'I am alone at the moment.'

'Oh.'

We spent a silent minute looking over towards the mainland. The streetlamps had won the battle for domination of the sky, and Bandol was glowing warmly, its ribbons of light festooning the dark landmass.

'You know,' I said, 'no matter what you think about humanity, we are pretty damn good at electric lighting. In fact, Earth might even be the only place in the universe that has electric light. I mean, I know it's overheating the atmosphere, but sometimes it looks fantastic, doesn't it?'

Lucky M couldn't hear me saying that, I thought. But Léanne nodded.

'Yes, I am sure that these toxic *algues* can also be beautiful to some people,' she said. Coming from M this would have been heavily sarcastic, but Léanne was simply joining me in my train of thought. Conversation with her flowed very easily.

'Are you hungry?' she asked, and without waiting for a reply, added, 'Will you have dinner with me?'

'Avec plaisir,' I said, and escorted her indoors.

The hotel's first floor was decorated with a mixture of medieval austerity and boutiquey excess. The lounge featured a stone fireplace and thick beams, combined with large panels of pure colour along the walls – tangerine, lime, blood and turquoise. Old armchairs and sofas had been re-covered with pale linen and scattered with pink and yellow cushions.

The restaurant itself was more formal, and although it

was early, a few people were already dining, talking in hushed tones. Our table was covered with a thick white tablecloth and topped with a bouquet of fresh flowers.

The waitress brought us menus and I opened the wine list first.

'You choose the wine before the food?' Léanne was amused at this breach of restaurant protocol.

'Why not? I like to drink the wine that was made closest to the restaurant. Look.' I pointed to a name that had sprung to my attention – a rosé, Domaine de l'île des Embiez. 'We should have that,' I said. 'It's from the other Ricard island. It was probably delivered by boat.'

Léanne didn't get the importance of this, so I explained my new-found obsession for reducing the carbon footprint of everything I ate and drank down here on the south coast.

'Not that I'm trying to tell you what to order,' I said. 'I mean, feel free to have the Argentinian beef and a mango salad.'

'Are you an ecologist, too?' she asked. 'What do you call them in English, a rainbow warrior?'

'Eco-warrior? No, I'm not that active. I'm just an eco-worrier.'

I then had to spend about five minutes explaining the pun, with all the associated pronunciation exercises.

I realized that I was letting myself be drawn in by Léanne. Letting myself be seduced – there was no other word for it. She was making me talk about myself, making me feel important. It was a classic guy's technique – by rights I should have been doing it to her.

The food came and we ate. She watched me eating, apparently thoughtful.

I was just staring at the menu for a third time, debating whether to follow my dessert with a *digestif*, when Léanne started rummaging in her handbag and produced a phone. She listened intently for a few seconds then turned to me, all seductiveness gone from her face.

'Sorry, I must go,' she said, standing up. First M, now her. Every woman I met wanted to leave me.

'What?'

'It is very urgent.' She paused and looked down at me. 'See you later.'

'OK,' I said, though I had no idea when this might be. I got up, preparing to say a French goodbye with a kiss on the cheeks, but she was already on her way out of the restaurant. I saw her stop to talk to the waitress, no doubt explaining why she'd left. I wished someone would explain it to me.

The waitress told me that my bill had been settled, and then I was on my own at the table, wondering what the hell had happened. Maybe it was the toxic algae in the Med, I thought. It seemed to drive all the women down here crazy.

I wandered downstairs and into the night, expecting to see Léanne being whisked away in a speedboat or something similarly dramatic. But everything was peaceful. The distant lights were winking at me across the channel as if they knew what was going on and didn't want to tell me.

I took a long, deep breath of the fresh night air, and was about to let it all out again when a black-clad arm clamped itself across my chest and pressed so hard that I thought my lungs might start bulging out of my nostrils. My hands were grabbed from behind and twisted up so that I had to bend forward to avoid snapping both my elbows.

I wanted to complain, but something warm and smooth was stuffed into my mouth, and I just had time to think, 'Gross – that's someone's leather glove,' before a French voice rasped in my ear that I was to shut my gob (difficult with a glove in it) and come with them. Not that I had much choice.

As I was (literally) frogmarched across the quay towards the fake Italian village, I tried to work out who could be doing the marching. The commandos, back for a second bite at the English cherry? Or, more likely, caviar bandits who'd heard about my snooping. Shit, they'd probably got M as well. But why? The closest we'd got to them was one alleged sighting of a fish somewhere in the Camargue.

We stomped between the cute fishermen's cottages, and I was shoved into a deeply shaded courtyard. I looked up to see that we were outside the Roman temple. I gave up thinking about why this was happening and concentrated on being scared. Suddenly the island had stopped being tranquil and become eerily empty.

I was spun expertly round and pulled into a sitting position on cold stone. The temple and its grounds were in total darkness, but the moonlight reflected off a window and lit up the face that was now thrust close to my own.

I recognized it. It belonged to the plain-clothes cop from Collioure, the guy in the leather jacket who'd been thrown out of the gendarmerie.

He breathed a mixture of pastis fumes and stale cigarettes at me, and informed me that he was going to remove the glove from my mouth and that if I shouted he would take great pleasure in hurting me.

I nodded. This seemed a fair exchange.

The leather was pulled out from between my jaws, and I turned to spit the bad taste into a flower bed. I tried, and failed, to get a look at another guy, who was holding my right arm in a wrestling hold to stop me running away.

'Bonsoir,' I said. I read this book once which said that wishing a French person 'Bonjour' or 'Bonsoir' is a kind of

Open Sesame. After receiving the greeting, they feel sub-consciously obliged to be pleasant to you.

'Ta gueule,' the leather-jacketed cop growled. Shut up. He obviously hadn't read the book.

Knowing that he was a policeman, though, made me feel slightly less afraid. After all, one of Valéry's uncles had told this guy and his mates to leave us alone. And he'd been forced to obey.

'How can I help you?' I asked.

'Ta gueule,' he repeated, and my arm was twisted slightly higher.

'Have I done something illegal?'

'Ta. Gueule.' This time he spat each word between clenched teeth. But – I noticed – he didn't resort to violence, or get his colleague to do so. Someone some-where had decided I wasn't to be roughed up. This was very reassuring, and I felt my heart rate slow to under two hundred for the first time in several minutes.

The grin on Leather Jacket's face was less reassuring, though. Seeing that I had apparently decided to shut up, he was looking decidedly cocky. Perhaps he was waiting for the person who had instructed him not to hurt me. Maybe they had told him that they wanted the pleasure of drawing first blood.

What was more, I now reasoned, there was nothing to stop a policeman moonlighting for the opposition. This guy could well be in with the caviar pirates. After all, M had said something about not wanting to tell the police, or any-one in uniform, about her search for illegal sturgeon. I heard footsteps behind me, and saw Leather Jacket look towards the entrance to the courtyard. My pulse started to pick up again. Here it comes, I thought, bracing myself as my heart neared explosion point.

But it stopped beating altogether when I saw who we'd been waiting for.

Léanne was standing in front of me, a denim jacket covering the top of her backless dress. She looked like a punk singer, half chic, half grungy. And her voice was as urgent as a punk song, too.

'Listen, Pol,' she said, before I could ask what was happening, 'Everything I will tell you is true. So believe me. OK?'

But as she spoke in slow, clear French, I shook my head, first in disbelief, and then to try and wake up from the nightmare she was pulling me into.

'Bollocks,' I said when she'd finished.

'Uh?' She didn't know the word.

'Conneries,' I translated. 'Merde.'

'No, it is true.' She repeated the central facts again. 'Your friend Gloria, or M – she is not a scientist. She has a very different job. She is visiting different criminals, trying to recruit an assassin.'

'Bollocks.' M was an expert on sturgeon, there was no doubt about that. She was obsessed with the poor, ugly brutes.

Léanne interrupted my thoughts. 'You have not noticed that she does bizarre things?'

'No. Well, yes. But of course she does bizarre things. She's a scientist.'

'She goes suddenly to all these meetings.'

'With other scientists, yes.'

'No, with criminals. We have listened to some suspect telephone conversations. We have followed her. We have followed you. This is why I was in Collioure. And the two men in your hotel there? They are police. And as you have seen, the man who interviewed you in the gendarmerie, he is in my team. Except –' she turned to glare at Leather

136

Jacket, 'that he has not obeyed my orders. He was not supposed to interview you.'

The guy folded his arms and looked away. He was a bit
of a maverick, it seemed.

'It was comic, though.' She lowered her voice. 'What you
said him to about the "big fish", you know? He thought you
were talking about a gangster. When you said the big
fish was from Iran or Russia, he was convinced he
had discovered the biggest secret in world crime.' She
laughed.

I saw the leather-jacketed cop straining to understand.
Léanne didn't enlighten him.

'So you're a policewoman?' I asked.

'Yes.'

'Where's your badge?'

'In this dress?' She ran her hands over her hips to
illustrate the lack of pockets.

'And you think M's hiring a killer? No way,' I said. 'To
kill who? A caviar pirate?'

'No.' Léanne took a deep breath. 'We were not
going to reveal it,' she said. 'But I must take a chance. We
supposed you were the accomplice, but now I am persuaded
that you are innocent. And maybe you can help to save
him.'

'Save who?'

She gulped. 'The President.'

'The President of what?'

'The President. Our President. *Le Président!*'

If I hadn't been choking, I would have laughed.

'You're nuts,' I said. This was way, way beyond bollocks.

'Nuts?'

'*Folle*. Why the hell would M be involved in a plot to kill
your President?'

'He has many enemies,' Léanne replied. 'The unions, the Mafia, terrorists . . .'

'And he is way too friendly with the Anglo-Saxons,' Leather Jacket chipped in, in French.

'Exactly,' I said. 'And M's English, so why would she want to kill a pro-English President?' What a steaming lump of merde. They'd got the wrong girl. She was hot-tempered, but not murderous.

'It is normal to be shocked.' Léanne stepped forward and started digging her nails into my biceps, staring into my eyes. 'Please, Pol, listen. M is not really English, she is half-French. She is not who she says.'

'Who is she, then?'

'I have no time to tell you. M is returning now, on the ferry. This is why I was obliged to interrupt our dinner. She will be here in ten minutes. So I give you the choice. You can help me to save my President. And say nothing to M. She cannot see us together. She cannot know we have met ourselves.'

'Met each other.' I corrected her English in a daze of denial. 'What's the other option?'

'If you do not promise to help, we must arrest you now, and her, and you will go to prison for twenty or thirty years.'

'*What?*' It was lucky she was holding on to my arms so tightly, because I felt like collapsing back into the flower bed. 'But you just agreed I'm innocent.'

'*I* think you are innocent. But I am not a judge. I do not want to arrest you now, because I need you. We do not know yet who will accept the contract, or who is paying M. We do not know exactly why they want to kill the President. So will you help us to find out?'

'I . . .' Until about ten minutes earlier, I'd been under the impression that my big dilemma of the night was going to be whether to give in and let this woman do naughty things to my body. And even that was going to be a toughie. This new set of options had come much, much too fast for my poor brain, which had been slowed down to even less than its usual snail's pace by my generous share of our bottle of rosé during dinner. Yes, she'd got me half-pissed, too, I realized. What a sucker I'd been.

'Please do not oblige me to arrest you, Pol,' Léanne said. 'My colleague here is impatient to recommence his interrogation. And in France, the judges are not troubled by a few marks on the face of a suspect.'

Leather Jacket nodded and grinned.

'What do you want me to do?' I asked.

'You must simply promise that you will tell M nothing about this. And you must quit the island tomorrow morning. Alone.'

'What?'

'You will take the first boat. You will be contacted and we will organize the – what do you say? – *la suite*.' She meant what came next, the immediate future. 'But first, you must call M now. She has left a message for you.'

'Oh.' I delved into my pocket. Of course, like a gentleman – especially one on a date with a lady other than his partner – I'd switched off my phone.

'Then you must dine with her.'

'Another dinner?'

'Yes. This is the natural thing to do. She must think you are waiting for her, alone.'

'But I can't eat another dinner. And this is the only restaurant on the island that's open in the evening. I can't go in there again. They've all seen me eating with you.'

'So you refuse?' Léanne looked sad, but in a very menacing way. She turned to Leather Jacket, and spoke to him in French. 'You deal with the suspect,' she said. 'I'm like the President – too friendly with the Anglais.'

5

The whole planet felt warped. Not just overheated by electric lights, but bent and buckled, spinning off-centre, heading for a collision with the moon. And I was alone with the knowledge, and not allowed to tell a soul.

I was down on the quayside, massaging my aching arm. Apart from the pain in my elbow and the taste of leather in my mouth, it was as if Léanne and her colleagues had never been there. As soon as I'd agreed to help them, they'd spirited away into the darkness, to be out of sight when M arrived.

The ferry docked in the miniature harbour, looking exactly as it had done when M and I had arrived the day before. Yet somehow it was profoundly different. At least one of the passengers on there, or a crew member, would be a cop. And M was no longer a lone scientist hurrying back from a meeting, she was caught up in a spiralling galaxy of people and events.

'Hi.' She strolled down the wide metal gangway and kissed me. 'We finished early. I told you we might.'

'Great. Did you learn anything new? Decide anything?' It was painful to look her in the eye.

'Bof,' she said evasively, and looked away. I was reminded of what Léanne had said about her not being English.

'Did you talk about the sturgeon in the Camargue? Getting an aerial survey?'

'Things don't happen that quickly,' she said.

Especially if you're not really trying to organize them, I thought.

'Weren't you going to tell them that you wanted out?' I asked. The idea came like a revelation. If she really was opting out, we could both offer to help Léanne. All I had to do was come clean with M, and we'd be off the hook.

She shrugged. Another French reflex. 'It's not that simple,' she said. 'They won't let me give up just yet. God, I'm starving.' She changed the subject brusquely. Or tried to, anyway.

'They can't force you to carry on if you don't want to, can they?' I asked.

'Force me? No. But you know how it is. When you've been working on a project for a while, you can't let people down.'

'I thought they were the ones letting *you* down, being too slow and not taking you seriously?' I blundered on, challenging her to convince me that she was for real. My theory about knowing when women were lying to me was being disproved before my very eyes.

She tutted. 'It's too depressing to talk about.' As usual, when it came to specifics, she clammed up. 'Have you eaten?'

Decision time.

What would happen if I told M all about my dinner with the mystery woman I'd seen in Collioure? Would she confess everything and appeal for help, or would she have some totally different explanation for what had been going on?

What if Léanne had simply got it all wrong?

So many questions, so little time to imagine the answers. I could only trust my instincts.

'No, I haven't had dinner yet,' I said.

It was done. The deception was beginning.

*

The same waitress escorted us to the same table as if she'd never seen me before in her life. The other diners, though, had not been briefed, and a few of them stopped in mid-chew to gape. One woman frowned disapprovingly, while her husband gave me a discreet nod. I understood why. First the tête-à-tête with a half-naked brunette, now candlelit supper with a curvaceous blonde. Smooth operator indeed.

'The wine list, Sir?' the waitress enquired.

'Why don't you choose?' I gave the list to M. I couldn't even face reading the names of all those bottles.

She began perusing the food and wine menus. I observed her, almost admiringly. She had to be under insane pressure, even more than usual if she'd genuinely told her bosses that she wanted out of her role in the assassination plot. And yet she was perfectly able to focus on what she was going to eat. Unless it was a displacement activity. Yes, that would explain her lapses into moodiness. What an idiot I'd been, believing that all her stress was caused by a fish.

'Are you having a starter?' M asked, and I felt my digestive tract whimper in pain.

'No, I don't think so,' I said. 'I had quite a lot of peanuts with my aperitif.'

'What are you having, then?' she asked, as I resigned myself to reading the list of tortures on offer.

'Just a salad. I don't feel too good.' Which was the first true word I'd spoken to her all evening.

'So how many aperitifs did you have with your peanuts?' She looked at me teasingly.

'Three Muscats at least.' I tried to look guilty. 'And I had some squid at lunchtime that wasn't all that fresh.' Back on the lies again.

'Shame. Because I feel like eating something big and bloody.' Was it my overheated imagination, or did she have a murderous glint in her eye as she said it?

'I'd have thought that you'd be a prime candidate for being a veggie,' I said. 'You know, an English ecologist working in London, studenty background.' I watched her carefully.

'No,' she said. 'There aren't as many veggies as before, I find. Not now there's so much organic meat around. And Brits are much more into the taste of things these days, don't you think?'

Good evasive answer, I thought. Like all her answers seemed to be.

'I fancy a nice juicy steak to put me in the mood.' M was leaning in close. 'Tonight, I'm going to be the hunter, you're the prey. I want your body.' I must have been blanching, because she looked hurt. 'Don't you want my body?'

'Yes, of course,' I said quickly. 'I'm just feeling a bit, you know . . .'

She examined my face. 'You do look rather pale – like you did after you got arrested. No one's arrested you here, have they?' She laughed, and then narrowed her eyes at me. Her joke had turned into a serious question.

I forced a laugh. 'Wine,' I said. 'I think I need to get drunk.'

'That's more like it.' M waved for the waitress and ordered a bottle of île des Embiez rosé. I saw the waitress bite her tongue so as not to say, 'Ah, Monsieur's usual?'

M devoured an undercooked steak with potato purée aux truffes, followed by a fruity mousse and a mountain of miniature macaroons with her coffee. I picked my way through a green salad.

On the way back to our room in the annex, M suggested a walk around the island.

'It's so quiet here,' she said. 'It feels like we're a million miles from all the headaches of life.' If only she knew that a headache for her was hiding behind every shrub on the island. 'Let's walk along the seashore,' she went on. 'It'll be dark, and there's no one about.' She slid her arm round my waist. 'We can make love on the rocks.'

Under normal circumstances, of course, nothing would have given me greater pleasure, but the idea of doing so while being observed – filmed, even – by a bunch of French cops would send anyone's libido diving for cover.

'Come on, lover,' M said, pulling at my arm.

'Oh God,' I groaned. 'Sorry.' I clutched my stomach, puffed out my cheeks, and tried to look green. 'That squid. And the wine.'

I turned and ran for the hotel, remembering at the last minute to limp like a man whose entrails are being attacked from within by squirming hordes of bacteria.

6

The sky was the lightest blue I'd ever seen, a shade so pale and transparent that a paint manufacturer would have got himself sued for putting the word 'blue' on the lid. Across this silky background, like an accident on a Fauvist's palette, lay a long splash of pineapple-yellow cloud, its edges tinged with coral pink.

It was seconds before dawn. I was sitting on the first ferry off the island, shivering slightly, both because of the cool air and the thought of what I was doing.

I was sneaking off. Something I hadn't done since I was a

student and owed a month's rent to a landlord who refused to fix my heating in the middle of February.

I'd left a note for M at the foot of the bedroom door, apologizing for the previous night's fiasco. I'd taken all kinds of stomach pills that the hotel had kindly provided, and made frequent noisy visits to the bathroom to spit them out before they did any damage. Poor M had not had the fun soirée she'd hoped for.

My note said that Elodie had called in the middle of the night, in floods of tears, and that I'd promised to catch the first boat to go and sort things out in Saint Tropez. I told M to call me as soon as she woke up, though I wasn't sure whether I'd have the guts to answer.

I was sorely tempted to give Saint Tropez a miss and head to the nearest airport. Like page two of my passport said, Her Majesty requires all those whom it might concern to offer the bearer assistance and protection in times of trouble. I figured that now was the perfect time for Air France to heed the old girl's request and find me a seat on the first plane out of there.

The ferry pulled away from the quayside, and I shot a guilty glance up at the window of the bedroom I'd just left. It was still dark. M was asleep in there, dreaming of either endangered fish or an endangered President. One day I might find out whether she was English, French, a scientist or a booking agent for assassins, but for the moment it hardly seemed to matter.

The boat picked up speed. I touched my passport in my jacket pocket, making sure my escape route was open.

'Bonjour, Pol. I am happy that you are here.'

Léanne had appeared beside me, and laid a denim-jacketed arm almost tenderly across my shoulders. She was wearing jeans now, and had washed off her femme fatale make-up, but seemed to be making an effort to appear less steely than the night before.

'I hope it will be a bon jour,' I told her. 'And I'm glad to see you, too. I want to ask you a few questions. And I warn you, I can always tell whether a woman is telling me the truth or not.'

I hoped Léanne wouldn't see through the lie.

On the mainland, a car was waiting for us, its engine running. It was a small grey Renault, driven by a large, snow-white man. He was one of the gay twins from the Collioure hotel, and nodded to me as I got in the back. The man in the passenger seat swivelled to scowl at me with a look that said 'I've got my eye on you'. It was the leather-jacketed cop.

'Take us to the *anse*,' Léanne said, getting in beside me. I hoped this wasn't a southern word for dungeon or torture chamber.

In fact, it couldn't have been further from a dungeon. It was a secluded, almost circular bay just outside the centre of Bandol. The sea was deep blue in the middle of the *anse*, and the lightest turquoise around the sandy edge, a colour so refreshing that I wanted to drink it, or at the very least lie down and let the cool, still water soothe away my worries.

The car dropped us off at the top of a small cliff overlooking the beach. It was edged with giant rounded pines so fragrant that the word could have been invented to describe this warm, green smell.

'Let us talk in peace,' Léanne said, pointing to a flight of concrete steps. She told the other two guys to wait by the car.

Below the pines were terraced gardens, one of which

belonged to a hotel built into the cliff. It had as many rooms below the road line as above – the guests on the ground floor could probably have reached out of their rooms and dipped their toes in the water.

Down on the beach, I took off my shoes and did just that, wiggling my toes in the chilly sea and feeling that at least ten small parts of my body were free.

Léanne sat on a rock at the water's edge and watched me.

'Why can't I just go and confront M?' I asked. 'It'd be a pleasant change to know what's really going on for once. And by the way, have you got some ID this morning?'

She smiled patiently and pulled out an ID card decorated with red, white and blue stripes. I went to sit beside her, to get a closer look.

'Brigade Anti-Criminalité,' the card read. 'Commissaire Cogolin, Léanne'. The mugshot was so grim that the ID had to be real. No faker would use that bad a photo of themselves.

'No, you cannot confront her,' she said. 'I understand that you want to know the truce' (despite my lessons, she still couldn't pronounce 'th') 'but it is not time for a confrontation yet. Imagine that you are a French husband.'

'What?'

'You are a French husband, and you have discovered that your wife has a secret lover. You must follow her, observe her, but not confront her before you find his name and you are certain that he exists.'

'It's not the same thing at all,' I objected. 'I know French lovers don't have a good reputation, but not many of them are planning to kill the President. This is a bit more serious than trying to find out if my wife's shagging her Pilates instructor.'

When I'd expressed this in simpler English, Léanne agreed.

'Yes, you're right, it is much, much more serious.' She picked up a handful of coarse, white sand and threw it into the water. A shoal of tiny green fish darted out of the way. 'Let me tell you some things about M,' Léanne went on. 'You believed she is English, yes?'

'Yes.'

'No. She is half-French. Her father was French.'

'*Was?*'

'He is dead.'

'How did he die? When?'

'You must ask her. It is not good if I tell you and then you accidentally reveal that you know it, you see?'

I nodded. I could see the logic.

'And you believed she was in London before Collioure, yes?' Léanne asked.

'Yes,' I agreed.

'No. She was already in the thouse of France, on a yacht in Saint Tropez.'

Now Léanne mentioned it, M's all-over tan did tally more with a couple of months on the Med than a rainy summer by the Thames.

'The first time we heard of her,' Léanne continued, 'was when a dealer was arrested, and he revealed some things to us that he had heard on the yacht.'

'What things?'

'I cannot tell you.'

'Well whose boat was it?'

'Sorry.' She shook her head. 'Let us just say, a person who has no reason to be happy with our President, or any part of the French government.'

'A terrorist? A criminal? The husband of one of the President's mistresses?'

In reply, she only shrugged her unwillingness to answer.

'And M was on this yacht?' I asked.

'Yes.'

'Doing what?'

'We do not know, exactly, but she was there, and when she quitted the boat, she started her mission.'

'And her mission is to hire a hitman?'

'Hitman?'

I mimed a sniper taking out a distant target.

'Yes,' she said.

'But why should M work for them? You said she has a reason to hate the President.'

'A President of any country has many enemies,' she said evasively. 'Anyway, I am more concerned by practicalities. We know who she sees when she goes to her meetings, but these are not the leaders. They are the – how do you say? – midwives?'

'Middle men.'

'Yes. We need for you to become an *espion* – how do you say?'

'Spy?'

'Yes, a spy. We know who the middle men are. You must try to find out who is their chef.' I guessed that she didn't mean their cook.

'How am I supposed to do that?'

'You must listen, ask some questions, try to discover when is her next meeting. Not too many questions, though. She must not – what do you say? – doubt?'

I was the one with doubts. If I'd still been working in London, I would have been sure that it was all a wind-up, a huge piss-take organized by some twisted bastard in the office. But the French don't go in for practical jokes like that. And Léanne's ID was no joke at all. Neither was her determination to use me. I wondered how far she would have gone to get information if she'd thought I was part of the plot. That backless dress hadn't just been for decoration.

I looked across the water, where a solo swimmer was doing a lazy crawl towards the open sea. It would be great, I thought, to dive in and follow him, and not stop swimming till all this nonsense had gone away.

'Wait here a moment,' Léanne said. She stood up and made a phone call, and a few seconds later, the leather-jacketed cop came bounding down the steps on to the beach. 'Keep an eye on him,' Léanne ordered. The guy nodded and came to stand over me as though I might suddenly leap into the sea and splash to freedom.

It was tempting. I saw that the lone swimmer had reached the edge of the bay. He was now having a rest, floating on his back and gazing up into the cloudless sky. I could imagine the sense of blissful achievement he would be feeling – the pure, tingling pleasure of being alive. A piercing envy shot through me, from my throbbing head to my impatiently twiddling toes. No, it wasn't envy exactly, it was an urgent need to share that all-over tingle, to prove to myself that I was, for the moment at least, still in control of my nerve endings.

Léanne had walked away along the beach and was speaking on the phone. The urgency and seriousness of her movements reminded me of M. Maybe they were involved in the same story after all.

'So you're going to play Mata Hari, uh?' Leather Jacket was grinning at me.

'Mata Hari?' I thought she was an oriental dancer.

'You don't know her? Famous spy. She fucked German generals and they gave her secrets. So you fuck your demi-Anglaise, and if you're good enough, maybe she'll tell us something useful.'

The cop spoke slowly and clearly, to make sure I understood his French.

I turned away, trying my best to ignore him.

'We call it *l'espionage horizontal*,' Leather Jacket went on. 'It is a noble French tradition. Mata Hari was not the only one. France has used lots of whores in this way.' He started to laugh, but broke off when Léanne began walking back towards us.

'What have you said to M?' she asked me. 'What reason have you given to quit the island?'

I told her about Saint Tropez and Elodie's wedding.

'This is good,' Léanne said. 'Yes. You leave her alone for a day or two. Maybe she will make some interesting calls. Maybe she will return to Marseille. We know that she has some problem there. You occupy yourself with this marriage, then you can begin the espionage.'

'Horizontal,' Leather Jacket added.

'Who will you see in Saint Tropez?' Léanne asked.

'Valéry,' I told her, 'the other guy who was arrested in Collioure.'

'Ha, ce petit con,' Leather Jacket spat. 'Him and his rich druggie friends. We'll get them.'

Léanne nodded. 'There are many arrestations in Saint Tropez,' she said. 'Lots of raids on the chic cafés. If your Valéry tries to buy cocaine, maybe he will get a bad surprise.'

'Valéry, cocaine? No way.' I tried my best to forget the drugs he'd offered me in the police car. 'He's a clean-living boy. Really close to his family, especially his dear old grandmother, and he still lives at his parents' home . . .'

As I stumbled on with my protestations of Valéry's cocaine-white innocence, it struck me how very far I was from anything you could call home. Here I was, defending the French fiancé of my French ex-boss's daughter, while being press-ganged into saving the life of France's President from a bunch of local killers.

I couldn't have been more embroiled in this foreign country's affairs if I'd been chained up in the deepest dungeon in the Bastille, with nothing to read except the rules of pétanque.

FOLLOW THE DEALER

Saint Tropez

1

THE FIRST PERSON I ever met who'd actually been to Saint Tropez was Elodie's dad, Jean-Marie. I'd recently arrived to work for him in Paris, and we were returning to the office after lunch. We were waiting to cross a posh street near the Champs-Elysées when we saw what looked like a hairy iguana scuttling towards us.

On closer inspection, it turned out to be a woman, though there was probably not much of her original DNA left. She was aged somewhere between sixty and six hundred, and had had so many facial operations that her nose was the size of a peanut and her lips could have been used as a sofa. Someone had glued several kilos of blond seaweed to the top of her head, and her body had been wedged into a leather catsuit made for a twelve-year-old, so that her industrially renovated breasts overflowed at the neckline like a pair of half-melted Camemberts. She was on the highest stilettos I'd ever seen, and looked in grave danger of breaking both ankles.

But she only had ten or so yards to walk, from the middle of the road, where she had abandoned her silver Smart Car, to the terrace of a restaurant that was so expensive it had as many parking valets as waiters.

The iguana lady was greeted with a syrupy smile by a hostess and shown to a table where a similarly reptilian woman was waiting for her. They did a mwa-mwa kiss, and then twitched their lips, which was probably as close as they got to smiling these days.

I'd never seen such creatures before, and asked Jean-Marie who, or what, they were.

He told me that they were a rare sub-species of French woman, and that I'd only see them if I hung about in chic areas like this one, because they spent most of their life cycle outside Paris.

'Where?' I asked.

'When they are not in Hungary for cheap surgery? In Saint Tropez,' he said. 'They all want to look like Brigitte Bardot in 1964. That whole town wants to pretend that it is 1964. Except for the people who fix the prices – they think it's 2064.'

Saint Tropez was, he went on, *the* place to go if you liked to watch rich old men pouring champagne over young girls' bikinis and see women pumped so full of silicone that they floated upright in the water. He hated it.

This was yet another subject on which he and Elodie didn't see eye-to-eye.

'Saint Trop's great,' she once told me. 'Best cocaine in France.'

Valéry's family's chateau wasn't actually in Saint Tropez – it was twenty kilometres southwest. It was a perfect Provençal mansion – a long, tall, chalky-white building, at least three floors high, with a gently sloping ochre-tiled roof. The windows along the top storey had rounded frames, and those on the floor below were stately rectangles with brick balconies. I couldn't see any lower because of the garden, which was even more stunning than the house itself. It was a luxuriant mass of vegetation – immaculate lawns, a jungle of flowers, the emerald finger of a cypress, a silver swathe of olive trees.

The driveway leading to this oasis was a double alley of date palms slicing through a field of grape vines. The branches of the palm trees burst upwards in vivid green fountains. The vines were turning a mellow yellow in the bright autumn sun.

And this paradise was set right on the shore, so that you could probably lie in bed and gaze past the palm trees to the glittering Mediterranean. Valéry's dad could call up his yacht crew in Saint Tropez and stay in his silk pyjamas until the boat appeared in the bay.

I pulled up outside the chateau grounds, between two massive green metal gates, and looked back along the coast road. Léanne had said that the cops would keep in touch, and I wondered if that included following me. One car passed, then another, and neither driver so much as glanced in my direction. There was no helicopter overhead, no glint of sunlight on binoculars in the woods. Maybe they were keeping their distance, I thought, trusting me not to fly away to a country where the Queen could protect me. Though reason told me that that wasn't the French style. Léanne and her men would be around here somewhere. They'd turn up soon enough.

The Peugeot I'd hired in Bandol crunched loudly along the driveway, between the trunks of palm trees that were chocolate brown and almost hairy, like elephant's legs. I was afraid one of them would deem the little car unworthy, and boot it into the sea.

It was around one thirty p.m., and I was starving. The purple grapes hanging on the vines looked so plump that I was tempted to stop for a picnic, but I'd just called Elodie to say I was at the gate, and she and Valéry were standing at the top of the drive waiting for me.

Elodie was gesturing at me to turn right, and I wondered why she would want me to slam into a date palm until I saw a small opening in the tree line. Steering carefully between two elephant legs, I turned on to a more modern, paved drive that led to the side of the house.

Elodie and Valéry reappeared, waving at me to carry on round to the back, into a well-hidden car park full of family-sized Renaults, with a red Mercedes sports car standing out from the crowd.

I parked with my bonnet snug against a huge bank of lavender, which was perfuming the air so forcefully that I felt a sudden urge to start sewing pot-pourri bags.

We said our hellos, and I noticed that Elodie had aged about ten years since I'd seen her in Paris the previous week. Not that she'd gone grey or wrinkly. It was her clothes. She was dressed as if she'd been invited to a frumps and geeks theme party. Her navy-blue skirt came down below the knee, and her blouse was cut to hide any sign that she might possess breasts. She was a nun on day release from the convent.

Valéry was looking pretty much how I'd seen him in Collioure – a big smile on his face, a pair of expensive sunglasses lodged in his floppy blond hair. Though he seemed to have *lost* ten years. His clothes were boyish, making him look like a kid on the verge of taking his baccalauréat. He was fidgeting with embarrassment.

'Uh, Paul, next time can you come on the new alley, not the old one?' He pointed towards the modern, tarmacked driveway. 'The old one with the palm trees, only my grandmother uses that.'

Oh dear. I wasn't even in the house and I'd already committed a gaffe.

'Sorry, Valéry. The big gate was open.'

'Yes, Bonne Maman arrived this morning. The gate is always open when she arrives. Anyway, you are just in time. Everyone is together in the salon for coffee.' With the rules of the house re-established, Valéry brightened up again.

'Coffee? Maybe I should have got a sandwich on the way . . .'

'Ah, yes, lunch is very early here,' Elodie said.

'It's Moo-Moo's fault,' Valéry explained.

'Moo-Moo?'

'My mother.'

'Her real name's Marie-Angélique,' Elodie informed me.

'Yes, here we eat at midday exactly,' Valéry said. 'She says we must respect God's timetable.'

'And He always has breakfast at eight and lunch at midday.' Elodie raised her eyes towards heaven in a plea for more flexible mealtimes.

'Oh, It is Bonne Maman who likes the early meals, really,' Valéry said. 'Moo-Moo is the pope who applies the laws, Bonne Maman is God. The rest of us are simply Adam and Eve.'

'I see.' The metaphor might be a bit scary, but I had to concede that the house looked like the Garden of Eden. The hellish goings-on in Bandol seemed an eternity away.

'You can meet Babou and Mimi, too, before they go to play golf,' Valéry said.

I turned to Elodie for help.

'His uncles, Charles-Henri and Dominic,' she explained.

Moo-Moo, Babou and Mimi. It sounded like a family of Teletubbies.

'Now, Paul, before you meet them, there is just one problem.' Valéry was looking pained again. 'Your clo-zez.'

'My clothes?'

'Yes.' Elodie took over. 'We must show the family that you are a good traiteur who will serve them champagne and grande cuisine. I do not want to be cruel, but today you look like the pizza boy.'

'Yes, well.' I couldn't explain that I'd practically been dragged out of bed in the middle of the night by the cops. 'Maybe I should get changed first, then?'

'I had to, so why shouldn't you?' Elodie led the way towards the house, lifting her skirt to show me where she would have preferred the hemline to be. She'd obviously had to frump down to please Moo-Moo.

'Ah.' A woman was standing in the doorway. She wore a pale-blue blouse with a rounded collar and a long pleated royal-blue skirt like Elodie's. Her dark hair was in a neck-length bob, topped off by a chunky felt headband. She was glowering at Elodie's exposed knees.

'Moo-Moo, voici Monsieur West,' Valéry announced. 'Il arrive de Londres.' I guessed he was exaggerating the length of my trip to excuse the crumpled state of my clothes. 'He's just going to change.'

Moo-Moo tore her eyes away from Elodie's knees, which had hastily been covered up again, and eyed me as if I was the snake arriving in her Eden.

'Hmm, well he must hurry if he wants coffee. No more after two o'clock, remember.'

'Oui, Moo-Moo.' Valéry spoke like a six-year-old.

The woman disappeared, and the three of us entered the

house in chastised silence, passing below a large, wrought-iron cross that was set in the wall, presumably to ward off vampires and bad caterers.

'No coffee after two o'clock?' I whispered.

'No stimulants,' Elodie replied, just as quietly. 'I think she is frightened that they will turn us into sex maniacs.'

We went up a winding staircase with peeling walls. It seemed to go on for hours. Eventually, we reached a narrow corridor with tiny round windows. The old servants' quarters, I guessed. I was being put in my place.

'This is now the children's floor,' Valéry said, and ducked into one of ten or so doorways.

I followed, and found myself in a musty room so small that Amnesty International would have started a poster campaign if a prisoner had been forced to sleep there. The ceiling was so low and sloping that Valéry actually had to reach down to open the skylight in the roof. It reminded me of the homes for midgets that I'd been shown when I first arrived in Paris and the estate agents thought it would be fun to take the piss out of a non-French-speaking immigrant. Except that those garrets weren't half-full of teddy bears and ancient kids' books.

'Sorry, it's the only free bed,' Valéry said. 'If it is too small, I will get you a room at the chambre d'hôte by the beach.'

'But politically, it is best to stay in the house,' Elodie added. 'N'est-ce pas, Valéry? Paul must be here to defend the marriage.'

'Yes, it would be good if you can stay.' Valéry bent down and swept a dozen or so teddies off the narrow bed so that it would, at a pinch, have been possible for a double-jointed yogi to lie down on it. He saw me staring at the mound of fake fur on the floor. 'There is one bear for every child in the family,' he said.

Wow, I thought, they say rodents breed, but they're nowhere near as prolific as the French upper classes.

'OK, I must go,' Valéry announced.

'Go?' Elodie was horrified.

'Yes, to Saint Trop. You know.' He clenched his facial features as if to communicate a telepathic secret.

'Now?' Elodie asked.

'Yes, it is arranged.' He kissed her on the forehead, shot a hearty grin at me and sped off down the corridor. Elodie stared after him.

'Urgent business?' I asked. 'Wedding stuff?'

She grunted. 'Huh! Stuff, yes, but not wedding stuff.'

A worry popped into my head. 'Elodie?' I tried to think how to put it diplomatically. 'He's not going out to buy coke, is he?' Balls to diplomacy. This was too important.

'Yes. I don't know why he can't wait until tonight.'

I remembered what Léanne had told me about dealers getting busted, and – even worse – the look of mean determination on the face of the leather-jacketed cop when he'd talked about Valéry.

'He's got to be very careful. The police are cracking down,' I began, before realizing that I couldn't explain how I knew so much about the Saint Tropez drugs trade. 'I overheard some people talking in Bandol,' I added. 'They said a big dealer in the white stuff had been caught red-handed and he was singing like a canary.'

'Uh?' Elodie's English was good, but the mix of colours was too much for her.

'Apparently the police in Saint Tropez are arresting lots of dealers and their customers,' I translated. 'Valéry ought to be careful.'

Elodie waved my concern out the window. 'Oh no, these aren't the sort of guys who get arrested in bars. To stop Valéry's dealer, the police would be obliged to annoy some very important people. He is – how do you say? – safe as a house?' She looked dubiously down at my shapeless bag. 'You must change quickly, Paul. We must take coffee with the family. Moo-Moo has told them you are here and she has probably said you are dressed like a tramp. You must show them different. You can show them different, can't you?'

'Well, I didn't bring my Paul Smith suit on holiday, but I do have a shirt that's been worn only ten or so times,' I told her.

'Well change, then.'

'OK.' I waited politely for her to leave the room while I disrobed.

'Come on, Paul, we have a lot to discuss and not much time. I have seen all of your body, with and without underwear, so don't try to play the timid schoolboy with me. Allez!'

It felt strange being ordered to undress by a nun, but I obeyed and began to hunt around for some decent clothes. I unravelled a pair of barely creased cargo pants and a white linen shirt that was designed to look artistically wrinkled. Elodie nodded her satisfaction.

'Now tell me about M,' she said as I stripped off. 'How is it going?'

'Ah.' I pretended to be preoccupied by a stubborn shirt button as a slideshow of photos ran through my head – M in the bathtub, M on the phone, Léanne in a backless dress and lecturing me on the beach. How much of the truth could I tell Elodie? None, was the simple answer. Telling her any secret was like starting a blog called 'Please broadcast all my secrets.'

'Great,' I said. 'Though she wasn't too pleased to be left alone in Bandol.' This much was true. I'd phoned M from the car on the way to Saint Tropez, and she had been highly suspicious. It was uncanny, she said, that I'd been sick as a dog all night and yet been able to get up at dawn to catch the boat. She said she thought I was trying to avoid her. No more than she was avoiding me, I retorted, by disappearing off to Marseille as soon as we got to the Island.

I felt a bit of a shit playing this game of emotional ping-pong, but it worked like a dream. With one short jibe I'd convinced M that I was just getting my own back on her. Léanne was right – you could explain away any weird behaviour simply by playing the disgruntled partner. *Vive les couples*, I thought.

'Why didn't you bring her with you?' Elodie asked.

'I didn't want to complicate things. It's best if I concentrate a hundred per cent on the catering deal, isn't it?'

'Yes, yes, true. What do you want?'

Her question was aimed at a miniature Valéry who had materialized in the doorway, his eyes riveted to my bare legs. The apparition was dressed in 1930s clothes – a blue checked shirt done up tight at the neck, and corduroy shorts that ended just below the knee with a kind of cuff that could be buttoned to grip long socks. This, plus the haircut – close cropped except for a long tuft at the fringe – convinced me that it couldn't be the spirit of Valéry as a seven-year-old. After all, he was too young to have been in the Hitler Youth.

'Maman says coffee is almost finished,' the boy said, still taking in my state of half-undress.

'OK, we're just coming.' Elodie shooed him away. 'One of Valéry's little brothers,' she explained when he had gone. 'Poor kid.'

'I can't believe this Moo-Moo's produced so many children. She looks like the archetypal spinster.'

'Oh no, Paul. In the grandes familles, you must not confuse looking totally unsexy with being unmarried. In fact it is better for the wife to be unsexy, because then the husband can be sure that she will not shag the dentist. Moo-Moo has six children. Or seven, maybe. The oldest is Valéry, and that boy is the youngest. She and her husband are so Catholic that they have to have a baby every time they fuck, or it is a sin.'

'So she hasn't had sex in seven years? No wonder she's a bit tense.'

'Paul, please. Put on your trousers. You cannot discuss Moo-Moo while you are nearly naked. It reminds me of once when I was on holiday in Italy. I met a boy who liked to make love during Mass. It was disgusting. I could feel the Pope watching us.' She smiled nostalgically, as if this sort of blasphemous action would have spiced up life in the chateau. The only sexy member of Moo-Moo's generation of the family, she went on, was one of the aunts, called Ludivine.

'She is a – how do you say? – *porte-parole*.'

'Spokesperson?'

'Yes, one of those, at the Elysée.'

I stopped in mid-trouser leg. 'She works at the presidential palace?' I asked. So here was someone who'd be directly affected if the assassination plot succeeded.

'Ludivine is an old friend of the President,' Elodie said. 'They were at school together. Valéry told me they screwed for the first time, you know, when they were virgins.'

'She was his first lady, you might say.'

Elodie laughed. 'You mock, Paul, but you see, this family

is at the heart of French society. And you know that France's heart is between its legs.'

2

It felt like riding through the streets on the back of a cart, taking in every detail before I arrived at the scaffold.

Filling an ante-room was a gilt-framed painting of a semi-naked young saint getting arrowed, his attacker shooting at him from no more than half a yard away. The archer was a pretty bad shot, too, because most of the arrows were embedded in the legs and arms, with only one hitting the torso, provoking a faint trickle of blood on the porcelain-white skin. Amazingly, the saint was looking only mildly pissed off with the guy taking pot-shots at him. I would have been furious myself. But I guessed that was why he was a saint.

Elodie stopped below the painting to put the finishing touches to her pep-talk.

'Now you must remember this,' she whispered. 'Bonne Maman, the bitch grand-mère, doesn't want the marriage, right? And Moo-Moo is always agreeing with her because she wants her part of the family to be the main – you know – *héritiers.*'

'Heirs?'

'Yes, and also because she is a bitch.'

'And what about the rest of the family?' I asked, looking around the walls at old framed photos of whiskered men and bonneted ladies, the ancestors keeping an eye on things.

Valéry's dad was always called Dadou, Elodie told me, though his real name was François-Louis, 'or some other royal combination'. There were three aunts, she thought, including one nun. A sizeable proportion of Moo-Moo's generation would be here at some point during the weekend, she said, because as soon as they had a spare moment they seemed to gravitate together, unlike Elodie's family who avoided each other as much as possible. It was, she conceded, the reason for their success as a clan, and as a class.

'And what do they all do?' I asked. 'Apart from banking and nunning.'

'Oh, Dadou is a director at the bank and has a post in the Ministère des Affaires Etrangères. Mimi is a director in the bank and with Total Fina Elf. Babou has a company that installs tennis courts. He is the richest but they snob him a bit.'

'What about the women?' I asked. 'Are they all nuns or President's girlfriends?'

Elodie shrugged. 'Don't know. The married women stop work as soon as they have a baby. Now come on, we must go and face them.'

She opened a warped door and let loose a babble of conversation and a smell of coffee and enclosed warmth.

I expected a polite silence when we walked in, but life went on as usual, and I got a good chance to study the crowd before we were noticed.

Moo-Moo was sitting on a bulky old sofa with her back to us, looking out towards the garden. She was nodding frantically, as if agreeing with every word uttered by the person next to her. I couldn't see who this was, because a girl with a rather attractive backside was bending over the back of the sofa, hugging someone who was hidden from view.

Two almost identical men standing by the French

windows had to be Valéry's uncles, Babou and Mimi. Although they were dressed for golf, their tall, gangly frames, jerky wrist movements and slight facial tics seemed to suggest that the sporting gene had been erased from their bloodline. And one of them had skin so white that he couldn't possibly have spent more than an hour out of doors since the previous winter. That had to be Mimi – Babou would be tanned to extol the virtues of his tennis courts.

There were various younger people in their teens and twenties lounging in battered leather armchairs or draped around the walls. Apart from a tendency for the females to wear prim collars and long skirts, and for the guys to iron their jeans too often, they looked a normal enough bunch.

Out on the terrace, a gaggle of children were chasing each other, wrestling and laughing. Only three of them were dressed as if they'd just got back from a summer camp in Bavaria.

'Ah!' One of the golfers had caught sight of Elodie and me, and was striding towards us. He took my hand in a tight grip and introduced himself.

'Charles-Henri de Bonnepoire. Enchanté, Monsieur.' Uncle Babou, then. He gave a small bow.

'Paul West. Enchanté.' I did the same.

'Venez, venez.' He pulled me into the room to meet everyone, and I did the rounds like you would at a party, introducing myself and instantly forgetting everyone's name. I shook hands with anyone who looked older than me, and was allowed to kiss some of the younger females on the cheeks, though I could sense Moo-Moo watching me, and I guessed she wouldn't approve. Kissing elevated me to the status of guest rather than tradesman.

Finally we reached the sofa and the young woman

standing behind it, who was just as attractive from the front as the rear. She told me her name was Sixteen, and that she was Valéry's sister.

'Sixteen,' I repeated, thinking it was a weird thing to call a kid. Perhaps she had so many siblings that her parents had resorted to numbers. 'An English name?'

'No.' She laughed and blushed.

'It's the chapel, Paul. At the Vatican.' Elodie was staring at me as if I was an idiot.

The penny dropped. 'Ah, we call it the *Sistine* chapel.' I laughed. 'The Vatican is so complicated, n'est-ce pas? We call the pope Benedict, you call him Benoit. I don't know why they can't just—'

A not-so-subtle kick in the ankle from Elodie warned me that religion wasn't a theme that I should try and develop.

'And you have already met Valéry's mother, Marie-Angélique,' Charles-Henri alias Babou said.

'Ah, yes, I have had the pleasure.' Moo-Moo's face stiffened as if a wasp had just landed on her nose. She clearly thought that merely saying the word was a sin.

'And this is my mother,' Babou announced.

I bowed low to shake the hand of the old lady sitting bolt upright in the middle of the sofa. Like all the best dictators, she was very small, a miniature grand. She had smooth powdery skin, hazel eyes much younger and brighter than her years, and a perfectly combed chestnut hairdo. She was dressed in an Austrian-green twin set and pearls. The expression on her face was one of benevolent superiority, as if I was a poodle that had been brought here to be house-trained.

'Enchanté, Madame de Bonnepoire,' I said, being careful not to squash her delicate hand. 'Or may I call you Bonne Maman?'

Elodie gave a soft moan beside me, and Sixtine giggled. I'd meant to show the grand-mère that I'd heard Valéry use the affectionate name for her, but I'd committed another gaffe. First the wrong driveway, and now the wrong name.

'No, you may call me Madame,' she said. 'And when you say Madame with the family name, you omit the *de*. So you may call me Madame Bonnepoire.'

'Enchanté, Madame Bonnepoire,' I corrected myself. 'Your family has a beautiful chateau.'

'Bastard,' Moo-Moo interrupted.

I tried to think what else I might have done wrong. Did she think I was trying it on with Bonne Maman?

'It's not a chateau, Monsieur,' Moo-Moo explained, noticing my confused expression. 'It is a typical large house of the region. A bastard.'

'Ah. Well you have a lovely bastard.' Who was I to argue?

'*Bastide*,' Elodie said, correcting my pronunciation.

'Ah.'

'You are too late for coffee,' Moo-Moo said. 'But we will make an exception. Sixtine?'

'Would you like—' Sixtine began, before Moo-Moo gave a cough like a bronchitic camel. Sixtine blushed and started again, this time using 'vous' instead of the familiar 'tu'.

I accepted a coffee, praying that it would come with a packet of biscuits and maybe a kilo or two of cheese.

'I am very happy that you have invited me to talk to you about the organization of Elodie's wedding,' I told Bonne Maman, speaking extra-slowly to get the grammar right.

'Bonne Maman did not invite you,' Moo-Moo corrected me. 'We accepted Valéry's request that you be received to discuss the possibility of an eventual ceremony.'

It sounded to me as if Elodie's plan to get married in under ten days was a touch optimistic.

'Well, I would be very happy to discuss the organization of the possibility of an eventual ceremony,' I said, turning back towards Bonne Maman. 'I have some ideas. I hope that they will please you.'

'You will discuss them with me first, Monsieur,' Moo-Moo said. 'We do not want to disturb Bonne Maman unless it is absolutely necessary.' The old dear in question was sitting there as if conserving her energy for a cross-Channel swim. 'Come, we will go outside,' Moo-Moo decreed.

'Ah, yes,' I said, 'you have a magnificent garden.'

'It is not a garden, it's a park.'

I was beginning to see why she'd only had sex six times in thirty years.

Moo-Moo didn't seem to notice the horde of sprogs charging around on the terrace, and they all seemed to possess a sixth sense that stopped them colliding with her as she moved towards the stone parapet. Every time an apparently out-of-control child careered in her direction, an invisible force seemed to wrench it to a standstill or make it veer to one side.

I, on the other hand, had to tread as carefully as a drunk in a minefield to avoid blundering into a junior Bonnepoire. I hardly had time to notice the splendour of my surroundings – the canopy of vines hanging from a trellis above our heads, the twisting branches and yellowing leaves intertwining to cast mottled shade over the marble flooring. In more peaceful times, I could have leaned back in a deckchair and let trained sparrows drop grapes into my mouth.

'Venez, Monsieur.' Moo-Moo had taken up a proprietorial stance overlooking the 'park' and was waiting for me to disentangle myself from a rugby scrum that had suddenly started up around my knees. Elodie was hovering nearby, looking anxious.

Not the best time, then, for my phone to start ringing. Especially because, to psych myself up for this meeting, I'd chosen 'We Are Family' as my ringtone, and its sudden eruption made all the kids prick up their ears. I guessed they didn't hear much disco around the bastide.

It was Léanne.

'Sorry to interrupt you, Pol, I hope everything is OK,' she began in a friendly voice, before clicking into Robocop mode. 'Tomorrow morning, at eleven o'clock, you must meet me. We have to discuss about M, OK?'

'OK. Where?'

'At Ramatuelle. It is a village near the Bonnepoires' chateau. You take the D93 road for Saint Tropez, and drive for about ten kilometres. You will see the signs. Meet me in the big café on the place du village, OK?'

'OK,' I said.

I went to join Elodie and Moo-Moo, apologizing for my impoliteness.

'I hope, Monsieur, that you are not one of those terrible people who answer their telephone every five minutes,' Moo-Moo said.

I thought it was lucky she didn't know that I was one of those terrible people whose girlfriends plot to kill the President.

'I am very sorry,' I said again. 'It was a client. I am the traiteur for a big wedding in England next month.'

Elodie almost squealed at this ridiculous lie.

'Ah, yes, which wedding?' Moo-Moo asked. Being a socialite, she wanted names, of course.

'Er, it is for a duke.'

'Which duke?'

'Oh, not a very famous duke.'

By now Elodie was preparing to leap off the balcony.

'We know some dukes,' Moo-Moo said.

Of course you do, you snooty cow, I thought. Why couldn't I have said it was for a millionaire plastic-cutlery manufacturer? Then she'd have been too snobbish to ask for details.

'He says that his name must be a secret.'

'Ah.' Apparently I'd come up with the right answer. 'English nobles know how to be discreet.' Moo-Moo nodded approvingly, and I realized how much the French haute bourgeoisie idolized English aristocrats.

'Anyway, the duke has given me a fantastic idea for Valéry's wedding,' I said, congratulating myself for seguing so smoothly into the key subject for discussion.

'We wouldn't want a second-hand idea,' Moo-Moo cut me off immediately. 'Even if it is for a noble English family.'

'Ah no, I am thinking that you must have the opposite idea,' I added quickly. 'A unique idea.' *Une idée unique.* I relished the sound of the phrase, mainly because I was so pleased that I was finally getting a chance to talk about my plans. Something positive to think about instead of all the police merde.

'Yes?' Moo-Moo asked, deigning to look almost curious.

'Local food,' I announced grandly. I still hadn't found out how you say 'carbon-neutral' in French. If they even had a word for it.

'Comment?' Moo-Moo looked and sounded under-whelmed. I wondered why. What better meal could there be than a succession of freshly picked, caught and cooked dishes from the South of France? Perhaps, I realized, I hadn't been explicit enough. It might have sounded to her French ears like suggesting a pizza party to a Neapolitan.

'Imagine an entrée of Collioure anchois marinés,' I said, feeling my mouth beginning to water. 'And vegetables of the season roasted in local olive oil.' My stomach pitched in with a loud grumble to remind me that nothing more solid than a piece of chewing gum had passed my lips since breakfast. 'An immense barbecue of fresh sea bream, cooked with local herbs and lemons from Menton. With this, we will serve a rosé, maybe from the île des Embiez . . .'

Moo-Moo cut me off again. 'Monsieur.' She flapped an arm across the vineyards towards the sea. 'We produce our own wine.'

'Encore mieux,' I said. Even better. 'We will serve your wine. With rice from the Camargue.'

'We have our own rice fields there,' she couldn't resist saying.

'Perfect.' Her snootiness was driving her into my trap. 'Don't you see, Madame, it will be a banquet that will be in harmony with your family, with the region, and ecology.'

'Ecology?' It seemed I'd said a naughty word.

'He doesn't mean the Ecology Party,' Elodie chipped in. 'In France, Paul, ecologists are seen as people with big moustaches who think that all cars must run on sunflower oil.' She turned to Moo-Moo again. 'What he means is that the food will come from nearby, so it will be fresh and seasonal. There will, of course, be champagne and amuse-bouches, won't there, Paul?' she prompted.

'Of course,' I conceded. 'The best champagne, with tapenade on toast grilled on the wood fire, small goat's cheeses marinated in olive oil. And for the pièce de résistance—'

'No, no, no.' Moo-Moo was shaking her head, her hands and large areas of the rest of her body in an all-over negative. 'Food, food, nothing but food. You think only of the pleasures of the mouth.' She shivered, and even managed to look almost sexy for once, because it is impossible for a French woman to say 'plaisirs de la bouche' without performing a spectacular pout. 'What about the tables?'

'The tables?' I asked.

'Yes, at the wedding of my niece Bénédicte, there was a terrible problem with the tables.' Moo-Moo trembled again.

'Ah yes?' Now that I thought about it, Valéry had mentioned this. 'Well, we will have excellent tables,' I promised. 'Uh, very solid tables, round tables?' I trod one step at a time into this unknown world of terrible tables. 'With, on top, white, uh . . . ?' I turned to Elodie.

'Nappes?' she said. Tablecloths.

'Yes, with white nappes.'

'It is not the colour of the tablecloths that concerns me, Monsieur.'

'No?'

'No. And if you don't even know the problem with the tables, how can you possibly organize everything in such a short time?' She raised her face to the skies as if she expected a team of angelic delivery men to descend with perfect dining-room furniture.

Before I could ask Moo-Moo or Elodie for more information, a double diversion came out on to the terrace.

First, sweet Sixtine, carrying a small tray with a large cup of coffee and – clever girl – a plate of madeleines – egg-shaped sponge cakes. I was reassured to see that, like me, she was forced to swerve her way through the scrum of kids.

'Ah, merci, you are like the angels in the chapel with your

name,' I said, earning a blush from Sixtine and a warning cough from Elodie.

Sixtine put the tray on the stone parapet and looked inclined to hang around, but Moo-Moo dismissed her with a pointed 'Merci, Sixtine.'

The second interruption was a guy who looked like a blend of uncles Babou and Mimi, except that he was even more spindly, and his hair was much longer. Instead of being parted on one side and combed across the head, his grey locks were brushed straight back, and stuck out over his ears as if he had grown wings out of the sides of his skull.

'I'm going to the golf club,' he announced to Moo-Moo. 'Ah.' He noticed me and introduced himself as François-Louis de Bonnepoire, Valéry's father. So this was Dadou, the banker and diplomat. I shook his limp hand.

'Golf?' Moo-Moo echoed. 'Ever since Babou and Mimi started playing, you have been going to that club at every opportunity. But you never play. I don't understand your interest in the place.'

'Come.' Elodie pulled me away. I grabbed my tray and allowed myself to be led to the far end of the terrace, where there was a Roman fountain, with a gaping sun god spouting water into a giant stone clamshell.

'Hang on,' I said, looking back at the bickering couple. 'Valéry's dad is one of the Bonnepoire brothers, right? So where does Moo-Moo fit in? Surely he didn't marry his first cousin, or his sister?'

'Stop staring, Paul, please,' she said. 'No. That is what is so shocking. Moo-Moo is only a pièce rapportée.'

'A what?'

'Moo-Moo is like me, or like I will be. She is not of the

family. She is only the wife of a Bonnepoire. She was the local doctor's daughter.'

'So how come she's so snobbish towards you?'

'You know, it's like what they say about immigrants. The newest ones are the most racist. She could be an ally to Valéry, but she prefers to lick the ass of Bonne Maman and go for the big inheritance. You know, even this house, it isn't hers and Dadou's yet. It belongs a hundred per cent to the old bitch.'

This shed a whole new light on Moo-Moo's holier-than-thou attitude.

'And what was all that about the tables?' I asked.

'I don't know. We must ask Valéry. If he ever comes back from Saint Trop. Ah, look.' Elodie nudged me. 'The coast is clear.'

Dadou was leaving the terrace, walking in a way that could only be called a mince. His shoulders and small buttocks were performing a wiggling dance of irritation, while his hands were flapping the various children out of his way. No, I told myself, you're being stupid. Six children, staunch Catholic? There was no way he could be gay.

While Elodie cruised the lounge doing PR, I went outside. Beyond the car park, I'd seen what looked like a vegetable plot and a small orchard. I was hoping to find enough ripe vitamins there to keep me alive for the afternoon.

Away from the cloying family atmosphere, it was a glorious day. The sky was an arc of pure blue, sweeping from the inland background of softly rounded hills to the seaward horizon of misted crystal. The small vegetable plot was divided up by tiny knee-high rosemary hedges so that it looked like a classical French garden, with beans, lettuces and tomatoes instead of royal rose beds. In one corner was a row of beehives, set between a stand of olive trees and a huge fig tree.

I could see no sign of a gardener, so I helped myself to a few cherry tomatoes and then headed for the trees. The olives smelt heady, and even though they hadn't been doused in oil or brine, I figured that they might be worth a nibble. I reached up into the silvery branches and began feeling for a ripe one.

'Paul!'

I turned to see Valéry standing up in his Mercedes sports car. Or rather, standing on it. He appeared to be perched on the boot.

'What are you doing?' he called out, laughing manically.

'Just admiring the garden. Sorry, the park.'

'What? Wait.' He leapt down from the car and came hurdling across the rosemary hedges. He screeched to a halt in a cloud of dust and squinted at me through the olive leaves.

'How did it go with Bonne Maman and Moo-Moo? Uh? Have you talked about the marriage? And the food? Have you talked about the food? Uh? What food have you suggested? Olives? Ha!' He cackled at the olives as if they'd just made fools of themselves. 'Moo-Moo, she's terrible, no? And you have met my papa also, yes? You know he is gay, no? He goes to the golf club to screw one of the gardeners. Funny, isn't it, no? Yes? Ha!'

Wow, I thought, if the leather-jacketed cop searched Valéry's nostrils, he'd probably find enough powder up there to charge him with wholesaling the stuff.

'Listen to me, Valéry.' I grabbed his wrists to try and focus his attention. 'Have you just been to town to buy some coke?'

'What? You know?' He looked around as if to pinpoint the person who'd ratted on him.

177

'Yes, it's a bit obvious.'

'Well, it's the only way I can support my family,' he said, mournfully quiet for a second.

'Support them?' So he did it for the money? He was a dealer? No wonder the cops were after him. 'What about your job at the bank?' I asked. I would have thought that would give him ample income.

'Oh, I never take it at the bank,' he said. 'Except maybe on a Friday afternoon. Ha!' He was back in manic mode again. 'What are you doing? Selecting olives for the marriage?'

'No, I'm hungry, if you must know,' I confessed. 'I was looking for things to nibble on.'

'Food? Oh, I will make you a meal. What do you want? A sandwich? Some ham? No, eggs! I will make an omelette. A big omelette with ham, yes? A giant one?'

He was growing so excited about the idea that I thought I'd better agree before he had an orgasm in the middle of the vegetable patch.

'Wait here!' He steeplechased into the house.

Doubting that I would ever see the omelette, I returned to inspecting the olives. They were hard, but some were black and shiny, and seemed to be crying out for a set of teeth to free all the smooth oil within.

I picked a likely looking one, bit into its flesh, and promptly spat it out again. How could something so sumptuous when marinated be so disgustingly bitter and woody? And what ancient tribe had been mad enough to crush such revolting fruit and expect rich, tasty oil to flow out?

'I see you do not appreciate our olives, Monsieur.'

It was Bonne Maman, who had come outside armed with a pair of vicious-looking secateurs. Not, I hoped, to attack olive poachers. She was smiling at me from under a wide-brimmed straw hat.

'In England, we don't have olive trees,' I explained.

'There are many things you do not have in England. And yet you think you can be the traiteur for a French wedding?' She gave a sabre-like flourish of her secateurs. Touché.

'Ah, but I have a salon de thé in Paris,' I said, 'near the Champs-Elysées. And my French clients are very happy.'

'Hmm.' She was thinking this over when I saw Valéry reappear in the car park behind her. He was waving a frying pan in the air.

'Two eggs? Three? Four?' he shouted.

Looking in the opposite direction to lead Bonne Maman off the scent of her crazed grandson, I held up a hand and made a V sign.

'Two? OK, two!' Valéry yelled, but by the time his grandmother had turned around, he had hurtled back indoors again.

'It was just some of the children,' I said, in answer to her look of enquiry.

'Ah. Yes, there are many things you do not have in England,' the little old lady said, 'but one thing you understand is class, n'est-ce pas?'

'Class?' I wasn't sure I did understand. Working in London, I'd found that loudness of voice and size of salary counted for much more than family background.

'Yes, origins,' Bonne Maman went on. 'You know who planted this olive tree? My husband. We have roots here. My husband bought the bastide during the Second World War. It was a ruin, but this was the unoccupied zone, so he moved his family down from Paris to safety. It was our refuge.' She made the place sound like a back-garden bomb shelter. 'He planted the vines, too, and insisted that we always have a vegetable garden. And around our estate in the Camargue, he bought rice fields and cattle. He wanted to protect his family from the dangers of history.'

And, I thought cynically, put his money into something solid like land instead of leaving it in a Nazi-occupied Parisian bank.

'Onions? Onions?' Valéry was leaping around in the car park, waving two globes by their long green stems.

'What is that?' Again, Bonne Maman was confused, and again I kept her that way by looking in the wrong direction. Meanwhile I held up an index finger and wiggled it in the French negative. Valéry lobbed the onions into the lavender patch and disappeared again.

'You understand class, Monsieur, and origins, so . . .' Bonne Maman paused as if she couldn't bring herself to say the next phrase, but I could tell that she was relishing every moment of her educational little speech. 'So you can understand that young Elodie is not of the right class. Her grandfather was a humble butcher, n'est-ce pas? And her father, well, he is the same except that the butchering is now done by machines instead of men.'

Given that Jean-Marie was not only my partner in the tea room but also my former boss, I guessed that Bonne Maman's class system put me even lower down the evolutionary scale.

'But Elodie is a beautiful, intelligent woman, and has a great future,' I said. 'She studied business in New York.' OK, most of the business had involved procuring hookers for a French pop star, but that was as traditional an industry as banking, wasn't it? 'And Valéry loves her,' I added, seeing with mild alarm that the man in question had emerged yet again, this time holding a smoking pan in one hand and a black circular object – presumably a cremated omelette – in the other. He was shrugging apologetically.

'And Valéry should think himself lucky to have her,' I wanted to add, 'because he is a total fucking cokehead.'

Instead, I managed to keep a wistful smile on my face. 'What can you do about l'amour?' I asked philosophically.

'Huh, l'amour,' Bonne Maman grunted. 'That is enough for poor people. Not for us.'

Valéry finally managed to connect pan to omelette and whooped with laughter as the black disc flew through the air and attached itself to the windscreen of a Renault.

'What is that?' Before I could distract her, Bonne Maman swivelled and caught Valéry in mid lap of honour around the car park.

'He is mad with l'amour,' I said, doing my best to protect the drug-crazed idiot. I mean, what fool gets coked up in the presence of the old lady who controls his financial future?

'Perhaps it is love,' Bonne Maman said. 'Or do you think it might be the cocaine?'

Leaving me to muse on the fact that she knew all about Valéry's bad habits, Bonne Maman cut some flowers and went back indoors.

I looked for Valéry, but he had disappeared, so I went to carry out a raid on the fig tree. The pale-green fruit was thick-skinned and slightly unripe, but that only meant that they were less messy to eat. I ripped open half a dozen of them, and chewed hungrily on the sweet red seeds.

After this zero-carbon-impact picnic, I spotted a hammock strung between two young peach trees, and, feeling like a true Mediterranean, I lay back and let my stomach gurgle a happy hello to the recent delivery of fresh fruit. I closed my eyes to enjoy the birdsong of every sort, from whistling chatter to deep cackles, and watched the alternate flicker of black and orange on my eyelids as the breeze parted and closed my parasol of leaves.

It was the perfect place to chill out and let the world get on with its business without me for a while. And to think about Bonne Maman. I'd been shocked but not surprised by what she'd said. After all, efficient dictators always know what everyone is getting up to. I half-expected her to announce that she was hiring the golf-club gardener to trim the vines, so that Dadou's antics wouldn't cause a scandal outside the family circle.

All in all, her comment about the cocaine seemed to suggest that if she had decided Valéry wasn't getting married, then he wasn't getting married. She was in total control, and all my speeches about local sea bream and marinated goat's cheese were just adding to the excess of carbon dioxide on the planet.

It was a shame, but that was that.

It was a realization that took some of the pressure off me. And, of course, left me free to panic about M.

I fell asleep dreaming of a president getting assassinated by a flying omelette, and woke again when his funeral service turned into a disco.

My phone was singing at me. I really ought to change that ringtone.

'I want to get off the island,' M told me.

'Why?' I wondered if she'd cottoned on to the fact that the police were watching her.

'I'm bored here without you.'

'But you never stay with me for more than ten minutes before you have to rush off to a meeting somewhere.'

'Yes, well I know it sounds naff, but I like knowing that you're here to come back to.'

'You're right,' I said. I'd been treated like a poodle enough for one day. 'It does sound a bit naff.'

'What I mean is, I miss you. Why don't I come to Saint Tropez?'

'It wouldn't be practical right now.' I did my best to tone down my horror at the suggestion. 'I'm staying with Valéry's family, and they're a bunch of fundamentalist Catholics. You know, no sex before or during marriage.'

'Can't you sneak me in through your bedroom window? It might be fun.' She giggled, sounding like nothing more sinister than a girl who fancied meeting up for a bit of sneaky sex. It took all my mental faculties to remind myself who, and what, she was.

'They've put me in a kiddie's room no bigger than a shower cubicle,' I said. 'I don't think I'm going to fit in the bed on my own, never mind with you there. Anyway, don't you have to stay on that part of the coast for all your meetings?'

'I can come away for a couple of days.'

'And what about the Camargue sighting? Have you followed up that lead?'

'Oh, Paul, do we have to talk about my work?' She tried to make this sound like a girlish plea, but all I heard was her evasiveness. She was hiding something, and making a pretty amateurish job of it. I'd been an idiot not to see through her before.

'Sorry, I've got to go,' I said, more harshly than I'd intended. I made an effort to sound warmer when I added that I'd call her later. After all, I was under police orders to stay on good terms with her.

*

It was dusk when I woke up, or rather when I was shaken awake. Elodie was leaning over the hammock, pinching and poking sensitive parts of me.

As soon as I opened my eyes, she began ranting at me in a hoarse whisper about tables. I suspected that she'd been sniffing at Valéry's perpetual-motion powder.

'I forced Valéry to tell me,' she hissed. 'And it is the legs – they must be covered up.'

'Pardon?'

'Yes. At Bénédicte's marriage, the table legs were thin, and metal.'

'So?' Not only was she speaking ultra-quickly, she also seemed to be straying off into Valéry's world of pop-eyed madness.

'The legs had lots of tables. I mean, the tables had lots of legs, and they were not covered by the tablecloths. They showed in the photos. Someone saw the metal legs in *Paris Match* and said that it looked like a common fête de village. Bonne Maman nearly had a heart attack at the shame of it all.'

'I get the picture.' The Bonnepoires had been out-snobbed by the snobs.

'So you see, we must show Moo-Moo a photo of some tables without legs, OK? Or with wooden legs. As soon as possible.' Elodie stopped talking and grinned insanely at me.

'OK,' I said. 'But there's a much bigger problem than tables.'

Before she could interrupt or object, I outlined the problem as I saw it. Bonne Maman was just too omniscient to let the wedding go ahead, I said. If it became necessary, I was sure she would take Valéry into a quiet corner and blackmail him about the cocaine.

'No, never,' Elodie said, but she looked less sure than she

sounded. 'She would not tell the police about that. She would never betray her family.'

'So you really think she'll let you marry Valéry?'

'Yes. If we can convince the rest of the family, then Bonne Maman must give her approval.'

We stopped talking. Both of us had heard men's voices drifting through the calm evening air. They were coming towards us.

'Rosemary,' one of them said. 'Of course I know what it looks like. I used to grow all sorts of plants out here, don't you remember?'

'Babou,' Elodie whispered. 'I think.'

'Don't you remember when Bonne Maman found your little plantation? We thought she didn't know what it was, but she just happened to find it when the leaves were exactly the right size for smoking.'

'That's Dadou,' Elodie said, even more quietly. They were very close now, and we were holding our breath so as not to be heard. I didn't really know why we were hiding, but subterfuge seemed to be the order of the day.

The two brothers were laughing, and saying something about keeping secrets in the family. I could make out their silhouettes clearly now.

'Which would be worse?' Babou said. 'That a child of yours marries a communist or a nouveau riche?'

Dadou laughed.

'With a communist,' Babou went on, 'at least things are clear. But this Elodie is the nouveau-riche daughter of a *butcher*.' Instinctively, I gripped Elodie's arm. I was afraid she might pull up a carrot and bludgeon them with it.

'You sell your tennis courts to those people,' Dadou pointed out.

'Of course I do. What does an intelligent man do when

he sees a cow? He milks it. But you don't want a cow marrying into your family.'

They both laughed again, and found their rosemary plant. They ripped off a few stalks and went back into the house, still chatting.

'Do you really want to marry into this family?' I asked Elodie.

'Oh yes,' she said. 'More than ever.'

4

Dinner got off to a shaky start when Dadou asked what route I'd taken to drive to the bastide. I remembered that I was meant to have arrived from London, and said I'd driven from 'Hee-air', my pronunciation of the airport just east of Toulon at Hyères.

This provoked a few sniggers amongst the dozen or so adult Bonnepoires who had assembled in the dining room. The kids were eating in the kitchen.

'Yairr,' Dadou corrected me, and then asked for more details, probably hoping that I'd cock up a few more place names. He wasn't disappointed. Cavalaire passed without incident, even Borme les Mimosas, but I came unstuck at the coastal village of La Bouillabaisse, which I attempted to pronounce two or three times, asking whether it was the village that inspired the fish stew of the same name, or vice versa. No one knew, but they all seemed highly amused at the way I said the name, except Moo-Moo, whose pale face became even whiter. Eventually Elodie put me out of my misery, whispering that it was pronounced with an 's' sound at the end, not 'z'. The way I'd said it made it sound like 'boiled fuck'.

'Can't you just stop talking for a while?' she begged me.

I kept my head down during the main course, but in a fit of optimism, while we were waiting for dessert, I pitched my idea for the pièce de résistance at Valéry's wedding. It might turn out to be a waste of breath, but it was better than listening to the family discussing the colour of a cousin's new pony, or the chances of getting a tenth Bonnepoire in as many years into the same elite school.

By chance or design, the dinner had been very local, with everything produced either in the grounds or by nearby farmers, so I was able to pick up the theme of a Provençal banquet.

I described my invention, a pièce montée – traditionally a giant pyramid of caramelized profiterole-style pastry balls – made out of fresh figs, which I've always seen as one of nature's more underrated gifts to humanity.

'It would be impossible, totally impossible,' Uncle Babou said.

Elodie, who had been placed next to him, looked likely to stab him with a fork at any moment.

'It's true that figs are not as solid as tennis balls,' I said, earning hearty laughs from most of the table. Babou pretended to be amused by this jibe about his profession, but I could see that I'd just made an enemy. Tough merde, I thought. After his little speech in the vegetable garden, he deserved all the punishment he got. 'I have already asked the manager of my salon de thé in Paris to make a miniature one as a test,' I said.

'Why are you not trying to persuade them to have an English wedding cake?' This was from one of Valéry's aunts, the presidential spokeswoman. She had introduced herself as Ludivine Saint Armand de Bonnepoire. A heavy handle to carry about. She'd obviously tacked her maiden name on the end when she got married, and now wasted a full minute every time she had to sign a cheque.

She was tall, thin and fine-featured, a younger version of Dadou, with dyed brown hair swept back in a simple pony tail. She was, if anything, the snootiest of the lot, and had the definite air of someone who had hit the jackpot in life with their very first shag. It was morbidly fascinating to look at the woman who would have to make the announcement to the press if the President did get shot.

'An English wedding cake? I don't think so,' I said. 'We English are very good at pop music and comedy films, but not at pâtisserie.'

'But this pièce montée, it is your idea, no? And you are English. So will it be any good?'

'The idea is by an Englishman, but it was inspired by France,' I replied, earning a short burst of applause from Sixtine.

Moo-Moo frowned at the poor girl, who winked at me. I didn't think it wise to wink back.

After dessert – a selection of fruit tarts made by one of the cousins whose names I'd forgotten – everyone wandered off with a cup of herbal tea in their hands. I accepted a mug of the rosemary that the two brothers had gathered. It tasted like soup with no salt, meat or vegetables.

I ambled amiably around the lounge, dishing out friendly smiles, and even risked a little banter with Bonne Maman, who was sitting next to Moo-Moo on the long sofa, sipping her cup while looking at a magazine's games page.

'Ah, Sudoku,' I said. 'I like that.'

The old lady almost spat her herbal tea into Moo-Moo's lap.

Elodie came up behind me and dragged me away. 'Please shut up now,' she pleaded.

'Why?' Since the boiled-fuck incident, things had gone very well, I thought.

'It's soo-doh-koo,' she said, saying the word almost exactly as I'd done.

'That's what I said.'

'No, you said the oo's wrong. Basically, you just told her that you like to sweat from your anus.'

That night, as I lay bent double on my bed, with my knees practically under my chin, I naturally started wondering what the hell I was doing there. Not just in my attic room, but in Saint Tropez, in France.

Most guys would have got up, thanked the family – no, the whole French nation – for their hospitality, and got as far away from the claustrophobic situation as possible. There had to be a reason why I stayed on.

And it was, I finally decided, nothing more complicated than friendship.

I had friends in need of help, and whatever happened to the President, his prospective hitman, the police and M, I had to keep my old chums in mind. Right now, my loyalties lay with Elodie and Jake.

Elodie had done some mean things to me in the States, but that had all been part of our American powerplay. It was a game I had lost, not because of her but because my own team was playing against me.

And Jake was a complete screw-up, the world's least readable poet and worst linguist, but he'd sent out a cry for help, and I had to heed it.

Deciding that I'd had enough of deforming my spine on the child-sized bed, I dumped the mattress on the floor, and heaped teddy bears together as a foundation for my pillow and my feet. From this lumpy refuge, I phoned Louisiana.

'Hey Pol, divine what I'm doing!' Jake meant guess, but I wasn't keen to do so. 'I'm taking a coffee in the diner we visited together. You recall yourself? The one where the people had no don.'

'No teeth?' Yes, I remembered the place, a friendly little truck stop near the Mississippi, where everyone had a baseball cap grafted on to their head, and the most dentured mouth had only enough teeth for half a smile.

'I have brung, uh, bringed – how do you say?'

'Brought?' I suggested.

'Yes, I have broot my estudients here to observe the veritable life of their region and inspire their posy. We are writing some on this diner. In Frinsh, of coose.'

'Well, that's just why I'm calling you, Jake. About your posy.'

'My posy?' He sounded suspicious. In the past, I hadn't always treated it with the greatest respect.

'Yes. I have an idea where you can get your grant.'

'Yeah? You have meeted, uh, mought . . . ?'

'Met?' I said, remembering that I was paying for this transatlantic English lesson.

'Yes, you have metted the Minister of Francophony?'

No, I told him, but Valéry's dad was with the Ministry of Foreign Affairs, and I was going to have a quiet word with him. I had high hopes that he'd be able to do something for Jake.

'Wo, genial!' Jake said. 'You want that I wrote, uh, written, uh?'

'Write?'

'Yes, merde, you want that I write a mel to him? Send him some of our posy?'

'No!' In a slightly less terrified tone, I explained that I

didn't think an email was necessary. I managed not to say that I thought it would be fatal.

'You want to listen at some of our posy?' Jake offered.

'No, thanks, I have to go,' I said. It was going to be hard enough sleeping on a pile of teddies. I didn't want to give myself nightmares as well.

5

A blond boy was sobbing in my doorway, wiping his runny nose on the long leg of the girl standing next to him. It was Sixtine, who was laughing and telling the kid not to cry. She was wearing pyjamas that she'd probably had since she was about thirteen. She'd grown slightly in the intervening five years, especially in the hip and chest areas, so that the fluffy pink T-shirt reached only down to navel level. The trousers, meanwhile, were short and tight, and perched on her hips so that the waistline dipped perilously low. I had to stop myself yelping at this dawn vision. I'd been afraid of nightmares and woken up to a dream. A very dangerous one. I reminded myself of the need to stick to loyalty-based priorities.

'He's jealous,' Sixtine said. 'He usually sleeps in this room with all the teddies. But he had to sleep with me.' Too young to appreciate his luck, I thought. 'Come, it is time for breakfast. You must be quick, you know.'

I thanked her and took a moment to compose myself before getting up and slinging on some clothes.

Hunting for the breakfast room, I came across Valéry, also in under-sized pyjamas, apparently offering a jam pot to Bonne Maman as a peace offering. She was swathed in a shapeless dressing gown, a pair of cork-soled sandals on her feet, and although she was a good two feet shorter than Valéry, he was the one cowering as they argued.

They were in the ante-room dominated by the picture of the tortured saint, and didn't notice me in the shadowy stairway.

'*Where* did you meet her?' Bonne Maman asked, clearly referring to Elodie.

'I told you – while renting a Vélib.'

'While doing what to a what?'

Valéry had a quick go at explaining Paris's communal bike rental system, shaking the jam pot as he searched for the right words. He'd come down from Planet Coke, but it had obviously been a bit of a crash-landing.

'Well, Valéry,' Bonne Maman replied. 'I don't know what your dear grand-père would have thought of that. For a start, he would not have understood why you should need to sit in or on any means of transport that does not belong to a member of his family. I mean, how many other people use these, these *fetid*?'

'Vélibs, Bonne Maman. It's short for vélos libres. They're for the general public.'

'How disgusting. Public bicycles? Surely your ancestors worked hard enough to ensure that no member of their family should ever be reduced to taking a means of transport with fewer than four wheels?'

'What about Babou's yacht? That has no wheels at all.'

It was a feeble comeback, and Valéry knew it. Bonne Maman gave him a look that would have sunk a battleship, never mind a yacht.

'Valéry may rhyme with *repartie*,' she concluded, 'but it also rhymes with *appauvri*, don't forget that.'

With this she swanned regally away, leaving Valéry

looking ten times more pissed off than the pin-cushioned saint in the painting.

I went and propped him up. 'What does *appauvri* mean?' I asked.

'Poor. Very poor,' he groaned.

'Ah.' Bad news. 'By the way, there's something else I need to talk to you about if you don't want to be poor – and behind bars.'

'What?' He looked the picture of saintly innocence.

I leaned in close. 'Don't go into Saint Tropez for cocaine. The police are cracking down. They'll catch you.'

Valéry opened his mouth to reply.

'Listen to the Englishman, Valéry. For once he has said something sensible.'

It was bloody Bonne Maman. She'd reappeared behind us, and her sandals must have been fitted with silencers because we hadn't heard a thing. We both stood gaping at her.

'Come to the table,' she said. 'We need that pot of jam.'

Various generations of the family were sitting at breakfast, all in their nightclothes. And all of them, except the youngest, had regressed about twenty years.

Babou, Dadou and Ludivine the spokeslady looked like wrinkled students. Valéry's generation were all in their early teens again, and the teenagers seemed to have mislaid their dummies. It had to be the effect of getting together as a family, and of Bonne Maman's tyrannical presence. They were all reduced to a state of passive infancy.

There wasn't enough room for everyone in the rustic breakfast room, where family photos of all sizes and ages hung crookedly on the pastel-yellow walls. The long table was covered with pots, jugs, bowls and crumbs, and everyone was indulging in a free-for-all of bread-slicing and coffee- or chocolate-pouring. As soon as one person had finished, they got up and left. Valéry and I slid into two seats left by a pair of departing Hitler Youth.

'You will be coming to Mass, won't you, Valéry?' Moo-Moo asked, from the end of the table. If the long-sleeved, high-collared garment she was wearing was her night-dress, it was pretty amazing that she'd had any kids at all. It was as grey and forbidding as a Scottish castle.

'Oui, Moo-Moo,' Valéry piped.

'And you, Monsieur West?' she asked, arching her eyebrows. The small crowd of Bonnepoires at the table stopped munching to hear my reply.

'Er, no,' I said. 'I am Eglise de l'Angleterre.' Being Church of England is such a great excuse for never doing anything religious.

'Ah. Perhaps there is an English church in Saint Tropez.'

'It's OK, thank you. I can listen to the ceremony on the BBC.' I commandeered a passing baguette, smothered it in butter and Valéry's apricot jam, and then got up.

'You are going to listen to the radio already?' Bonne Maman asked.

'No, excuse me, I would like to eat in the garden – er – park, if that is OK. The weather is so magnifique.'

'Good idea,' she said. 'We will be needing your seat for one of the family.' Putting me in my place again.

In fact, I'd seen Dadou leave the table, and had decided to do something practical about helping my friends. I caught up with him in the courtyard as he was lighting a cigarette.

'Are you going to the golf course?' I asked.

'Not in my pyjamas, no.'

'Ah, no, of course not,' I said. 'I just wanted to tell you that I . . . I have a friend.'

'Lucky you.' He smiled, obviously enjoying knocking my conversation gambits into holes.

'He writes poems.'

'Really?'

'Yes. He lives in Louisiana.'

'How very interesting,' he lied.

'And he needs money.'

'What?'

'I mean a – how do you say? Yes, *une subvention*. A grant. Perhaps you can pass his request to the correct person in Francophonie? That department is in your ministry, n'est-ce pas?'

'Yes.' Now he was looking pissed off at my overt begging.

'What's your email?' I asked. 'I will send you his co-ordinates.' That's what the French call addresses.

'My email address?'

'Yes.' I stood my ground, not even acknowledging the possibility of a refusal, and he dictated it to me.

'Merci,' I said. 'Bon golf.' As I walked away, I could feel him watching me, wondering what the hell had just happened.

Now all I had to do to finish my morning session of loyalty to my chums was find Elodie and convince her to tie Valéry to the bedpost so that he wouldn't go into Saint Tropez and get himself arrested. And I knew from personal experience that anything to do with the bedroom was no problem for Elodie.

I tracked her down on the terrace. She was clicking through her text messages.

I looked around to check that Bonne Maman wasn't lurk-ing anywhere nearby, and in my most discreet whisper, begged her to keep Valéry in check today, especially if, as he said, he was not only buying but dealing.

'Dealing?' she shrieked. 'Who told you that?'

I told her what he'd said about it being the only way to support his family.

'Oh, you idiot,' she laughed. 'Support doesn't mean support. It means stand.'

'Pardon?'

'Supporter sa famille. Stand his family. It's the only way he can stand them. When he's . . .' She lowered her voice again, 'high on something. A dealer? Pah! Anyway, how do you know all this stuff about the police? Is M a dealer? Has she been arrested? Is that it?' Elodie's eyes were sparkling. She thought she was on to a juicy secret.

If only she knew, I thought, if only she knew.

There are some opportunities in life that you would be an idiot to miss. A free trip to the moon. An invitation to tell the G8 leaders what you think of them (with a guarantee that you won't be arrested afterwards). Time travel anywhere.

Well, swimming with one of the most luscious human beings on the Côte d'Azur was one of those opportunities, and yet I turned it down. I was obliged, I told Sixtine, to go out to an important meeting. Her pout of disappointment alone was the most sensual experience I'd had for days.

And so I drove, inwardly sobbing, down the tarmacked drive and away from temptation. It was time to go and see Léanne.

The road to Ramatuelle was a dizzying snail shell of a ride. The village was one of those hilltop postcard places, a gaggle of tall beige houses perched so high on a pinnacle that you wondered whether the original inhabitants didn't choose the spot in an attempt to discourage their in-laws from visiting.

I guess it is the fate of anywhere like this to be turned from a farming community to a command post for the local tourist industry. But on this off-season Sunday morning, the village-square café was quiet, and I estimated that a good quarter of the people sitting on the olive-shaded terrace were French. The waiter even had a strong local accent, which was a change for me after the posh Bonnepoires.

There was wi-fi, too, thanks to the nearby tourist office, and while I waited for Léanne to arrive, I bashed out a message to Jake, asking for the details of his poetry festival so that I could email Dadou.

In my inbox was a message from Benoit with news of the pièce montée experiment. He'd got Gilles, the tea room's cook, to make a miniature fig pyramid, but it had collapsed and become a sort of leaky green beret that had taken them an hour to scrape off the base of the oven. I told him I couldn't believe that pâtissiers cooked their traditional, three-foot-tall pièces montées in a giant oven, and asked them to try baking and caramelizing the figs first, then piling them up afterwards.

Once I'd zapped all the emails offering me watches, medication, sex and the opportunity to reveal my bank details to criminals, I started to wonder where Léanne had got to. I was on my second coffee, and she was half an hour late.

Even though it is not polite to hassle French women, I called her. She was in her car, and in a rush somewhere. Not to meet me, as it happened.

'I am sorry, Pol,' she said. 'I cannot see you today. But anyway, you must return to Bendor.'

'What?'

Léanne paused before answering, presumably to negotiate traffic. 'We think that M has finalized the deal,' she went on. 'This is why she wants to leave the island and come to you. But she must not go away. She must take us to the organizers, and to the assassin. It is the only way to protect the President. So you must be with her, observe her. You must return to the island.'

'Now?'

'Tomorrow at the latest. Call her and tell her you are coming. I will talk to you before you go. Sorry I cannot come now. There is a special operation, I must go to Saint Tropez.'

As soon as she rang off, I speed-dialled Valéry – no answer. Elodie – no answer.

Shit, I thought, if this special operation was what I thought it was, they might not be getting married for a few years yet.

I folded up my laptop, ran to the car park and swung my car down the snail-shell road, trying my best not to take an accidental short cut through the olive groves.

What was more important, I wondered, saving the Bonnepoires' favourite son from arrest or respecting their stupid code about which driveway I should use?

The entrance to the new tarmacked drive was blocked by an empty Renault Espace. My only option was to back up, open the big green gates and use the date-palm drive. There didn't seem to be anyone about. With a bit of luck, the snootier members of the family would still be at Mass.

To reduce the actual time spent on the forbidden drive, I gunned the engine and kicked up a lot of dust, which probably explained why, when I came to the place where I had to manoeuvre between two palm trees, I saw a gallery of Bonnepoires watching me from the terrace. Arms were waving, heads were shaking. Too bad, I decided.

I pulled into the car park and dialled Valéry again, all the while shouting for Elodie in case she was in earshot.

'Monsieur West!' Someone was calling me, with even more urgency than I was managing.

It was Dadou, marching across the car park, followed closely by Moo Moo, who was performing a sort of stately trot to keep up with her husband.

'Have you seen Valéry?' I asked.

Dadou opened and shut his mouth, as if to gobble my question away.

'Did Valéry not tell you which driveway to use?' he snapped. 'And at such speed! Do you know how much damage you could do to the old drive, and to one of the date palms if you crashed into it? Do you think the bastide is a rally circuit?'

Moo-Moo gave her husband a congratulatory 'ho!' They might be totally different people – the religious prude and the shagger of golf-club gardeners – but they shared the same goal in life, to defend the famille.

'The other way was blocked,' I told him, pointing across the gardens to the large Renault which was now, I noticed, driving sedately up the tarmac towards us, as if to show me how it should be done. 'Have you seen Valéry?'

'Valéry? He went into Saint Tropez. Why?'

'Oh shit,' I said, and Moo-Moo's gasp proved that she understood English swearwords. I saw Bonne Maman coming over, a look of satisfaction on her face, as if I had finally revealed my true colours.

'Honestly, Monsieur, I don't know what you are trying to do,' Bonne Maman said. 'You parade in your underwear in front of the children, you contradict us when we try to explain why this wedding is premature, you try to seduce poor Sixtine . . .'

'Moi?' I was going to defend myself, but gallantry got the better of me. There was no point revealing who'd invited whom for a morning dip.

'And,' Bonne Maman went on, frowning, 'I don't understand this affair with Dadou and Louisiana. You do realize that France sold Louisiana to the Americans in 1803? We can't pay its bills any more.'

The three of them shared a self-congratulatory smile at this witticism, and Moo-Moo and Dadou went to greet the fresh batch of Bonnepoires arriving in the Renault. Bonne Maman held back to finish lecturing me.

'I think you will agree,' she said quietly, 'that there is no reason for you to stay here any longer. Perhaps you will fetch your things and leave?'

'Of course,' I said, stopping myself from saying what a pleasure it would be to escape from her clutches. 'But if you will permit, I would like to see Valéry and Elodie first. Have you seen Elodie?'

'She went to the beach, I think, with Sixtine. But I don't think you need to bother them.'

'Sorry, but I must,' I said.

I would just have to drive along the beach road until I spotted the girls, I decided. I couldn't leave without warning Elodie about the police operation. I might not have won the contract to prepare a feast for her wedding, but at least I could do my best to ensure that her fiancé didn't meet up with my old friend the leather-jacketed cop.

What happened next was a bit confusing.

Valéry's parents and Bonne Maman had left the car park. I was trying one last time to get through to Elodie when I heard a squeal of brakes and the wrench of a badly timed gear change. Valéry's red Mercedes came swerving towards me.

He slewed to a halt and started babbling. Drugs, panic or both were making him about as comprehensible as a gibbon on helium. I went over to his car to listen more closely, and gradually, words started to take form.

'Police . . . Dealer . . . Cocaine . . . Merde' seemed to be the basic gist.

'The police are after your dealer? Or after you?' I asked.

'Yes,' he replied.

'Which?'

'Both. I think.' He stared down the driveway as if he was expecting an army of zombies to come chasing after him.

'Have you got any drugs on you? Or in you?' I asked.

In reply, he just started to twitch in the driver's seat, as if he couldn't decide whether to start up the engine again or jump out of the car and run for the hills.

I turned and saw what he was twitching about – a black BMW with impenetrably tinted windows had just come racing into the date-palm driveway, and was beating my own speed record on its crazed trajectory towards the car park. This, I presumed, was the dealer.

A good-looking young guy got out of the car. He was smartly dressed in a gleaming white shirt, clean jeans and designer sunglasses. He looked a pleasant sort of bloke, the kind with classic features and a square chin who could put on a white coat and play a TV surgeon.

His words, though, were less those of a lifesaver than a serial killer. He was swearing at Valéry, using images that I only half-understood but which sounded extremely painful. From what I gathered, the guy was under the impression that Valéry had brought the cops along to their latest meeting. Already, I thought I could hear sirens in the distance.

'Non, non, je te jure que non,' Valéry was saying, swearing his innocence.

But he was obviously not convincing, because the dealer cocked his ear towards the approaching sirens, gave an especially wide grin, and produced a phone-sized plastic package from behind his back.

'Here,' he said, 'a present for your family,' and he threw it into the lavender bush.

I saw what was happening. The cops were going to arrive and search the place, and this dealer-sized pack of drugs was going to land Valéry, and his whole clan, in the merde.

The dealer wished us a 'bonne journée' and returned calmly to his car, which was still running. He did a quick tyre burn as a farewell gesture, and skidded away, peppering us with pieces of gravel.

The air was still thick with dust when, about two seconds later, we heard a loud thud, a blast on the horn, and then the metallic plonking sound of a small shower of dates landing on a car bonnet. The dickhead had driven into a date palm.

It took us a few moments more to realize that, given the lack of any activity from the BMW, the dealer had obviously knackered his engine, hurt himself, or both.

The sirens were still no more than a faint wail in the distance, but there was not much time to act. I jumped up into the lavender bed. I'd seen more or less where the drugs had landed, and the bush was so thick that the shiny package was resting in full view on top of a clump of purple flowers. Great marketing concept, I thought, lavender-scented coke – drugs that keep your nostrils fresh.

Luckily, the bag was undamaged. I grabbed it and ran for the BMW.

'Come and help me,' I told Valéry, who climbed out of his own car, still in a daze.

Sure enough, the dealer hadn't had time to put on his seat belt, and had knocked himself out on the windscreen. A bulbous red lump was pulsing at the bridge of his nose.

'Pull him over to the passenger seat,' I told Valéry.

With me shoving from one side and Valéry hauling from the other, it took only a few seconds to free the driving seat. The dealer moaned loudly, but didn't wake up.

'Now go and flush any other stuff you have down the toilet,' I told Valéry.

'OK, OK,' he said, and sprinted into the house.

Praying that I had enough time, and that the car would work, I turned the key. The engine growled to life. Yes. It had only stalled. I backed gently away from the date palm.

The dealer had dented the brown tree trunk, which was a shame, but it was nothing compared to the dent in the Bonnepoires' fortunes if I didn't get the BMW and the drugs out of their garden – sorry, park – before the police arrived.

So, defying family policy yet again, I drove down the driveway as fast as I could, and pulled out on to the road, checking in my mirror to make sure there were no flashing lights in sight.

I resisted the urge to gun the engine, and set off on a sedate cruise parallel to the beach. I could hear sirens much more clearly now, but they didn't seem to be following me. In any case, I told myself, I was just another daytripper out for a spin, with his friend enjoying a quiet nap in the passenger seat.

The next hurdle was to park without attracting attention.

I didn't want witnesses sending the cops after the tourist who'd abandoned an unconscious man in a dented BMW and gone for a walk along a beach that was completely free of hiding places.

There were plenty of cars parked along the seafront. Several of them were flash sports models, too. A BMW was nothing out of the ordinary down here. What's more, no one on the beach seemed to be paying any attention to the traffic. The sunlit Mediterranean was way too good a spectacle.

I slid into an empty parking space, wiped my fingerprints from the steering wheel and the gear lever, checked that no pedestrians were coming my way, and stepped out of the car.

After a shaky start, I was getting good at this spying stuff, I thought.

The dealer was mumbling, as though he might wake up pretty soon. When he did, he'd find that his gift had been returned to him. If, that is, he searched under the seats.

6

We were sitting on the terrace, overlooking the scene of the family's latest victory over history. It was well after two p.m., but Bonne Maman didn't seem to care. She pointed to my empty cup, and Moo-Moo, trembling only slightly at the sinfulness of it all, was forced to pour out another dose of fresh coffee.

I, meanwhile, was having to re-tell the story of the drugs in the lavender, and the date palm that had saved the family, to a rapt audience of Bonnepoires. Adults only, of course – even Sixtine had been deemed too young for this little coffee party.

The all-knowing Bonne Maman had of course seen me driving away in the BMW, and demanded a full confession from Valéry. He'd been given a right aristocratic bollocking, and was now sitting, chastened but relieved, holding hands with Elodie, who was smiling for pretty well the first time all weekend.

After dumping the car, I had found her and Sixtine swimming, and told them about the narrow escape in the BMW. Elodie had immediately rushed to a call box to inform the police anonymously where to find a groggy dealer and his stash. Consequently, she was also a heroine of the hour, and had even dared to change into an above-the-knee skirt.

The police had arrived at the bastide, sirens blazing, mere seconds after I'd driven away. They'd received a tip-off, they said, that drugs would be found in the grounds of the house, and they had a search warrant that even the Bonnepoires' good connections couldn't override. A collection of shirt-sleeved men and women were now poking about below us in shrubs and flower beds, accompanied by straining dogs that would – Valéry had promised – go home frustrated.

'It seems that you do understand the importance of family after all,' Bonne Maman told me gravely, to a flurry of nods from the others. It would have been cruel to tell her that I'd done it for my friends, not her family. 'You can imagine the potential scandal for us. Drugs are not well viewed by the Elysée . . .' She held out a hand towards Ludivine the presidential spokeslady. 'By the banking community . . .' She nodded to Mimi. 'Or by our government's ministries . . .' She smiled at Dadou. 'Furthermore,' she went on, ignoring the plea in Babou's eyes to include the tennis-court industry in her little speech, 'Dadou has kindly agreed to look into this Louisiana matter for you.'

'I can't promise anything. Send me an email,' Dadou said. It pained him to offer, but he knew that family obligations couldn't be overlooked.

'Valéry has assured me that this will put an end to his bad habit,' Bonne Maman said, and her grandson nodded in furious agreement. 'He has been a young imbecile, but perhaps with this shock he will at last become an adult. And Mademoiselle, also, has proved her loyalty.' She nodded gratefully to Elodie. 'Now, I am not a snob...' at this point, a thunderbolt really ought to have come down from heaven and welded Bonne Maman's tongue to her dentures, but someone up there was clearly in an indulgent mood today, 'so I am willing to overlook her, uh, humble origins...' I glanced at Elodie, who was managing very well under the circumstances to control her desire to murder the old bat, '... and, on behalf of the family, to consider the viability of her marriage to my grandson.'

There was a little ripple of applause at Bonne Maman's boundless generosity, except of course from Moo-Moo, whose body contained no positive cells at all. Valéry gave Elodie a discreet peck on the cheek.

'Providing that you change the arrangements,' Bonne Maman added. 'It is unthinkable that a grandson of mine should get married anywhere but in one of our family homes. So the reception must be held aux Chefs.'

'Their chateau in the Camargue,' Elodie whispered to me.

'And speaking of the reception...' Bonne Maman turned to me. 'If Monsieur West can guarantee that it will be of the required excellence, I think that he has proved himself a capable young man, despite his tendency to contravene certain standards of common decency.'

I smiled in acknowledgement of this glowing testimony. 'It would be a pleasure,' I said, only remembering when Moo-Moo whimpered that uttering this word was one of those indecencies.

'Naturally you will agree, Valéry,' Bonne Maman concluded, 'that you are obliged to change the date.'

This froze the smile on Valéry's face. 'But I've sent out the invitations,' he objected.

'New ones can be sent,' Bonne Maman decreed.

'I've made an appointment at the town hall for the ceremony.'

'It can be cancelled. We know plenty of people in town halls.'

'But Bonne Maman, the date has been set.' Urged on by Elodie's elbows, Valéry was putting up a fight.

'Do you still persist in trying to contradict me, young man?' Bonne Maman inquired with acid calm.

'Well . . .'

Grandmother and grandson locked horns in a new round of argument, while Moo-Moo and Dadou made diplomatic noises in both directions, siding with Bonne Maman and trying to appease their son.

I didn't really see what the fuss was about. So what if Valéry and Elodie had to wait a few weeks or months to get married? It wasn't as if they were desperate to end a lifetime's virginity. Just give in, I wanted to tell them, keep the old girl happy and life will be much sweeter.

But it wasn't my problem. I took a long, tasty draught of coffee. With the sun reflecting gently off the distant sea, the softest of breezes wafting through the protective date palms, and the birdsong almost completely drowning out the disheartened yelps of the police dogs below us, I decided that, after a few scares, things were on the up again.

All I had to do now was keep tabs on M, so that I could stop her whacking the President.

And, from the look of things, prevent Elodie hiring the same hitman to take out Bonne Maman.

THE BEST-LAID PLANS
OF VIBRATING MICE AND MEN

Marseille

1

UNPLEASANT AS IT IS to admit it, some of the world's most famous ballads started out as chansons françaises. 'My Way' was originally 'Comme d'Habitude', by the squawking French crooner Claude François, the man who would have won a worldwide contest to find the voice least like Frank Sinatra's. And the song that we Anglos know as 'If You Go Away' is a translation of 'Ne Me Quitte Pas' by Jacques Brel.

I knew about 'My Way', but it was M who put me right on 'If You Go Away' when we were in Collioure. We'd just enjoyed our erotic bathtime and she'd found a radio channel on the hotel TV. 'Ne Me Quitte Pas' came on, and I said it was a clever translation, especially the way the French singers pronounced the extra syllable on the end of 'quitte' – 'kee-ta', to fit the rhythm.

When she realized I wasn't joking, M told me that Brel's was the original version, and ran me through the French lyrics. They begin very poetically, she said. If his lover will agree not to leave him, Brel promises to give her pearls of rain from countries where it never rains. He says he'll create a brand-new country for her, where love will be king and she will be queen.

'But then he starts getting desperate,' she said. 'He promises to tell her a story about a king who died because he never met her, which is just plain silly. And he ends up on his knees saying that he would be content just to be near her, to be the shadow of her shadow, the shadow of her dog.'

'The shadow of her dog?' I couldn't believe it. 'He doesn't sound much like a Latin lover to me.'

'No,' she agreed. 'A typical Frenchman would tell the woman, OK, bugger off then, I've been shagging your best friend anyway.'

Then she explained why the song was so untypical – Brel wasn't French at all. He was Belgian, with a self-destructive combination of French poeticism and Flemish insecurity.

Now, a week or so later, I was thinking back to that conversation in Collioure. I had just phoned M and told her I was coming back to Bendor to be with her. She was still a bit miffed that I'd told her not to come to Saint Tropez, and didn't sound very keen to see me again.

Trouble was, as far as I knew, I had no Belgian blood in me at all. So I doubted very much that I was going to be any good at begging M not to leave me.

On the morning after the dramatic events at the bastide – the Monday – Elodie woke me up to tell me that I was to take her as near to Marseille as possible. She intended to get the TGV from there to Paris, and wanted a chat on the way. Most of the weekending Bonnepoires had either left the previous night or at dawn, so breakfast was an intimate affair, with Bonne Maman in benevolent mood, but obviously impatient for her troublesome guests to leave her in peace.

Valéry and Elodie were surprisingly muted, and said a low-key but saliva-sodden farewell, whispering together for several minutes while I hung around. Valéry, it seemed, was staying down south to try and finalize the wedding arrangements.

At last they managed to let go of each other, and Elodie and I were on our way along the coast road. It really did feel like cruising through one of those 1960s films when the South of France was the chicest place on Earth and the movie cameras had trouble cramming all the colours on to their tiny squares of celluloid.

Of course, in those films, an open-top sports car zooms along deserted coast roads, overtaking only a Rolls-Royce and a comic 2CV, a manoeuvre it usually carries out on a hairpin bend over a thousand-foot drop. More mundanely, almost as soon as we left the bastide, Elodie and I got stuck behind a German campervan and a gas-bottle delivery truck, a duo that chugged westwards so slowly that we could have counted the rocks on the sea shore below.

In the end, Elodie got too impatient with trundling along in our queue of cars and jammed her fist on my steering wheel to give a long blast on the horn.

'Connards!' she yelled. Dickheads.

I laughed and she told me to shut up with more than her usual assertiveness.

'What's up with you?' I asked. 'I don't get it. Bonne Maman gives you her permission to marry but you're still in a mood. You didn't expect the family to turn into angels, did you? To survive with that lot, you've got to do what

Moo-Moo's done and rise to their level of snootiness. You can't expect them to come down off their mountaintop. They won't, they only survive because they're up there. They're like a high-altitude breed of llama.'

'You don't understand a thing about France,' she snapped. 'Haven't you noticed how they still don't accept me? The old bitch still calls me *vous*.'

'I thought it was a kind of respect,' I said.

'Not in this case, imbecile. If she thought I was equal to Valéry, she would call me *tu*. I am young, it would be a kind of acceptance in the family. Then maybe some of Valéry's aunts and uncles would call me *tu*, as well. Maybe I would call them *tu*. Although not Moo-Moo. Yuk.'

She was right, I didn't understand a thing about France.

We swung through the easily mispronounceable town of La Bouillabaisse, which didn't cause Elodie to crack a smile, and she spent the next few kilometres in total muteness, only breaking her vow of silence when our snake of cars caught up with an even slower-moving tourist coach.

'Merde!' she swore. 'Did you have to choose such a stupid road? Why didn't you take the autoroute?'

'And why didn't you get a lift with Babou?' I grumped.

'That bastard!'

'*Bastide*, you mean,' I said, and at last the storm subsided.

'I'm sorry to be angry with you, Paul,' Elodie said. 'It's because there is something you do not know. I promised Valéry that I would not tell you, but I must. It is about the date of the wedding. It *is* important. Very important. And the old bitch knows this.'

I drove, changing gears about every twenty yards, and she explained.

'You see, Valéry discovered that there is a contract. One of his aunts – the wife of Mimi – revealed this to him. She was not born a Bonnepoire, so she is less, you know, faithful to the family. She is originally from—'

'A contract?' I prompted her before she could go off on a genealogical tangent.

'Yes. Valéry must marry before his thirtieth birthday. If he does not, his share of a *donation* – a present made for tax reasons, you know?'

'Yes. A lifetime gift, I think they call it.'

'Yes. His share of this lifetime gift made by his grandfather to all of his grandchildren returns to Bonne Maman. The grandfather died ten years ago, and Bonne Maman refuses to make any gifts. She wants to own everything. When she dies, it will be la merde fiscale – total tax shit.'

'And when's Valéry's thirtieth birthday?'

'The day after we were due to marry.'

I had to laugh.

'So he's marrying you for his own money? That's a new one.'

Now I understood. I had never been able to work out why Elodie was so cynical about marriage and yet so keen to tie the knot with this bunch of snobs.

'It's not just the money,' she defended herself. 'It's the independence. The *donation* is enough to buy a fantastic apartment in Paris, and escape from his family's house.'

'Valéry still lives at home?' I thought I'd been exaggerating when I said this to the cops.

'He has an apartment in their hôtel particulier – their mini-chateau in the seizième arrondissement. With this money, he can be free. *We* can be free.'

I couldn't take my eyes off the road to check for signs of irony or cynicism in Elodie's face, which was a pity. All I could do was ask her, cruelly perhaps, whether she was on a percentage. OK, not the kind of question you should ask a bride-to-be, but Elodie was not your average fiancée. She was the daughter of Jean-Marie. Scheming was in her genes.

Instead of pinching my earlobe or punching me, she just started to make a sound that, if it hadn't been Elodie, I would have mistaken for sobbing. Elodie didn't do that kind of thing. When life hit her hard, she didn't buckle – she hit back.

'Oh Paul, this is my tragedy,' she said finally. 'I have become weak. I have discovered with Valéry that, underneath this tough exterior, made hard by constant battles with Papa since the age of twelve, is hidden a very sensitive woman.'

Pretty well hidden, I thought.

'You know,' she went on, 'I have realized that I really want to get married. It is a romantic idea, after all, to be joined by a ring and a name, rather than just by sex.'

Yes, very romantic, I agreed.

'I've been single a long time,' she said. 'We call it les quatre cents coups. You could say the four hundred hard times, or the four hundred shags. Well, with me there have not been four hundred men.' She seemed to be doing some mental arithmetic to make sure. 'But it gets a bit boring, meeting someone, starting a relationship, breaking up, all that merde. I want to stay with Valéry. He's fun, he loves me . . .'

'He's rich . . .'

'Yes, OK, he's rich, but no one can deny their background. My family is rich, too. I am not physically capable of living in poverty. I am a delicate flower.'

'That needs watering with champagne.'

'Yes, I am a luxury flower.'

'And you don't just want to marry Valéry to get revenge on the snobs?'

She thought about this for a moment.

'OK,' she said, 'I do more than ever want to defy them. But we want to get married. It is very simple. And if we can get Valéry's money, too, why not? It is a lot of money, a very good wedding present. The sort of present that can last a lifetime, even for a girl like me with a platinum credit card.'

We were on a stretch of road that curved around a bay lined with dreamy villas. With their balconies overlooking the Med, and little staircases leading directly from their gardens down to the sea, they looked like very good reasons to get rich. I could see Elodie's point. Especially because, if what she said was true, she was going to get true love into the bargain.

'OK,' I said. 'So we have to think of a way to stop Bonne Maman changing Valéry's arrangements. A way of forcing her to let you get married on the right date.'

Elodie laughed. 'That is as simple as forcing Moo-Moo to get "fuck me here" tattooed on her ass,' she said, a remark which very nearly ended both of our lives.

'No, no, there might be a way,' I said, swerving back on to the right side of the road again. 'I think we need to have a word with your dad.'

'Papa? No, please. If you tell him about the money, I will lose it all.'

'We *have* to tell him about the money. It's the only way. Get him on the phone,' I said.

Moaning loudly, she did what I asked.

2

I pulled into the lane leading to Bandol's cute little railway station, and stopped in the tiny car park. It felt almost like a homecoming. Only – what? – three or four days earlier, I'd arrived here with M, thinking that my biggest problem in life was how long we would have to wait for the ferry to Bendor. Things had changed slightly since.

'There are trains about every twenty minutes. It's half an hour to Marseille,' I told Elodie.

'Hmm,' she said.

'I'll help you with your bag.'

'Hmm.' It was as if she'd had her tongue pierced and couldn't talk for the swelling.

'What is it?' I asked.

She looked suddenly mischievous. 'Why don't I get a later train? I want to meet M.'

'But you'll lose your reservation on the TGV.'

'I can change it.'

'Are you sure? Some TGV tickets are non-exchange-able.'

'You're forgetting I have a platinum card.'

I tried to think how to tell Elodie that her meeting M was not a good idea. My reunion with M was not just boyfriend and girlfriend meeting up after a short separation. There was no room for Elodie in the game of I Spy that I'd been ordered to play.

'What is it?' Elodie asked. 'You want to keep her secret? Don't tell me she's ugly.'

'No, she's not ugly.'

'She's bisexual.'

'She's not bloody bisexual. Well, not as far as I know.'

'Well then, come on, let's go and say hello.'

It wasn't Elodie's fault, I reasoned. For once in her life, she had no idea what was at stake. And there was no way I could explain.

Trying to banish negative thoughts from my mind, I started the engine and steered us downhill into town.

M had moved off the island and taken a room on the mainland, at the hotel overlooking Bandol's *anse*. She said it was more low-key here. She didn't know, of course, that binoculars, cameras and microphones were being pointed at her from all around the bay.

We found her in the garden, reading a French political magazine. She was lounging on a teak armchair, with her feet up on the rail overlooking the beach. I wondered how many cops were staring up her skirt.

I hadn't warned her that Elodie would be tagging along, so M's first reaction was a questioning frown that could almost have been jealousy. Perhaps she really did care about me, I thought. But her look could also have been plain distrust. Who was this strange woman, and what was she doing, hanging around with me?

Elodie did her usual thing of giving new people a long, frank stare of sexual assessment. I would have liked to know her conclusion.

'So you couldn't stay away from me, after all?' M asked me, keeping her eyes on Elodie.

'Only long enough to get the wedding fixed up,' I said. 'This is Elodie, by the way, the bride-to-be.'

M looked relieved to hear the name.

The two girls gave each other a polite *bise*. They could almost have been sisters, despite the apparently different courses their lives had taken. Elodie had leapt on to the rich-kid, fast-money corporate bandwagon, and M had opted for an only slightly less aggressive career in political assassination.

'It's good to see you again,' I told M, though it was less than half-true. I was pretty sure I would have got the hell away from her as fast as possible if Léanne hadn't ordered me to do otherwise.

M pulled me down to give her a kiss, and held on to me for several seconds when I tried to break away. Elodie raised her eyebrows, impressed by this show of passion.

'So they call you M because of the James Bond films, right? Are you a spy?' Elodie laughed, not noticing that M was reddening.

'No, I was just the bossiest in my office,' she replied, deadpan.

'And with Paul, do you have to dominate him? Is he a typical cold Englishman with you?'

'Only when he's had too much Muscat on an empty stomach,' M said, meaningfully.

'Well, you can be assured he was a good boy in Saint Tropez,' Elodie said. 'Despite all the temptations in his bed.'

M shot me a questioning look, and I did my best to shrug my innocence.

'Teddy bears,' Elodie finally said, enjoying the effect she'd created. 'Paul was forced to share a bed with about a hundred of them. It was like an orgy in a Disney movie.'

M laughed. 'So you've sorted out the wedding, have you?' she asked Elodie. 'And you're sure you want to hire Paul to feed your wedding guests?'

'I'm hoping he'll poison some of them,' Elodie answered.

Again, only I noticed M's blush. One more gaffe like that, I thought, and she'll smell a rat. I was going to have to get rid of Elodie, and fast.

*

Elodie insisted on treating M and me to lunch, and we walked along the coastal path to a restaurant nestling in a rocky inlet.

More fresh fish and more pale rosé, at a table that you could have used as a diving board to jump into the crystal-clear sea. These southerners sure knew how to live, I mused, as I savoured the taste of a crème brûlée perfumed with orange-blossom essence.

Elodie, however, decided to sour the sweetness in my mouth by carrying on with her seemingly endless series of allusions to killing people. She outlined her plans for guillotining the snootiest members of the French upper classes, and then segued straight into asking M about her work, as if the two subjects might be related.

Was there really money to be made from oceanography, Elodie wanted to know. Was black-market caviar as good as the legal stuff, and where could she get some for her wedding?

M laughed, fortunately, and gave Elodie her standard speech about sturgeon extinction.

'You are wasting your time with this fish ecology,' Elodie lectured her. 'You should go into a real business where you can make big money. Paul, why don't you go into partnership with M?'

I already am, I thought. I'm the pilot fish, glued to her as she sharks her way towards her target.

'Paul's a good partner to have on your side in times of crisis,' Elodie went on, and cajoled me into giving M a blow-by-blow account of how I'd saved the Bonnepoires.

'Quite the undercover operator, aren't you?' M teased me. I shrugged as modestly as possible, not wanting to appear too much of a man of action in her eyes.

'He does diplomacy, too,' Elodie added. Was she trying

to marry me off to M or what? 'If Paul was not here, I would be dealing direct with my father. Agh!' She gave a silent-movie scream of horror.

'Elodie and her dad don't exactly get on,' I explained to M. 'When they're not shouting at each other, they're throwing fruit.'

'You should make the most of him, Elodie,' M blurted out. She seemed to regret it instantly, but Elodie was on to her like a flash.

'You mean your father is . . . ?'

'Yes,' M said. 'When I was three.'

'Oh.' Elodie put a consoling hand on her shoulder, but couldn't resist fishing for info. 'How did it happen?'

'An accident.'

'A car accident?' Elodie asked.

'No, boat.'

'Was he a fisherman?' I asked. 'Did he have a yacht, or what?'

'Honestly, Paul, can't you see you're upsetting M?' Elodie had suddenly morphed from chief interrogator into M's protector. Damn her, I thought, it was practically the first time M had revealed anything about herself.

And then Elodie made things even worse.

'This is a fantastic place,' she sighed. She took a deep breath of olive-scented sea air and smiled out across the sunlit sea that was as smooth as a mirror. 'I think I will stay here tonight. Do you think they can put an extra bed in your room?'

M and Elodie joined forces to slap me on the back and dislodge the crème brûlée I'd inhaled. 'It's a good idea, Paul,' M said. 'Elodie can get a room at the hotel, then we can all go to Marseille together tomorrow. You can drop her at the station while I go to my meeting.'

'You have another meeting there?' I asked, when I could speak again.

'Yes. Why don't you phone the hotel and ask if they've got a room?'

I went outside to book a second room. I also took the opportunity to put in a call to Léanne.

'A meeting tomorrow? This is it.' She sounded very pleased. 'We are coming to the climax.'

'Great,' I said, though I was feeling a lot less orgasmic than she clearly was.

After lunch, we crashed out on the small deserted beach below the restaurant. I could sense waves of envy flowing down from the terrace above. How did the Englishman do it, they were thinking, how come he gets to lie there between the two topless babes?

I didn't want to be ungrateful, but I would have liked to tell them that our carefree appearance was slightly deceptive.

I was dozing fitfully when the pebbles by my head began to vibrate. All three of us reached for our phones, but it was Elodie who came up trumps.

'Uh? Who? Qui?' she answered. 'What?' She listened to a long, droning question. 'No, of course Valéry's uncle has not responded,' she snapped. 'Paul has posed the question yesterday only.'

Now I knew who was calling. Only someone having Jake's Franglais inflicted on them would start to talk like that.

'What? Honestly! Without doubt your festival of posy is important to you, but I am in the middle of a catastrophe with my plans of marriage.' Elodie grimaced, presumably at the way her ability to speak English had so suddenly evaporated. 'No, I will not pass you Valéry's number. Leave him tranquil with your festival! What? Come to the marriage? Lobby direct with Dadou? T'es fou ou quoi?' She wailed the last sentence, but using French seemed to have a magical calming effect on her, because she suddenly began to smile and speak in a conciliatory tone. 'Sorry, yes, why not come? Bon idea. If you can get a plane ticket. I will tell Dadou to expect you . . .' She hung up and giggled. 'It's perfect,' she said. 'Dadou loves the raggedy, grungy type. I will give him a hint that Jake is gay and we will all have a lot of fun.'

As if to prove it, she laughed loud enough to scare every fish out of the inlet.

After a day of good food, sun, wine and swimming, it's only natural to feel mellow when you finally get to bed. You've showered off the salt, the hot water has relaxed your muscles, and you can wiggle your toes beneath the sheets with a real sense that life is worth living. Having a naked woman lying next to you would, to most men I know, count as a definite plus.

To me, though, M was a threat. I almost wished she wasn't there. Which was a horrific first in my life. Ever since I'd realized that there were more things that guys and girls could do together than play tag and pull each other's hair, I'd dreamt of ending every day next to a girl shaped exactly like M.

And now here I was, living the dream, and I wished I was back with the teddy bears. It was like a punishment invented by the Greek gods. Except that it had been invented by people even crueller than Zeus and co. – the French police. I could have howled in frustration. Instead I asked M, who had just settled into bed and was probably wondering what, if anything, would happen next, 'Have you told your people you want to get out of the project?'

She groaned. 'I really don't want to talk about work, Paul.'

'Does that mean you've tried but they won't let you?'

'Kind of,' she said. 'Look, do we have to talk about that? Or anything? I don't want to talk. All I really want is to make love. Can we make love?'

She shifted towards me, and I froze.

'Elodie's just next door,' I objected. 'These walls are paper-thin. I'm sure I heard her drop her knickers on the floor.'

'I won't ask how you know what it sounds like when she drops her knickers.' I could almost hear M smiling. She moved even closer, and an arm slid across my belly. 'Come on, Paul. We don't have to rock the foundations. We can be quiet. I bet there have been times when you had to keep the volume down. When you brought a girl home and you didn't want your folks to know?' The hand began sliding lower down my body, fingers flicking lightly across my skin. 'Or maybe you're on a plane, everyone's asleep or watching the movie, you're wrapped up in your airline blanket and your girlfriend reaches under it and starts to give you a little massage?'

M was now doing things that would definitely have distracted me from the in-flight entertainment.

'Or you go back to a girl's place and she shares a room with a friend, so you have to get under the sheets and make love slowly and quietly, without waking up the other girl?'

Now her whole body was softly caressing me. It seemed to be hovering over my skin like the warm rays of the sun.

I didn't move – I didn't have to – as she climbed on top of me. Then, gently, almost soundlessly, except for faint creaks from the bedframe, restrained moans, and – finally – a pair of almost simultaneous gasps, with my body remembering why it enjoyed doing things like this, I became Mata Hari.

I fucked for France.

M exhaled deeply and let her whole weight press on my chest. Both of us were silent for a full minute.

'Don't worry about me,' came a voice through the wall. 'You can do it again and make all the noise you want.'

3

When I got up next morning, M was on the beach below the hotel, phoning. She was listening, nodding, pacing back and forth. I looked down on her from our window.

My phone started to buzz by the bed. It was Léanne.

'Bonjour, Paul. At last you wake up. You have slept a long time. Does this mean you had a good night?'

'So you're watching my hotel window?' I asked, avoiding her question.

'Yes, you can say cuckoo to me if you look at the garden over the beach. But please don't do this, because M is looking at your window right now.'

So our every movement was being observed. I wondered if the surveillance included infra-red binoculars, because we'd left the window open last night, and the cops could well have been peering in from one of the buildings on the other side of the bay.

'She is talking with Marseille,' Léanne said. 'She is arranging her rendezvous.'

'Who with?'

'We are sure it is with the man who will accept her . . . commission.' She meant the hitman.

'What do you want me to do?'

'You drive M and your friend to Marseille, OK?'

'OK.'

'I know today was the end of your car-hire contract, but we have – how do you say? – elongated it for you. So you leave as soon as M wants you to, OK? No time for swimming and such luxuries.'

'OK.' The passivity of last night's lovemaking seemed to have done something to me. My body had decided to do nothing except take orders from women.

'Come on, Paul, breakfast, then we leave.' It was Elodie, bursting into the room as if she hoped to interrupt M and myself in the middle of something naughty. 'I must go to Paris to buy a dress. I will get it today and then return down south to support Valéry.'

'Why don't you buy one in Marseille?'

'What, buy a wedding dress outside Paris? En *province*? Quelle idée!' I might as well have suggested getting married in a mud hut and serving cockroaches at the reception. 'Allez, Paul, let's go.'

'OK.' This morning, a female wish was my command.

We were on the outskirts of Marseille when Elodie's phone rang.

'Ah, c'est toi,' she grunted, and then listened for a few seconds before tapping me on the shoulder. 'He wants to talk to you.'

'Who does?'

'My father.' She held the phone to my ear and I heard a very smug-sounding Jean-Marie telling me how brilliant he'd been.

'I have talked to some important friends, I have used my influence, I have contacted my, uh, contacts, and I think that I have something,' he said.

Yes, I thought, an ego so puffed up that it could fly him across the Atlantic.

'You know that the President and I have certain things in common?' he asked.

'Yes?' The ego, plus the belief that the world would be a better place if everyone spoke French and drove Renaults.

'Yes. For the first thing, we live in the same part of Paris. Before he was President, he was our major.' He meant mayor. 'And you know that I represent his political party here?'

'Right.'

'Yes, but not extreme right.'

'No, I meant right, as in OK.'

'Uh?'

'Go on, Jean-Marie, what were you saying?'

'I don't know, you have interrupted me.' I'd forgotten that you don't cut in when a Frenchman is asking rhetorical questions.

'You have things in common with the President . . .'

'Ah yes.' He was happy again. 'For the second thing, we are both very interested in, you know, immobile, uh, how do you say?'

'I have no idea,' I said, wondering if this boasting was going to last much longer.

'*L'immobilier*. Houses, apartments.'

'Property,' I said. 'Real estate.'

'Yes. We are both part of a deal in our district that is, shall I say, not one hundred per cent *conventional*.' He chuckled. He liked that word. 'We are, if you want, *associés*, how do you say?'

'Partners in crime?'

'Crime? Who mentioned crime? The President cannot commit a crime. He is immune. It is illegal to accuse a president of crime. And anyway, do you think I could be implicated in something illegal?'

Which was a bit like asking whether pigeons ever poo on statues.

'Oh no, of course not,' I said. 'Sorry I mentioned it. Please go on.' Both of the girls were staring at me, wondering what the hell we were talking about. I had no idea myself.

'OK, OK.' Jean-Marie slowly unruffled his feathers. 'This means that I can maybe have some influence on the President. You understand?' This wasn't a rhetorical question.

'I'm beginning to. Go on.'

'You know he is a friend of these aristocratic imbeciles the Bonnepoires? One of them gives him – how do you say? – *des pipes*. Before the press conferences.'

'Blowjobs?' Now M and Elodie were even more curious about what was going on. 'You mean Ludivine, the spokeslady?'

'Yes. And you can criticize French presidents if you want, but they are always grateful to the women who give them . . .'

'Blowjobs,' I prompted.

'Yes. Blowjobs.' He memorized it, as if it might come in useful one day in his political career.

'And this, in combination with our, uh, immobile deal together, can be very useful. Now, I am going to see the President at a soirée tonight. I think that if I talk to him, maybe he can influence the family to keep the marriage on the correct date, the day before Valéry's birthday. Voilà.' I could almost hear him applauding himself.

'That's great, Jean-Marie, but why tell me? Why didn't you tell Elodie?'

'Huh, we are still officially fâchés. Angry. You can tell her. To me, she would shout and say that I am doing this only so we can get the old vache's money.'

'Well, aren't you?'

He was still chuckling as he rang off.

4

M suggested that I drop her off at the Vieux Port, where she'd reserved a room for us, then take Elodie on to the railway station.

For the first time that morning, I disobeyed a female order, and as soon as M had disappeared into the hotel, I started a rapid-fire apology to Elodie.

Really, really sorry, I said, but would she be pissed off if I left her to get a taxi and doubled back?

'Why?' She was surprised more than annoyed.

'It's M.' I'd rehearsed my explanation in my head. 'She's been coming to Marseille a lot, and every time she comes here, she shakes me off and goes to meet someone. I'm sure it's another man.'

'Oh.' Elodie put a consoling hand on my arm. She had clearly noticed the tensions between M and myself. 'You think she's going to meet him now?'

'Yes.'

'OK, just drop me on the corner of the main street. I'll get a taxi.'

Léanne's trick had worked yet again. In France, you only had to hint at relationship problems and you could act as erratically as you wanted.

'Call me and tell me how it goes,' Elodie said as we unloaded her case. 'And remember – it might not be a man. It could be a woman.' She poked my ribs to show that she was joking. Or half-joking.

I left the car in a side street, ignoring the parking meters. Then I nipped back to the Vieux Port and found a doorway from where I could see the entrance to our hotel.

The hotel itself was four storeys of balconies pointing straight along the harbour. I didn't know which was our room, but M had said it was high up, to give us a good view and reduce the noise from the bustling nightlife below. She must have checked in by now, I calculated. She was probably in the room, unpacking her essentials, changing into more urban clothes.

If you had to hang around on a street corner, it was a pretty pleasant spot to do so. The early-afternoon sun was shining straight at me, and a large pleasure cruiser was just arriving at the nearby jetty, idling up to the harbourside with its cargo of smiling boat-trippers.

I wondered why they call it the 'old port' – on the whole, it looked pretty recent. Half of the water space was taken up by rank upon rank of new yachts. There were thousands of them crammed into the rectangular basin. One side of the harbour was lined with angular modern apartment buildings, and between the wide café terraces and the waterside was a busy road, constantly growling with traffic.

The distant entrance to the port was obviously older, though – an ancient castle with sheer walls and a stubby tower that was a sunburnt version of Collioure's historic willy.

M stepped into the street, and I shrank back into my doorway. She was wearing sunglasses, and had changed into jeans. She looked right and left, as if checking for observers, then walked briskly towards the nearest junction.

Next minute, I was swearing in fluent French. 'Oh merdy putainy crotty shit.' Well, fluent Franglais, anyway.

She was getting a bloody bike. Marseille had Vélibs, like Paris, and she was going to pedal off on one.

What's more, she obviously had a subscription, because she swiped a card at one of the bike stands, wiggled the saddle and the handlebars to make sure everything was in working order, and pushed out into the traffic.

I had no time to fiddle about with a credit card and do likewise. Keeping up a steady stream of bilingual swearing, I jogged after her. Luckily, the bikes were the same heavy model as in Paris, so she was having a bit of trouble getting up speed. I reached the street corner only a few yards behind her, and had a little laugh at what I saw next – a hill, leading to an even steeper hill, topped in the distance by a giant golden statue of the Virgin Mary, waving down at me from a veritable mountaintop.

There was no way M was going to speed up there.

Sure enough, she began to wind through a grid of dark, right-angled streets. It reminded me of when I'd had to risk my life to keep up with Elodie in Paris. This time, on foot, I was much safer, but I couldn't say the same for M. Cars were parked on both sides, and the streets were danger-ously narrow. She was having to concentrate hard on keeping ahead of the impatient drivers behind her, and there was no way she could look back and see me behind her, dodging past dawdling pedestrians.

She rode by the Roman-temple Palais de Justice, and didn't even glance at two bizarre statues of golden cherubs apparently trying to stop themselves falling into a rubbish-strewn fountain. The road was flatter here, and she began to get up speed. I did my best to keep pace, but lost sight of her just before a roundabout.

The central reservation was a grassy mound with a statue of a frock-coated politician receiving something from Marianne, France's female equivalent of Uncle Sam. Either she was handing him a parchment or trying to stab him with a baguette. I trotted around the mound, gazing along each exit to try and spot M's pedalling backside, and drew a blank. A very sexy blank, though.

On the corner of one exit was something I'd never seen in France before – a women's sex shop. I'd seen the men's versions all over Paris, of course – glitzy windows with posters of pouting women, offers of cheap relief in a 'cabine', a curtain of plastic streamers protecting passers-by from the sordid goings-on inside.

This place was completely different. It was a wide, double-fronted shop window, with an uninterrupted view of the interior, and the overriding colours were clean pink and purple rather than the dingy black and red of the guys' dives.

On one side of the entrance was a hanging garden of undies, with the emphasis on transparency and strategically placed holes. On the other was a row of little bottles of flavoured lubricants, and a display of things to tickle, massage and penetrate women's intimate parts. Some of the vibrators had animal heads and faces, including a smily pink dolphin and a grinning blue mouse. Who, I wondered, would want to get shagged by a vibrating rodent?

'You want to go inside, Monsieur?' A tall girl in a tight black T-shirt and low-cut jeans was standing in the door-way, smoking. One of the shop assistants, I guessed. 'Because normally, it's interdit for unaccompanied men,' she added apologetically.

'Ah, merci, non, je—' I stopped in mid-stutter. The thing

was, I'd seen M inside the shop. She was standing near the back of the store, between the corsets and the furry hand-cuffs, as if she was waiting for someone to bring out the split-crotch cycling shorts she'd ordered.

So this was her meeting point – a women's sex shop. What could it mean?

The shop assistant was taking the last puffs of her cigarette, keeping one eye on me, so I waved an innocent goodbye and walked away. She would assume I'd been scared off by the display of electronic penises with animal faces.

In a way she was dead right.

'Why have you followed her, Pol? Merde!' Léanne was doing her best not to sound furious, but making a pretty bad job of it. '*We* follow her. You don't do that. I have told you this was an important meeting.'

The call had come almost as soon as I walked away from the shop. The buzzing in my pocket almost got me killed, because I stopped in the middle of a street to answer, and a car swung round the corner and screeched to a halt. The four young guys in the car yelled and gestured insults at me. I got out of their way.

'But you told me to watch her in Marseille,' I said to Léanne, 'so that's what I'm doing. I need to know what's happening. I'm the one that has to be with her all day. And night.'

There was a long silence, but I could hear how frustrated Léanne was. She wanted me to be the puppet and I kept pulling strings.

'It's the money,' she said at last. 'We think she has come for the money to pay the *man*.' I presumed she meant the hitman.

'Hey, toi, t'es cong?' The driver of the car was keeping

pace with me as I walked, and insulting me in the strong local accent. But I didn't have time to retort. What Léanne had said was much more urgent.

'She's picking up cash?' I asked. 'I would have thought they'd do it by bank transfer. Much cleaner.'

'Huh, no, some people do not like the – what do you call it? – the electronic bank. They prefer to feel the paper in their fingers. She will pick up the money, and she will hide it. So please go to your hotel now and give me the number of your room safe.'

'Hey toi, l'Anglais, là? Tu m'écoutes ou quoi?' Now the driver was asking me whether I was listening to him. Which I wasn't, because Léanne was letting me in on some secrets at last.

'You know, we have a big problem in France,' she was saying. 'Our frontiers are very open, and the euro is the best money for paying crime. The five hundred, it is the biggest value note in the world. A million euros is only as big as two tablets of chocolate or a small computer. It is very easy to hide. This is also, we think, why M takes the bike. She does not want to walk in the street with so much money. She prefers to pedal fast to the hotel. The streets can be dangerous.'

As I was just finding out. The car had pulled up in front of me, and the driver, quite a large guy, was getting out, presumably to ask more insistently whether I had been paying attention to him. He had a very silly haircut – short at the front and sides, with a kind of black chicken crest on top of his skull – but he still looked pretty tough.

'Er, Madame la commissaire, there is a car, number nine two seven . . .' I read out the whole registration, speaking in loud, clear French. 'I think that the driver is going to attack me. Is one of your men in this street?'

The guy laughed, but I'd sown a seed of doubt in his mind. He called me a 'cong' again, shook his crest and got in his car. As he pulled away, the back wheels screeched on the tarmac to show me that he wasn't a wuss.

'What was that?' Léanne asked, and I gave her a brief account. 'I told you the streets can be dangerous here,' she said.

'You haven't been to an English city recently,' I told her. 'I'd have been dead by now.'

I've never been one for cheating on girlfriends. Well, not deliberately anyway. There has been the odd infidelity incident when I was literally blind drunk, or under the impression that I'd been dumped. But a long-term double-dealer? No. It's too complicated.

Now, though, I was rapidly learning what it felt like to be cheater and cheatee, because M and I both had plenty to hide.

'Am I acting natural enough?' I kept asking myself. 'Or is my naturalness unnaturally natural?' And I was thinking, 'I don't think she knows I know. But I do know she *thinks* she knows what I know, and she doesn't. Know, that is. I think.'

We were in a restaurant one street in from the Vieux Port. Sitting at our corner table, guzzling an over-pink Côtes de Provence while we waited for our entrées, both M and I must have seemed uncannily carefree.

M was chatty, telling me that she'd spent most of the afternoon cycling around the city, puffing up hills and getting hooted at. As she spoke, I was sure – well, almost – that she was watching me for signs that I might have doubts about what she'd really been up to.

I was being equally breezy, telling her all the stuff about the Bonnepoires that I hadn't dared to mention in front of

Elodie, and scrutinizing her for any hint that she might have seen me following her that afternoon.

Early on in the meal, I realized I'd made a mistake when I ordered a bouillabaisse, Marseille's trademark stew. I'd only done it so that I'd be able to tell M the story of mispronouncing the name. The thing is, a real bouillabaisse should contain three or four types of local fish, caught and served the same day. A good one costs a fortune. And mine was the main dish in a very cheap three-course menu. It was basically a lumpy, none-too-fresh fish soup. I poked at a doughy potato, and tried to raise my spirits by picturing the fresh food I was planning to serve at Elodie's wedding.

'I wonder how Benoit's getting on with my fig pièce montée,' I said.

'Why don't you call him and ask?' M said.

Naturally, as we were in mutual-suspicion mode, I wondered why she'd suggested this.

'In the middle of dinner?' I said. 'I'm way too polite.'

'But if you're really worried about the wedding, you should call. You're obviously worried about something.' She gave me a bright smile, and rubbed the back of my hand as if this would magically cheer me up.

'I'll call him later,' I said, thinking, Does she want me to phone now so I'll leave the table and she can send someone a text message?

Mutual suspicion had turned me completely paranoid. If this was what it was like to be a full-time adulterer, give me boring old monogamy any day.

We wandered back to the hotel through the kind of area that has been sanitized out of existence in Paris. Groups of guys were hanging around, engulfed in aromatic clouds of dope smoke. Women in ultra-short skirts were standing at the entrance of every dark bar. Very friendly women, too, engaging passing men in chummy banter. One of them, a tall middle-aged lady in PVC thigh boots, was on the phone, commiserating loudly with a friend who'd been arrested, and letting all passers-by know that it was unfair to prevent a woman doing her job of hiring out parts of her body. All this just yards from the main tourist hub.

Our hotel room was small and muggy, so I went to open the window. A rush of traffic noise and café-terrace conversation burst in from below. The view was great, though, straight along the lattice of lights running down each side of the Vieux Port, and away to the floodlit castle.

'Hey.' M was standing by the bed, her hands on her hips, scanning the furniture.

'What?'

'Someone's been in our room.' She looked inside the small wardrobe, and pulled at the padlock on her case.

She was probably right, I thought. One of Léanne's mob had almost certainly been in here looking for the money M had collected from the sex shop. But I couldn't say so. I had to try and imagine what someone would say if they had no idea who might want to search their room.

'Anything missing?' I asked. Yes, that wasn't bad.

'I don't know,' M said, and I watched her carefully, wondering whether she might look where she'd hidden the money.

She opened her bag, and seemed satisfied that the lock and the contents hadn't been interfered with. I tried to see what the combination on her padlock was, but she was too far away and I couldn't afford to be obvious.

'You're not checking your stuff?' she asked.

Damn, I thought. That's exactly what an innocent person would do.

'Nothing worth stealing in my bag. Not unless you're a dirty T-shirt fetishist.' Blast – had I made it obvious that I knew she'd been in a sex shop? 'My laptop's in the safe,' I said. 'Is that OK?'

M opened the safe, the combination of which I'd already given to Léanne. Not that the money was in there. I'd looked.

'Hmm,' M said, not entirely satisfied.

'You want me to call reception? Or the police?' I was especially proud of this last idea. No one who was dealing with the police would suggest calling the police, would they?

'Police, huh,' M said. 'I thought you read the local papers. Down here they're all crooks, in league with the Mafia.' Which, of course, was exactly what someone who was in league with the Mafia would say. Or someone who *wasn't* in league with the Mafia. Shit, it was all getting too complicated.

'I need a drink,' I said. 'Let's go and find a bar.'

'You want to go out? But I got us a staying-in present.' M was kneeling by her bag, holding up a little golden sachet with a pink ribbon on top.

'What is it?' Please, I thought, don't let it be what I think it is.

Smiling enigmatically, she tugged at the ribbon and dipped her fingers inside the bag, which rustled as she pulled out a transparent plastic box.

'Holy shit.' I couldn't stop myself.

'You know what it is?' She looked disappointed at my reaction.

'I think so.'

She took it out of the box to give me a better view, and I came face to face with a smiling pink dolphin. She twisted its tail and it started to buzz, while its little head nodded a manic hello.

'I thought it would be fun,' she said. 'They're not just for women, you know.' She was walking towards me, pointing the dolphin at me, and her thin jacket was already slipping off her shoulders. 'Some men get great pleasure from one of these, you know, if a woman pushes it up—'

'You're not sticking that fish up my backside,' I told her. 'It'd traumatize me for life. I'd never feel safe snorkelling again.'

M was suddenly deflated. Her arms fell to her side, and she threw the dolphin on the bed, where it carried on thrashing about as if it wanted to jump off the balcony and into the harbour.

'You don't fancy me any more, do you, Paul?'

'Course I do. You're beautiful, you're sexy,' I told her, truthfully. I just couldn't add that I was shit-scared of who she was and who her friends were.

'But I don't turn you on any more. I practically had to rape you in Bandol.' She looked genuinely sad. 'Maybe we should call it a day.'

'Call it a day?'

'Go our separate ways.'

'Merde,' I said, failing to act like a guy who loved his girl-friend and didn't want the relationship to end. No, I sounded exactly like a man who has been warned that if he and his girlfriend break up, they are both going to be arrested and thrown in jail.

I spent most of the night lying flat on my back, examining the problem from all angles. I had to find a way of staying with M. And I didn't think I was capable of going down on my knees in the morning and singing 'Ne Me Quitte Pas'.

At about four a.m., I had one moment of frightening lucidity. I was waking from a brief nightmare in which Jean-Marie was boasting about his political connections, and stressing his point by doing unspeakable things to the President, when I had an idea that was either sheer genius or total lunacy. I needed a second opinion. Staring at the ceiling, I waited impatiently for dawn.

As soon as there was a decent amount of light and noise in the street, I snuck out of bed and went downstairs to call Léanne. I left a note for M, saying I'd gone for a coffee. I didn't want her thinking I'd taken her at her word and called it a day.

Out on the waterfront I found a fish market that seemed too authentic to be authentic. It was a single row of around twenty small stands, each one fronted with the registration number of a fishing boat. Sometimes the boat itself was moored at the quay behind the stall, with a fisherman on board mending nets or doing other trawlery stuff

The fishermen looked like gnarled peasants, their hands swollen and their faces wrinkled by years of sun and sea water. And, I guessed, booze to make the long nights go quicker.

The women selling the fish were dressed shapelessly in layers of pullovers and plastic aprons, but they looked decidedly land-bound, with hair-dos dyed blond or the colour of Côte du Rhône wine, like Paris boulangères. All of them were speaking in the strong local accent as they asked their middle-class customers if they wanted their sole and sea bream gutted.

Several of the stalls, I noticed, were selling live fish. Grey sole were flapping, and rougets – red mullet – were gaping in surprise at their human audience. It was hypocritical to be squeamish, but I did feel sorry for the little poissons de roche – small, colourful aquarium fish, my mates from my snorkelling trips in Collioure and Bendor, who had been kidnapped in the middle of their fancy-dress party. Two stalls had little piles of them, still alive, flapping like M's pink dolphin up in the hotel room. I thought of buying them all and setting them free in the harbour, but they looked exhausted. If I returned them to the polluted harbour water they'd probably lie side-up on the surface and get pecked to death by the seagulls.

I turned away and dialled Léanne's number. She answered quickly and told me to look up at the hotel. It sounded as though she was standing in a wind tunnel.

I did as she said and, Christ, there she was on the roof, repeating the balancing act that I'd seen in Collioure.

'Be careful,' I told her. 'M's in the room, asleep. She'll hear you and wake up. She's already suspicious because you searched the room. You did search it, didn't you?'

'Yes, yes,' she said. 'Please wait, I will call you in a minute.'

'But I need to talk to you. M wants us to split—'

'Monsieur, Monsieur.' An old woman was tugging at my arm. She was wearing a shapeless green cardigan and a bright-red headscarf, and was trying to thrust a bag of lemons in my hand. 'Des citrons, Monsieur?' she said, and gripped my elbow almost painfully as she pulled me towards her little citrus fruit stall.

'Non, merci,' I said, but she wouldn't let go.

'Stop calling Léanne,' she hissed at me. 'Des oranges, alors?'

I looked closer and my mouth fell open so wide you could have stuck a kilo of lemons in there. It was one of the ghostly gay twins from Collioure. A cop in drag.

'We think your girlfriend hid the money on the roof. Un

kilo de citrons?' he added for the benefit of an old man buy-ing a headless angler fish from the next stall.

'So Léanne is going to take it? Er, yes, a kilo, please.'

'No, she's going to bug the package. If she finds it.' He began choosing lemons and putting them in a flimsy plastic bag.

'But I must talk to Léanne,' I said. 'M says that we must separate . . .'

'No, no. You must stay with her and follow the money. Anything else, Monsieur?'

'But if there is this bug in the package, I am not necessary. Non, merci, Monsieur, er, Madame. How much for the lemons?'

'We still need you to stay with her. What if Léanne can't plant the bug, or if your girlfriend finds it? You must be there. A million euros, please.'

'*How* much?'

He laughed. 'You can afford it,' he said. 'Or your girl-friend can, anyway.'

M came down and joined me at the fish market before I had a chance to talk to Léanne again.

'I saw you getting beaten up by the old lady,' she said. 'I thought you might need some help. Shall we go and get some coffee?' Behind her jokey tone, I could hear resig-nation. This was probably going to be our Last Breakfast.

'Sure.' I steered her away from the lemon seller and towards the sunlit café terraces on the other side of the harbour. If my suspicions were correct, I had only a minute or two before M gave me the 'You're dumped' speech and set out on her solo career as a money-delivery girl. But I had had an idea. The only problem was that I had no time to ask Léanne if she approved of the scheme that I'd cooked up while lying awake in the night.

We sat down, ordered two crèmes and croissants from a gruff waiter, and I closed my eyes, turning my face to the sun to get the speech straight.

'Paul—' M began, her voice heavy.

Merde, I thought, here goes.

'Hey, guess who I just talked to,' I said, and like a rhetorical Frenchman I didn't give her time to reply. 'Jean-Marie. And guess what he told me.' Yet again, I left no room for her to interrupt. 'It's amazing. Not only is the wedding going to take place on the date Elodie and Valéry want, but there's going to be a very special surprise guest. You'll never guess who.' She couldn't have, anyway, because I carried straight on talking. 'The President.'

'The President?' She looked gobsmacked.

'Yes, Jean-Marie talked to him, and because the President's, you know, a friend of the family, he had a word with the old bitch grand-mère.' Slow down, I told myself. I was gabbling, getting the lies out as fast as possible in an attempt to make them sound convincing. 'And at first she said that the date had to change, but then the President said he was going to be down in the Camargue next weekend – on a secret visit,' I added, in case M and her chums had plotted the President's known movements. 'And when he told her he was going to come along to the wedding in person, she had to give in, even though it means Valéry will be getting married on the day before his birthday.'

'So the President will be there, in the Bonnepoires' chateau?' M asked, apparently testing the story for freshness.

'Yes.'

She thought about this.

'Wow,' she eventually said. 'So when is it?'

'Saturday. Four days' time.'

'Saturday,' she repeated, and I could almost see the plans gelling in her head.

'So it's going to be a mad rush to buy all the ingredients for the reception and get the staff down here. You will help me, won't you?'

'Er, yes, of course I will.'

There was to be no more talk about breaking up, it seemed. My crack-brained plan had worked.

And even though I said so myself, it was a minor stroke of genius. All Léanne's people had to do was set up a fake wedding, and the hitman would go along thinking he was going to whack the surprise guest. But hey presto, the only surprise guests he'd find would be a few bus loads of plain-clothes police.

Alternatively, if the wedding did go ahead on the Saturday as Elodie wanted – which still seemed a pretty slim hope – the cops just had to stake out the family chateau and nab the hitman when he arrived.

The shimmering beauty of it was that, whatever happened, the killer was going to try and whack a president who wasn't even going to be there. I'd baited the perfect trap. Léanne was going to be deliriously happy with me. No more threats of prison now. They might even let me off income tax for life.

'Hey, I must call Benoit about the pièce montée,' I said. 'Got to get things moving.'

'Yes, good idea,' M said. 'Excuse me, I must go for a pee.' She left the table. Off to call her paymasters, I assumed, setting up the job for next Saturday. Excellent.

'Bonjour, Pol,' Benoit answered, sounding his usual sleepy self.

I asked him how the fig experiments were going, playing my part to the full.

'Oh, not bad,' he said. 'But now I am with Papa. He was waiting until you woke up to call you. He has news for you.'

'Paul?' Jean-Marie came on the line, and I could hear a huge grin in his voice. 'Great news. Great news. Great, great . . .'

'News?' I ventured.

'Yes. I was at the city hall last night for a dinner.' Ah yes. The soirée he'd told me about. 'Very, very chic, everyone was there. The major of Paris, the Minister of Justice – she is very sexy, you know – and Johnny Hallyday . . .'

'So what's the news? Are you all going to make a record?'

He laughed good-naturedly. It had to be very good news indeed if he didn't mind me poking fun at his pomposity.

'The President was there, too, of course, with his friend Ludivine, you know, the one who gives him the blow . . . ? Merde.'

'Blowjobs, Jean-Marie. A blow merde would be something very different, and I doubt if a Bonnepoire would do it.'

He laughed again. 'I had a word with the two of them,' he said, 'and the President said – the President said . . .' He was so self-satisfied that his tongue had got entangled while hugging itself.

'Yes?'

'That he guarantees that the wedding will be next Saturday. He will persuade the family. Young Valéry will be rich, after all.'

I didn't reply.

'Excellent news, no?' Jean-Marie sounded disappointed at my lack of response.

'Yes, excellent,' I agreed. I was thinking how this would make the police job more difficult.

'But that is not the only thing. The best is yet to come.' He paused dramatically.

'Yes?' I prompted.

'Well, later on in the soirée, he came back to me. He said that he had consulted with his staff, and . . . and . . .'

'And?'

'He will do the ceremony himself.'

'The President? No, he can't!'

'He can. As an elected official, it is one of his powers. Isn't that excellent? My daughter Elodie married by the President. The honour. And the photos. Think how much *Paris-Match* will pay for the exclusive photos. Isn't this *merveilleux*?'

I was too shocked to say anything, especially because he was right. The photos were going to be worth a fortune. The President arriving incognito at the society wedding. The President marrying the beautiful young couple. The President's head exploding all over Elodie's posh Parisian wedding dress.

I could see the captions already – I now pronounce you man and splat. Till death him do part. The head of state's brain as confetti. Photo opportunity organized by Paul West.

Bloody *merveilleux*.

A Mata of Life and Death

The Camargue

1

I DID A WEB SEARCH for French presidential deaths. There were some spectacular stories. Best of them all had to be the demise at the Elysée palace of Félix Faure in 1899, supposedly while getting a blowjob from his mistress.

Marguerite Steinheil arrived at the palace and was ushered up to the President's apartments. Some time later, she rang for assistance, and servants found fifty-eight-year-old Monsieur Faure unconscious on his bed, his hands – so it was alleged – still clinging to Madame Steinheil's hair. The affair caused a massive scandal, and also one of France's most famous puns. It took me quite a while to work it out, but to understand it, all you need to know is that the word *connaissance* can mean consciousness or acquaintance:

When the priest arrived to give Faure the last rites, he asked one of the servants whether the President was conscious – 'Le Président a-t-il toujours sa connaissance?'

The servant misunderstood. 'No,' he replied, 'we sneaked her out the back door.'

Faure died a few hours later, apparently of a brain haemorrhage.

Not all the country's leaders died such pleasurable deaths. There was, I discovered, a long tradition of presidential assassinations.

Marie-François Sadi Carnot, a man despite his name, became President in 1887, and was reaching what one website called 'the zenith of his popularity' and being hotly tipped for re-election when he was stabbed by a twenty-one-year-old anarchist called Santo Geronimo Caerio. The killer was tried and guillotined within two months.

Paul Doumer met a similar fate. In 1932, he was invited to the opening of a book fair to promote the works of First World War veterans. A noble cause, but it was here that Doumer was shot by a 'mentally unstable Russian émigré' called Gorguloff, who was also swiftly tried and guillotined.

Jacques Chirac was luckier. During the 2002 Bastille Day parade in Paris, he was riding down the Champs-Elysées in an open-top car when a right-wing fanatic pulled a hunting rifle out of a guitar case. He managed to fire off a single round before a Canadian tourist grabbed the gun and saved the President, an event which has to be one of Canada's few contributions to world politics.

And now, somewhere out there, a much more professional hand was getting ready to take a potshot at the current President, and it was up to me to be the Canadian.

'Please forget what I said last night,' M told me. 'When a girl says things like "We ought to call it a day," she doesn't always mean it, you know. Sometimes it's just a test. You're meant to say, "No, don't leave me, ne me quitte pas," then the girl feels loved and everything's OK.'

She leant across the café table and stroked my cheek. Her eyes were moist with sincerity. She was like the desperate housewife whose boring hubbie has just won the lottery. Life was about to have its compensations.

A reconciliation was all very well, but right now I needed a long, undisturbed phone conversation with Léanne. She had to stop the President coming to the wedding. Too bad for Elodie, who would just have to be married by a bog-standard mayor like any other French girl.

Trouble was, suddenly M didn't have any more meetings to rush off to. She said that she was totally free to hang out with me in Marseille or leave for the Camargue.

'No meetings for the next four days?' I asked. 'Are all the sturgeon experts stopping work for Iranian New Year or something?'

It sounded aggressive, and I could see that M was tempted to bite back, but she controlled her instincts and said that no, she'd finished her discussions for the moment. Which seemed to suggest that she must have met her hit-man already. I guessed that her next appointment would be to hand over the dosh to him when the job was done. I really needed to get this information to Léanne.

'I can help you out with your work, like you helped me,' M said.

I did my best to look grateful. In desperation, I took a risk and walked her back past the fish market, where I managed to fire off a meaningful gesture at the lemon seller.

Call me, I mimed, my thumb and little finger held up to my cheek. But the cross-dressing cop had been replaced by a real old lady, who, to judge by her lascivious wink, thought I was a wrinkle groupie.

Léanne's roof-clambering operation was over, it seemed, and the cops had melted away into the shadows again. I knew that they'd be watching, though, so I hung back slightly behind M, and started to mouth a message, in French and English – 'Call me . . . appelle-moi . . . call me' – sweeping my head from right to left so that the distress signal would be picked up anywhere around the Vieux Port.

'What are you doing? You look like one of those poor fish.' M was staring at me.

'Er, yeah, I must have been gaping in sympathy. I've got to order a couple of hundred sea bream for the wedding. It's a heavy weight to have on your conscience.'

'Why don't you just buy a whale and give them steaks?' M said. 'Then you'd only have one lot of blood on your hands.'

She laughed. I didn't.

We packed and left our room. I was with M the whole time, and she showed no sign of wanting to climb up on the roof, or even go out on to the balcony. The money, I guessed, had to be in her luggage somewhere.

While we were checking out, I opened up my laptop and emailed Benoit. The pièce montée was now the least of his problems, I told him. He had to get moving with his share of the organization – hiring waiting and cooking staff, ordering some of the food, renting crockery and cutlery, maybe a marquee too. It was all incredibly last-minute. I said he'd have to motivate reluctant suppliers by telling them that the President was going to be there. I just wished I could tell him to take out insurance against bullet-ridden tables and blood-stained tablecloths.

I also sent Benoit my ideas for the menu, the carbon-neutral banquet that I'd been refining ever since I tasted my first Collioure anchovy. I cut and pasted it into the email window.

Amuse-bouches of tapenade on toast soaked in olive oil.
Goat's cheese à l'hulle.
Barbecue of daurade (order from nearest harbour) on vine wood fires (wood suppliers??). Skins brushed with Camargue salt and Menton lemons.
Camargue rice provided by family.
Tomates Provençales, plus other seasonal, local vegetables.
Sorbets – lavender, honey, Muscat.
Pièce montée of caramelized figs. Must contain at least 200 figs.
Wine from family.
Champagne – I'll contact supplier.

It was either blind optimism or blind stupidity that made me push on as though a wedding reception would actually happen, but it was also therapeutic. Re-reading the list lifted me almost physically out of the merde I'd got myself into. My head was temporarily emptied of stress and filled with the sights, sounds and smells of the banquet. The crackling fire, the glistening green oil, the prickle of thyme and rosemary sprigs, the pungent stickiness of fresh caramel.

'You know a champagne supplier?' M had settled the bill and was reading over my shoulder.

'Yes, a little guy near Reims,' I said. 'Makes organic champagne. I've got his phone number.'

As we walked to the car, I told her the story. I'd been having a picnic with my old girlfriend Alexa (I told M diplomatically that it was with 'a few friends') at the Cité Universitaire on the southern edge of Paris. It's one of the few places in Paris where you can really hurl a frisbee and not be afraid that it'll land in the middle of a traffic jam or on a grumpy park-keeper's head. After an acrobatic game of catch, we opened the bottle of champagne that Alexa had brought – a brand I'd never heard of, made in a small, family vineyard. I noticed that the farmer's name was at the bottom of the label, and there was even a mobile phone number. I decided to call him and congratulate him on his excellent bubbly.

'Allô, oui?' A man answered, against an echoey background of wind and open space. He sounded surprisingly un-chic.

I asked him if he was the guy on the label, and he said yes, warily, as if he was afraid of a practical joke, especially from someone with a shaky foreign accent like mine.

'I just called to say that your champagne is excellent,' I told him.

'Uh?' He sounded as though he couldn't quite believe it was that simple.

'I am having a picnic in Paris, with your champagne, and it is excellent.'

'Oh, merci beaucoup,' he said, brightening up.

'Yes, I just wanted to say this.'

'Merci,' he said again. 'Is it chilled enough? At a picnic, I mean.'

'Oh yes, we have carried in it a, you know, cold bag,' I told him. 'It is cool and excellent. Or it was, we have almost finished.'

'I am happy,' he said, and he sounded it.

'Moi aussi,' I said. There was nothing else to say, really, so I thanked him again and we said goodbye.

'Oh.' M was looking choked up. I thought it was because we'd arrived at the car to find a parking ticket stuffed under the wiper. But no. 'That was really cute,' she told me. 'I bet he went home and told his wife, guess what just happened. Someone called me up just to say he liked our wine.' She seemed to be on the verge of tears. 'Don't you think it'd be great to have a simple life like that?'

Well, I thought, it does sound much cooler than sneaking round the back streets of Marseille picking up blood money.

'Yes, and I think they'll be even happier with their lifestyle when I call them up to order three hundred bottles,' I said, ripping the parking ticket in two. I didn't need to bother with it. The policeman had effectively given himself a fine, because his colleagues were the new hirers of the vehicle.

'Hadn't you better keep that?' M asked. 'The hire people will want it.'

'Oh, shit, yeah,' I said, remembering that I was supposed to be a normal car-hiring tourist.

No such luck. As I folded the two halves of the ticket together, I saw that there was a note scribbled inside, signed 'L'.

The only way to read Léanne's note, I realized, was to risk my life.

We headed northwest out of Marseille and I pulled into the first motorway layby we came to and ventured into the concrete toilet block.

Bracing my nostrils, I tried to avoid eye contact with the seatless metal receptacle at the back of my cubicle, but even as I blurred my vision, I saw that the toilet had been used more for long-distance target practice than precision bombing. The unmentionable impacts of failed operations were splashed around the floor, back wall and the metal itself.

I focussed on the note, praying that my oxygen supply would last long enough for me to read it.

'It's OK,' Léanne had written on the inside sheet of the ticket. 'We have noted presence of l'invité d'honneur. Call me when it is safe. I can't call you if you are not alone. Do not take risks.'

I crumpled the note and threw it into the toilet bowl. There was no point flushing it away, I thought. Only a suicidal rat would dare go diving for it. I unlocked the door and got out, my lungs at bursting point.

M probably wondered why I had to bend over and get my breath back after a brief visit to the loo, but we weren't quite intimate enough for her to ask for news of my digestive system.

'That's better,' I said, getting back in the car, and she looked as though she believed me. I saw out of the corner of my eye that her phone was sticking slightly out of the top of her bag. I hadn't been the only one dealing with my messages.

I asked her to drive – I wanted to put in a call to Valéry and get the address of a good hotel near Bonne Maman's chateau in the Camargue. I needed a base camp from which to marshal operations.

Valéry answered after the fourth or fifth ring. He was over the moon. By which I mean not just happy, but actually flying out in space, his brain having been launched skywards by some chemical or other. So much for his resolution to keep off the powdery stuff.

'It is super, Paul, super,' he sang. I could hear a strange creaking noise – the wings, perhaps, of his makeshift spacecraft. 'The good date, with all my family, and le Président himself. Super.' He sighed and seemed to forget for a moment that he was meant to be speaking to someone.

'Yes, Valéry, it's fantastic. Now I need to ask you something.'

'Elodie is so happy. I am so happy. Are you happy?' The creaking got louder. Perhaps he was altering course to go round to the dark side of the moon.

'Yes, I am bloody happy, Valéry. Now—'

There was a thud. 'Oh merde.'

'What is it, Valéry?'

'I am just falling from the hammock,' he said, as if he was still in mid-air. 'Ay, mon bras. I have not dropped the phone, but I have hurt my arm. Ay.'

'Valéry! Valéry!' This was not my voice. It was a woman calling out to him. Or rather getting up the momentum for a good bollocking.

I heard Valéry say 'Oh là' and then he rang off. I was none the wiser about a hotel, but at least I now knew the name of one guy I couldn't rely on for help.

M had just joined a convoy of trucks heading north towards Avignon and the Rhône valley when Valéry's number showed up on my phone.

'Have you managed get back in the hammock?' I asked him.

'Monsieur West?' It wasn't Valéry, unless he'd turned into a plummy-voiced woman.

'Oui,' I answered.

'Un instant,' she said, and the phone rustled loudly in my ear.

'Monsieur West?' It was another woman. They seemed to be queuing up to check my identity.

'Oui?'

'Oh là là, are you on an aeroplane?'

'No, in a car.'

'You are not driving, I hope?'

'No,' I said, 'I am a passenger.'

'Well it is very difficult to hear you. Honestly, it is impossible to have a conversation.'

Well why did you bloody call me, then, I thought, but managed to apologize politely. I'd recognized the voice. It was Bonne Maman. The first woman must have been Moo-Moo, playing secretary. They seemed to have confiscated Valéry's phone.

'Can I help you?' I asked.

'You know about the President?' Bonne Maman said, sounding slightly gruff. She had been outwitted, after all, forced to agree to the date she didn't want.

'Yes, excellent news. What an honour for your family.'

'It is an honour,' she conceded. 'And the reception must be à la hauteur.' Meaning, of an appropriately high standard. 'So I am obliged to ask you whether you are capable of organizing a wedding of this calibre?'

Incredibly arrogant, but straight to the point.

'Oh yes,' I said. 'I am driving to the Camargue now. My staff in Paris are beginning preparations.'

'But do you have enough people to organize an event of national importance?'

National importance was right, I thought. If I couldn't persuade Léanne to keep the President away from the wedding, it was going to go down in French history. It'd be listed on the web alongside Faure's blowjob.

'Certainement,' I said. 'We are going to employ many, er, employees.'

'And what about the tables?'

Ah, yes, the non-vulgar furniture.

'We will find excellent tables, classy ones, with wooden legs,' I promised her. 'But what I must know is the number of guests. Valéry told me two hundred. Is that correct?'

'Ha!' She barked a laugh as though she had just seen Valéry fall out of the hammock again. 'Two hundred might have been enough for his little private arrangement, but he has seventy cousins and second-cousins, you know, and half of them are married with children, and now that the President is coming, we must say, oh, at least three hundred and fifty.'

Wow, I thought. I'd have to give Benoit the bad news pretty damn quick. And Jean-Marie, too. As father of the bride, I assumed he'd be footing the food bill.

'I will do the table plan myself,' Bonne Maman said. 'I, of course, will be placed next to the President.'

'Of course,' I said, thinking that if the poor guy actually survived till dinner, Bonne Maman would have to watch where she put her feet. One false move and she might kick Ludivine the spokeswoman, who'd no doubt be under the table keeping the head of state amused between courses.

It wasn't till we stopped to have a sandwich in the Roman amphitheatre at Arles that I managed to get in a quick call to Léanne.

Despite its antiquity, the amphitheatre is a living stadium, and blood is still shed there – these days it's bulls who get sacrificed to the crowds rather than gladiators and Christians. For this reason, inside the old walls, there are towering metal grandstands around a modern sandy arena. I clanged to the top, telling M I wanted to get a good view of the city. She stayed down below, stretched out on one of the original stone steps that still serve as seating.

As soon as I reached the highest point in the metal grandstand, I took out my phone as if I'd just received a call.

'Ah, Valéry,' I announced loudly, to test whether this was one of those ancient theatres where you could hear someone farting from a hundred yards away. No, my voice trailed off towards the blue horizon.

Turning my back to M so that I faced the thick grey arches of the outer wall, I speed-dialled Léanne. She answered straight away.

'You are going to stop the President coming to the wedding?' I asked.

'No.'

I felt a stab of panic.

'But you must. He does know what's going on, doesn't he?' It struck me that secrecy is such an integral part of French life that the police might not warn him until the gunman actually had him in his telescopic sight.

'Naturally he does. Do you think that he accepted to go to this marriage because your friend Jean-Marie invited him? It is our plan.'

Of course. How stupid of me to think that any of us mere citizens of the world might be influencing events. Just looking out over Arles, you could see that France never really changed. The ancient square-topped spires, the distant blue of the Rhône, the low horizon of evergreen trees. There were modern details in there, but the view had probably changed little in two thousand years.

'My plan was that he *wouldn't* turn up.'

'That would not work. Criminals are not stupid. This way we are sure that the criminal will come.'

'But the President might get shot,' I said.

'No, no.' She laughed. 'His plan is, he will go there, survive, then tell the media of his courage. At the moment he suffers a little in the sondages.'

'The polls?'

'Yes. He will win ten, twenty per cent for this.' She laughed again. 'Chirac had this when he was attacked. And he did not know of the attack on him. A President who knows the danger, and takes the risk? He will be a hero. Impossible to defeat in the next election. It is an intelligent tactic.'

Bloody hell, I thought, these politicians really will do anything to get elected.

'So you, Pol, you must simply stay with M, yes?'

'I'm trying.' I turned to make sure M wasn't watching. Which she was. Damn. I waved down, and shrugged an apology that I was on the phone. Again, I hoped I hadn't overdone the naturalness.

'Do not follow her if she goes to a meeting, please. It is more interesting for us to see the people she does *not* meet. Maybe she will pass a man, just look at him, you know, eye-to-eye, to give a signal. Maybe in a hotel or restaurant, a man who says nothing, just like when I was there in Collioure, you know?'

'Yes.' I remembered those naive days when I thought that she was simply a lonely woman who was coming on to me.

'It is difficult, I know, Pol. It must be hard to stay with her now that you know everything about her. Especially at night, yes?'

'Yes, it is,' I said. 'Bloody difficult.'

'I know, and I regret this, honestly. I would prefer really

that you were not forced to play Mata Hari for us. Especially because . . .'

'Yes?' I didn't like the way she had trailed off in mid-sentence.

'Well, you know the way it went for Mata Hari.'

'No.' I knew she'd been an exotic dancer and a bit of a high-class hooker, but I didn't think I was in danger of becoming either of those.

'Ah. Well, when she was a spy for France, she was arrested.'

'By the Germans?' No danger of that, either, in my case.

'No, by the French. She was a – how did you say? – a caterer?'

'She was arrested for *catering*?'

'No, no, how do you say, you know – someone who is *un traître*.'

'A traitor?'

'Yes, of course.' Léanne laughed at our old confusion.

'So what happened to her?' I asked.

'Oh,' Léanne said dismissively, 'she was shot.'

2

I came down from the Arles skyline feeling somewhat light-headed.

'Problems?' M asked me when I joined her on the warm stone steps.

Yes, a big one, I wanted to say – you.

'Oh, it's Valéry,' I told her. 'He's coked up again. I just hope he comes down for the ceremony. We want it to be a great day for Elodie, don't we?'

I looked closely into M's eyes to see if she would flinch. She didn't disappoint.

I wondered again why the hell she was doing this. She didn't strike me as profoundly evil, or violent. She seemed to like sturgeon more than people, but I'd never heard stories of the President torturing fish or filling jacuzzis with illegal caviar. And surely no one would kill a French leader for political reasons – they hardly seem to bother with politics. They're much too busy enjoying their presidential chateaux, getting their photo in *Paris-Match* and going on sunny foreign trips.

So why the sudden need to off the chef d'état?

It would have been so wonderfully simple to ask.

On the western side of the Rhône, the shadows seemed to lengthen, as if they had more room to spread out in the flat, expansive landscape of the Camargue. The straight road ran between empty, swaying beds of wispy-headed reeds. To right and left there were boggy rice paddies and meadows. Milky-grey horses, grazing hoof-deep in the swamp, looked up to watch us pass. One of them was being ridden by a gleaming-white egret, pecking insects from the horse's back. A huge cloud of starlings swirled across an immense flat sky that was like a sheet of blue-tinted glass propped up on the horizon. It was a good, moody background for a heart-to-heart, I decided.

'Do you mind me asking about your dad?' I asked, studying M's profile for a reaction.

She continued to stare out of the windscreen for a few seconds before answering. 'What about him?'

'How old were you? Three, you said?'

'Yes. I can hardly remember him. Most of my memories come from photos.'

'It was an accident, right?'

'I'd rather not talk about it.' She shook her head. 'But in case you're wondering, he's the reason why I won't use black pens any more.'

I remembered that she'd insisted on using a blue one in Collioure. 'Why?' I asked.

'Well, before his, er, accident' – she obviously didn't like the word – 'he wrote a letter. My mother got it after he died. She showed it to me when I was old enough to read. And it was written in thick black felt pen. So now I only use thin blue pens.'

'And what did it say? If you don't mind my asking.'

'The ink had soaked through the paper, you could hardly read it any more. But basically he was saying that he missed me and Maman, and—' She stopped speaking suddenly. She'd given away too much.

'Maman? She was French?' I asked.

'Yes.'

'So that explains how you knew those crap French songs in Bandol,' I said, teasing her.

She laughed. 'Yes. My mother's record collection would make you weep.'

'And that's why you speak such good French.'

'Yes.'

I didn't remind her that she'd explained away her excellent French by trying to tell me that it was the language of international oceanographers, or some such bullshit.

'Why was your dad writing to you?' I asked. 'He was away somewhere, was he? On his boat?'

'Yes. On the other side of the world. But it wasn't his boat. He was a photographer.'

'Underwater photography?' I hazarded, but it was a question too far.

'I really don't like talking about it, Paul, sorry. Now where are we headed exactly?'

I studied the map and let out a whistle of admiration. The chateau was such an important landmark that it warranted a little rectangle of its own, with its name alongside, the Mas des Chefs. The Bonnepoires were an integral part of French geography.

We saw it coming from at least a kilometre away, when a jungle suddenly sprang up in the flat emptiness, hemmed in by a high, moss-covered stone wall. There were more trees in the family's grounds than in the rest of the Camargue put together.

A faded sign, gold on green, pointed us to a gap in the wall. The gates were open. This time, there didn't seem to be a second driveway, so M turned in, and once we'd broken through the ring of trees, the grounds opened out to reveal what looked like a Mississippi plantation – a huge house set on a river bank, surrounded by a patchwork of meadows and deep drainage streams. A lone black bull with long, pointed horns, grazing in a fenced-off enclosure, observed our arrival.

'Bloody hell,' I said. 'The Saint Tropez bastide was a cottage compared to this.'

'Do we just drive up to the front door?' M asked.

'Why not?' There didn't seem to be any other option.

She edged the car respectfully along the gravel driveway that was lined not with closely planted date palms but with tall, airy plane trees.

'If anyone asks,' I said, 'don't call all this the garden, will you? It has to be a park at the very least. The old bat probably calls it her savanna or something.'

'Where will you hold your barbecue?' M asked. She was looking right and left, taking it all in, and it suddenly occurred to me that I was being an idiot. How could I have been mad enough to let her case the joint?

'I don't know yet,' I said. The least I could do was keep her guessing about where exactly her man would have to aim his rifle.

Beside an outbuilding bigger than most French family homes, we saw a leaf-strewn tennis court – no doubt Uncle Babou's contribution. And then, a mere kilometre or so later, we pulled up outside the chateau and got a close look at it.

It was a proud triple-cube of a building, three storeys high and made of sand-coloured stone, with a small central tower that was festooned with chimneys shaped like castle turrets. It was too bulky and angular to be especially beautiful, but it was somehow very sure of its importance. A lot like most of the Bonnepoire family members I'd seen.

Getting out of the car, I saw that the house had humorous little touches – grinning, clownish faces carved into the façade and, sticking out at roof level, long gargoyles in the shape of cannons – or maybe penises. Poor Moo-Moo probably got hot flushes every time she came here.

Lizards were scampering up the walls and diving behind the spiky palms that were growing in huge pots on either side of the double front doors. There was a large metal bell-handle set into the doorframe, but before I could grab it, there was a crunching sound on the driveway behind me, and a bull-like roar.

I turned to see some kind of cowboy marching towards me. He was wearing tight black trousers, a black shirt and a trilby hat.

'There's no visit,' he shouted.

'No, we're not tourists,' I answered.

'It's private property.' He rolled his Rs and pronounced every bit of every syllable. His was the strongest southern accent I'd heard so far.

'Yes,' I agreed, 'we know.'

'There's no visit,' he repeated, as if I was deaf. He walked right up to me, and came to breathe horsily in my face. Or my chest, anyway. He was a little barrel of a man, about sixty years old, red-faced and red-eyed. The only thing preventing him from coming any closer was his stomach, which stuck out above a thick belt and held him at bay. I saw now that his bulging black shirt was in fact white, with a crowded motif of tiny black bulls. He was eyeing me as though I was an Apache walking into his saloon.

'We have come for the wedding,' I said.

'What wedding? There's no wedding.'

'Hasn't Madame Bonnepoire called you?'

'Madame Bonnepoire?' He looked doubly suspicious now. I was not just an intrusive tourist. I knew things about the family.

'Yes, Bonne Maman,' I said, and he blanched. Like Moo-Moo, he clearly thought the use of the nickname was blasphemous. 'Valéry will marry here on Saturday,' I added quickly. 'I am the traitor, er, caterer. I would like to look and see where we can have the barbecue, the place for the tables, everything.'

The cowboy shook his head.

'It is new news,' I said. 'Ask Bonne – er, Madame Bonnepoire.'

He puffed like a bull about to charge. 'Madame tells me everything. If she has not told me there is a wedding, there's no wedding.'

Time for a diplomatic change of tack, I thought.

'You must be the guardian of the chateau,' I said. 'So I

understand your, er . . .' I didn't know how to say caution, but it didn't matter, because he was puffing even louder.

'I'm not a guardian. I'm a guardian,' he said, somewhat confusingly.

'Ah.'

'You understand?'

'Yes. Er, no.'

'I'm a guardian.'

'Right.'

'You understand?'

'No, not yet.'

'You don't understand anything, do you?' He called me *tu*, as if I was one of the lizards peeking out at us from behind the plant pots.

M stepped up to save the day.

'He's not a *gardee-an*, a concierge,' she explained. 'He's a *gardee-on*, a Camargue cowboy.'

So it was an accent thing.

'Biyeng, biyeng,' he congratulated M. 'You understand now?' he asked me, his mouth still only a few inches below my chin.

'Yes, I understand,' I said. 'Now can we look at the chateau, please?'

'Non, foutez le kang,' he said, the local way of telling us to get lost.

It was my own fault. I should have asked Bonne Maman to call the guy and set him straight.

'Well, can you recommend a good hotel?' I asked him.

'What do you take me for, the tourist office? A travel agency? The chamber of commerce?' He herded us to the car, savouring every word of his parting speech. He was still listing possible sources of hotel information as we drove back towards the road. I just wished he could have recited the phone numbers as well.

We headed towards Saintes Maries de la Mer, the nearest coastal town.

'That's where the commando told me he'd seen a sturgeon,' I reminded M.

'Yeah.' She didn't seem especially excited.

'Will you be going out to have a scout around?'

'Maybe,' she said. Her mind was clearly on bigger fish.

Only a few clicks down the road, we found a hotel. It was a typical Camargue place, a huddle of low white buildings on an oasis of solid ground in the marshes. The driveway was a ribbon of tarmac between two lakes, and flamingos were wandering around on either side of the track, squeaking and grunting like a gang of impatient parking attendants. They strutted along on their stiff, gaudy-pink legs, their long necks hoovering up food from the inch-deep water. As we passed, one of them flapped its wings, showing a sudden flash of black and blood-red.

Behind the main hacienda-style building, there was a horse-training enclosure, and a faint whiff of dung was blowing across the car park. I was afraid that we were in for another cowboy-style welcome, but the guy at reception was incredibly pleasant, and said he had a perfect little room looking out across the nature reserve.

'The flamingos will be your alarm clock,' he said.

'We won't need one.' M laughed, and I was reminded that in the past, she had been my wake-up call, climbing on board for one of her dawn quickies.

Our simple, whitewashed room was in one of the out-buildings. Its windows faced out across an unbroken expanse of grassy banks and sea-blue lake.

'You can walk for miles out there,' the hotel owner said. 'Right up to the main road or down to the sea. When I was a boy we used to go out and hide in the marshes, and no one would ever find us.'

'It's perfect.' M was gazing thoughtfully at the horizon.

Too damn perfect, I thought. I was making the business of assassination all too easy. Not only had I given her the President on a plate, I'd done it in the middle of a perfect getaway zone. He was going to be a sitting flamingo.

4

Since arriving at the Camargue ranch hotel, M and I had made love twice.

The previous evening, it had been a kind of consolation shag, like the last time before you break up, an intense flash of closeness and emotion before you start trying your best to be indifferent. I got the feeling that we were both doing it to relieve our stresses, too, plunging ourselves into physical sensation to forget the mental complications.

That, in any case, was how I interpreted M's noisy, Tour-de-France-style wake-up quickie this morning. My body was an exercise bike, and she pedalled herself – and me – to exhaustion. We didn't use her new dolphin, I must stress. It stayed in her toilet bag. I fished it out while I was brushing my teeth, and couldn't resist giving its tail a twist so that it started its manic headbanging.

'Hey!' M called out from the bed.

'Sorry, sorry.' It was like when I'd touched her laptop that time. She really hated people meddling with her things. I switched it off and put it back in the bag. As I did so, I saw a small brown bottle in there. It looked as though she'd bought some flavoured oil from the sex shop, to go with the vibrator. I was tempted to open the bottle and sniff. If it was a tropical flavour, I thought I might annoy M by asking her whether she shouldn't have bought something with a smaller carbon footprint.

She barged into the bathroom, a bundle of (literally) naked anger.

'Paul, please!' She reached out, grabbed the little brown bottle and her toilet bag and took them into the bedroom.

Not a good time to make a joke about eco-friendly sex oil, I decided.

The wedding arrangements suddenly gathered momentum, and I started to feel like a novice water-skier. I was constantly on the brink of disaster, but if I slowed down I would sink.

I had a long, absurd conversation with a furniture-hire company. They couldn't understand why I needed to see close-up photos of their table-legs before I would agree to the hire. In the end I had to play things the French way and tell the woman I had 'une cliente chiante' – a customer who was as annoying as shit. This she understood, and sent me photos of some perfect, snooty-legged tables. Now all I had to do was hope they arrived in time.

I had a much shorter, but equally absurd, conversation with Jean-Marie, who was livid about the sudden doubling of the guest list. He wanted me to call Bonne Maman and ask how many kids there would be, so he could reduce the amount of food accordingly. Sure, I told him, and I'll ask if any of the nuns in the family have taken a vow of starvation.

Back at the tea room, Benoit was infuriatingly calm. He

talked me through the latest attempt at my fig pièce montée. I could almost feel the caramel hardening in real time as he spoke. Well, did it bloody work or didn't it, I wanted to scream, but he just kept on saying, Wait, wait, before describing the next step in the process.

At last, after ten tooth-grindingly slow minutes, he ended the suspense. It had worked. The tiny kitchen at the tea room was home to a metre-high mound of caramelized figs that was too big and wide to get up the winding stairs to street level. He would have to dig a tunnel to get it out.

Before he could go and buy a pneumatic drill, I told him not to worry. He should just get himself and Gilles the cook down here, and pick up some figs on the way. They could make a new pièce montée at the chateau.

Valéry resurfaced, like a dolphin coming up for air before diving back down into a drug-infused sea. He seemed to have been thrown into a total panic by the idea that his wedding was actually going ahead, and that he might, for the first time in his and probably anyone's life, be about to win a battle against his tyrannical granny.

He phoned me from his car. He was driving to Marseille to pick Elodie up from the station. But I was afraid he'd never get there. He had plugged his iPod into the car radio and wanted to play snatches of music for me. He seemed to think that as well as getting married, he'd also have time to DJ at his reception.

Between each burst of disco, chanson française and horrific vintage French rock 'n' roll – and the accompanying hoots of the drivers around him as he took his eyes off the road – I tried to tell him to forget it and book a professional, but he just whooped and told me to 'check out this', and put on another song. In the end, I lost my temper. I yelled at him to hire a DJ and tell the guy to cue up at least one waltz to start the evening, because Elodie had been practising.

'One what? Wulss?' he chirruped.

'A waltz. Une valse!' I shouted.

There was a screech of brakes, a frantic hooting, and he rang off.

I didn't have time to call back and see if he'd survived. I'd find out when – if – he turned up at the chateau with Elodie.

Apart from the spat about the toilet bag, things with M were relatively peaceful. In a matter of days, we'd gone from box-fresh love to adulterous suspicion to reconciliation, and now we were like middle-aged, long-term marrieds who hardly bothered talk to each other.

During one of my marathon phone sessions, she announced that she was going for a walk. It was only when I noticed the breeze that I saw she'd gone out the window, straight into the marshes. She was striding purposefully along a track towards the main road and the chateau, her small laptop backpack swinging from one shoulder.

I went to the wardrobe and looked down at her soft kit bag. The padlock was on it, but that didn't stop me having a feel. Without pulling the bag out of its nesting place, I probed and prodded like a pianist looking for the right chord. And yes, I could feel the hard outline of her laptop in there amongst the clothes. I remembered what Léanne had said about the money taking up so little room. M was probably carrying it with her now. To hide it or deliver it?

I called Léanne and told her about this new development. She said that M was being watched from the road, and begged me not to go arousing suspicion by following her.

'We still do not see any sign of the man she will meet,' she said. 'He is not here yet. You must not fry her.'

'Fry her?'

'*Effrayer.*'

'Frighten. No, I don't intend to frighten her away.' Though I wished I could.

Léanne told me that Bonne Maman had arrived, and that I should go and visit the chateau. Her men were having to keep a low profile, and she wanted me to make a list of all the entrances to the main house and the outbuildings.

'Bon courage,' she told me. It's what French people say before someone does something unpleasant like go to the dentist or host a birthday party for fifty kids with attention-deficit disorder. What I was doing felt like a mix of the two.

'Chateau? Chateau? It is not a chateau, Monsieur, it is a gentilhommière.'

I'd made the mistake of trying to compliment Bonne Maman on the beauty and size of her house, and been put in my place yet again. I'd never realized there were so many nuances of French chateau-ness. It was as bad as their business with vous and tu, and when to say the 'de' before Bonnepoire. Nothing in France was ever simple.

'It is the home of a gentleman,' Bonne Maman went on. 'In this case, my dear, late husband.' She held out a pale hand towards the portrait hanging in the hall. It was a painting of a white-haired guy in a dark suit. He was sitting on a velvet armchair with a brown speckled dog at his feet, both of them looking very pleased with life. In fact, Valéry's granddad looked like quite a mischievous old bloke, and probably gave the servant girls the runaround. He was even giving the eye to the painting on the opposite wall, an ornately framed picture of the Virgin Mary, who bore a suspicious resemblance to Bonne Maman herself.

She was showing M and myself around the house, giving us a rundown of where she wanted various things to happen.

I had intended to drive over alone, but on my way I'd come across M walking by the roadside. I'd waved hello, not planning to stop, but she'd flagged me down and climbed into the passenger seat. She was obviously keen to have a snoop around inside the chateau, and I'd dished up the opportunity on a plate. Not a good move.

The salon, Bonne Maman said, was where she would receive the President. No one else was to be allowed in here.

This news appeared to interest M a lot, and she went over to the window as if to inspect the thickness of the glass. I could imagine it shattering into the President's eyes as a bullet crashed through. I'd have to tell Léanne not to let him admire the view.

'Can we see the kitchens?' I asked.

'Of course.' Bonne Maman led us into the corridor again, and past a gigantic carved staircase. Lodged beneath it was a wire-fronted, wardrobe-like gun cabinet, stocked with half a dozen rusting old shotguns. No danger to the President there, I thought. Pull the trigger on one of those and you'd probably lose your face.

We went through a double door into a cool, chequer-tiled zone of the house. First there was a square serving room with a long wooden table and, against one wall, a chunky metal safe.

'For the silver,' Bonne Maman told us. 'We won't be using it for Valéry's wedding. Except at the President's table, of course.'

There was also a large panel of bells, maybe twenty of them, each labelled with the name of a room. Grand salon, petit salon, salle à manger, several chambres – there were even bells for the bathrooms.

The kitchen was dominated by an immense fireplace, maybe ten feet wide. It was basically a giant rôtisserie under a chimney. There was also a central range with at least ten cooking rings. In its heyday, the kitchen could have served up a dozen different types of porridge to the family every morning.

Off the kitchen was a door with an ancient keyhole big enough to get two fingers in.

'The wine cellar,' Bonne Maman said. 'Only I have the key.'

'Can we get directly from the kitchen into the, uh, park?' I asked, and was relieved to find that I'd actually used the right word for once.

'Yes, come.' Bonne Maman led us through a glass-paned door, and we emerged at the back of the house, in a small kitchen garden. There was a path around to the grounds at the side, where I intended to put the barbecue. It would be relatively easy to transport food to and fro during the reception.

'And that is the chapel.' Bonne Maman was pointing beyond the kitchen garden to a cuboid building with a small cross at the centre of its pyramid roof. 'That is where Monsieur le Président will perform the ceremony. The civil ceremony, that is, which will be followed by the religious ceremony. We are lucky,' she added. 'Until recently, we Catholics had to go to a town hall first, then to a church. These days, God still comes in second place behind a bureaucrat, but fortunately the rules have eased about where one can hold the civil ceremony, so we no longer have to go to some administrative office.'

'You will all be in there?' I asked. The chapel was tiny, no bigger than a bandstand. Knowing Elodie, there would hardly be room for her dress.

'Yes, the President, the curé and the immediate family.' The old girl seemed to be delighted at the way the architecture of her house was going to impose the required elitism on proceedings.

I was pleased, too. No one was going to pop the President during the wedding vows. Unless the priest had agreed to do the job. I'd have to remind Léanne to frisk his cassock.

'Excellent,' I said. I thanked Bonne Maman, and told her we would leave her in peace for now.

'Oh, would it be possible to take a short walk around the park?' M asked. 'It is so beautiful.'

Bonne Maman smiled at her, clearly appreciating M's perfect French, and – I thought – assessing her suitability as a potential source of new gene material for the family. There were probably dozens of horny young male Bonnepoires who would love a blonde wife like her.

'No, no,' I told M in French. 'You must come with me. I need your help.' I took her arm and escorted her gently but firmly from the scene of her future crime.

'What was that about?' she demanded as we got in the car. She was looking suspicious again.

'Let's quit while we're ahead. We've got to keep in the old bitch's good books,' I said, pretty convincingly. 'Besides, I really would like you to come along. I want to go and taste some oils. I mean olive oil, of course, not one of those perfumed oils you're so fond of.'

She pretended not to know what I was talking about.

*

When we got back to the chateau, Benoit and Gilles the chef were being given a hard time by the cowboy, the *gardian*, whose name, we found out, was Monsieur Yena. No one had told him to expect two strange men bearing crates of figs, and he was trying to hold them at bay with a long pole that ended in a pointy, crescent-shaped metal tip.

I sidetracked him by asking what he thought the weather was going to be like on Saturday, a question that had him almost bursting out of his bull-motif shirt with self-importance. He launched into a long speech about the way the bull was facing, and how far from the river the egrets and herons were hunting frogs, and concluded that the weather would be sunny and 'tranquil', adding that his favourite TV weather girl agreed.

All of which gave Benoit and Gilles ample time to colonize the kitchen with their fruit and equipment.

Monsieur Yena and I unloaded the olive oil, and I gave his wife a couple of bottles as compensation for usurping her in the kitchen.

When I came out again, I saw that M was making use of her free time to inspect all the main house's exits. I even thought I caught sight of her filming something with her phone. A trickle of sweat chilled my spine.

I interrupted her research by asking her to check out the large green van that was heading slowly towards us down the drive. She went and met the driver and pointed him towards me. It turned out to be the champagne-maker. He'd driven all the way down with my order. Not very carbon-neutral, but it was worth it to see the smile on the guy's face.

I realized, of course, that he hadn't come just to meet his satisfied English customer. As he said hello, his eyes were flicking around for signs of presidential presence. And he told me that he'd been interviewed by a man at the gate, who said he'd come to take photos of all the wedding guests and suppliers as they arrived. The guy had asked him if he knew when the President was arriving.

Oh merde, I thought. The photographer hadn't been there – or hadn't shown himself – when M and I came in. He must have been hiding. He might not be a photographer at all. I asked M to show the champagne guy to the wine cellar, and snuck off to call Léanne.

She wasn't in a good mood.

'You have *told* everyone that the President is coming?' she snapped.

'If I hadn't, most of the suppliers would have told me to get lost. They would have said it was too short notice. Do you know who the guy is on the gate?'

'Yes,' she said, 'a photographer from the local newspaper. Others will come soon. Probably TV. In a way it is not bad, because now we can put visible police there. Everyone will think it is normal security. But you must not discuss the President's visit with anyone else, *please*, Pol. We must not give M or her associates the idea that there will be too many police around the chateau. They must not be afraid to come.'

I agreed and apologized, but I was thinking the opposite. Wouldn't it be great if the place was so overrun with guests, media and security that the killer called the job off? Elodie and Valéry could simply get married, have a dance and a meal with their family and friends, and not spend their wedding night being interviewed by police and forced to watch security footage of the President getting his head blown off.

I wondered how Elodie would feel if she knew that her only chance of marrying Valéry on Saturday and pocketing his inheritance was by exposing the President to possible assassination.

Actually, I could guess her answer.

Let him get shot, she would have said, as long as he marries us first.

THE BEST MARRIAGES
END IN DEATH

The Camargue

1

IT WAS FRIDAY, the day before the wedding. For the past twenty-four hours, family members had been turning up at the chateau in vast numbers. I quickly stopped saying 'Did we meet in Saint Tropez?' because except for Valéry's closest uncles and aunts, I had no idea who was who.

As soon as Moo-Moo arrived, she attached herself to Bonne Maman, and the two of them toured the grounds dishing out kisses and head-pats to family, and showing the deliverers of furniture and food who was boss.

Dadou, meanwhile, dressed up in gardian gear and went off riding, his too-clean trousers bouncing up and down on his shiny saddle as he and Monsieur Yena disappeared into the marshes.

That was where M had disappeared, too. After two days of trying to keep her in my sights, I'd had to give up and concentrate on getting things organized. In any case, the only people she was likely to be exchanging furtive glances with now were Bonnepoires, and none of them were going to whack the man who was about to bestow the ultimate honour upon their family.

Elodie arrived, with a semi-coherent Valéry lolling in his own passenger seat. They'd stopped for a night at the chateau where he had originally planned to hold the wedding, and Valéry had apparently spent the whole evening alternately feeding himself with uppers and downers, until his brain was as scrambled as if it had been bouncing up and down a lift shaft.

I couldn't let Bonne Maman see him like that. I had to get him either cleaned up or out of sight. Looking at the fixed smile on his face – like a baby that's just realized it can fart – the second option seemed easier.

Luckily, the lovely Sixtine had appointed herself my personal assistant, so I gave her and Valéry the task of fetching a few sacks of the family's famous Camargue rice from a nearby farm. Valéry would probably use one of the sacks as a pillow, or try to buy drugs from it, but at least Bonne Maman wouldn't see him screwing up.

'What shall I fetch them in?' Sixtine asked. 'The Mercedes is too small.'

I laughed and swept an arm around our immediate surroundings. There were enough Renault Espaces parked there to supply a refugee camp.

The drivers and passengers of all these family cars were obviously used to keeping themselves amused. An army of kids was rampaging about, falling in drainage ditches, trying to pull the bull's tail, tumbling out of trees. None of the adults seemed to mind much – they had kids to spare.

Meanwhile, one of the uncles I didn't know, who looked like a mildly disturbing mix of Valéry and Bonne Maman, had rounded up the adults and older teens for a game of

Bonnepoire Trivial Pursuit. They were sitting on the grass in front of the main house, gathered round their question master like disciples at a sect meeting, and as I helped Gilles and Benoit to set up the barbecue, I caught snatches of the game.

'Who sat on Bonne Maman's hat at Ludivine's fiftieth birthday party?' he asked, to howls of nostalgic laughter. 'Where did little Paul-Emmanuel use to hide his food when he didn't want to finish his dinner?'

They were a world unto themselves. They'd probably written a Bonnepoire Book of World Records and held Bonnepoire Olympic Games.

I just hoped for their sakes that the next round of Bonnepoire Trivial Pursuit wouldn't start with 'Who was hit in the crossfire when the President got shot?'

One of Valéry's aunts showed particular bravery, I thought, by agreeing to go and fetch Jake from the airport. Deciding who to ask had been a tough call, and I had finally opted for the nun, Eve-Marie. I couldn't send a male, because Jake would only have started asking him about shaggable sisters and nieces, or enquired whether the guy had ever slept with a Bulgarian. I figured that Eve-Marie would be safe from his advances. She was way too old, even for his undiscerning libido, and wore clothes that had the magical effect of convincing the onlooker that sex didn't exist.

So I was surprised when she arrived back at the chateau and almost fell from the car, pale with shock.

Jake jumped out after her, looking deliriously happy.

'Success immediate!' he proclaimed, grabbing me in an American hug.

'You haven't started shagging different religious orders?' I asked, horrified.

'Uh? No, man. Are you malade? She will contribute to my fon.'

'She's giving money to your cause?'

'Oui. I am reciting to her some of our Cajun posy, and she says, "Stop, enough, I will contribute." And every time I recite another posy, she offers more. Formidable, huh?'

'Yes, formidable,' I agreed, watching the poor woman stagger off for a lie-down.

'Now where is the Prayzidon?' he asked.

'Well he's not going to turn up early to help lay the tables, Jake.' I told him that he would have to wait until the next day for the chance to lobby the head of state. 'You're looking, er, good,' I said. My hesitation was caused by the fact that his natural tendency towards slobbishness had been enhanced somewhat by a year living in a Louisiana swamp. His matted blond hair was long and style-free, his clothes were no doubt what the hippest shrimp fishermen were all wearing this season. He needed tidying up fast if he was going to be allowed within nibbling distance of the wedding buffet.

'Good flight?' I asked, wondering where I could get him some clothes that wouldn't terrify a French audience.

'Oh, oui, man. I got a freebie to Paree with Iran Air. I had to go via Teheran, but so what?'

'Iran Air? How come?' I asked, fearing the reply.

'Oh, I once boned this Iranian hôtesse de l'air. So I appelled her last week and she said, "Sure, I can give you a ticket." Oh man, she was formidable. She had, like, all this caviar, and we—'

It was too much. 'Please, Jake, stop. I've had enough of fucking caviar these past couple of weeks.'

'You been fucking with caviar? Hey, that's exactement what we did. I inserted it in—'

Five minutes later, I tottered off in search of Eve-Marie the nun. Maybe the sight of her clothes would hypnotize me into forgetting the gruesome details of Jake's sex life.

My own sex life hit a new low on the night before the wedding.

M kissed and caressed me, talked dirty, and even got her dolphin in on the act, but I was too tired and tense to perform.

'Sorry,' I apologized, putting my arm around her as she lay down, frustrated, beside me. I really was sorry, too, not just for making such an anti-climax of what was no doubt our last night together, but also because of the trap I was leading her into.

I did my best to recall the various deceptions and humiliations she'd put me through, directly and indirectly – the endless lies about sturgeon, getting me roughed up by the police on Bendor, using me so that we'd look like a normal holidaying couple travelling along the coast. She'd been playing with me. She deserved what she was going to get. It was payback time.

But you can't – or I can't – feel aggressive towards someone you're in bed with, and who you feel comfortable putting your arm around.

Over the past few days, she had been much more silent than usual, and when she hadn't been snooping around the chateau, she'd often sat alone in the shade of a tree, looking around at the chatting Bonnepoires as if she envied them.

She seemed to have a conscience about what she was doing. It was almost as if she was caught in a trap herself. Perhaps she was being blackmailed? Something to do with her dad, maybe, or her French mum? If only, I thought, we could get it all out in the open and talk.

But we'd gone too far with our deception. And besides, I had Léanne and her leather-jacketed sidekick on my back, threatening me with a long holiday in a French prison if I clicked out of my Mata Hari role.

'I understand. It's the stress,' M said, forgiving me for under-performing. I was relieved that she'd given up with out trying out her lickable oil. After Jake's description of what he'd done with caviar, mixing food and sex had totally lost its appeal.

2

It was Saturday at last, the morning of the wedding.

A whirring flight of flamingos was my wake-up call, after all. I drew the curtains to see a layer of dawn mist hanging over the marshes. It looked as though the pink birds were landing on snow. Outside, the air was as chilly as our silence during the drive to the chateau.

My brain was on overload. Léanne's team still had no leads on the identity or whereabouts of the hitman. But he had to be on his way now. For all I knew, M might even have paid him already. I was almost certain that she didn't have the money with her. She just had her party frock – a dark-blue dress that she took everywhere – and her make-up bag. Which meant that she'd either hidden the money or handed it over during one of her walks across the marshes.

'You look as nervous as I feel,' I told her. 'We'll have to cheer up or we'll spoil Elodie's wedding day. We wouldn't want to do that, would we?'

She met my innocent look with inscrutable eyes.

OK, I thought, that was our last chance. Now we've both got to go through with it.

At the chateau, the biggest threat to the wedding seemed to be the Bonnepoire kids. Like an infestation of cackling elves, they were attacking the furniture, and using the tables that we'd had so much trouble procuring as tents, climbing frames and capsized boats.

M went upstairs to help Elodie get ready for her big day, which was either the worst case of hypocrisy I'd ever witnessed or just the executioner being kind to the condemned.

I dived into the kitchen in search of Léanne. She had said that she would be coming as a waitress, along with several of her men.

I found her in the serving room, holding a little confab by the silver safe. She was dressed in a short black skirt and tight white shirt, with a tiny apron tied low on her hips. She looked, even to my stressed eyes, very tasty indeed.

With her were the leather-jacketed cop – he snarled a sort of hello – and four other officers in waiter's uniform. There was the lemon-seller – in trousers and white shirt – along with his semi-identical twin from the hotel in Collioure, and two younger guys.

Léanne told them to make room for me to enter their huddle. She made sure no one else was listening, and continued her briefing.

'No one knows we are cops. Even the presidential security must think we are waiters. OK?'

Her men nodded.

'If we need to search the house, I stay here, you others go

around the rooms. When a room is clear, you pull the bell. It will show up here.' She pointed to the bell panel on the wall. 'We will use phones as little as possible. Everyone on earth will be listening in tonight.'

The men nodded again.

'Pol,' she went on, 'anything new to tell us about M?'

'Not much,' I said. 'I don't know where the money is. Have you seen her meet with someone?'

'No.' Léanne looked thoughtful. 'We watched her go for walks alone, once from the chateau to your hotel – five kilometres – and once through the marshes as far as the Rhône. That is all.' I noticed that her soft southern accent had got stronger. She was obviously making an effort to bond with her men.

'You still don't know who the assassin is?' I said.

'If we did, he'd be dead,' Leather Jacket snorted.

'No, he wouldn't,' Léanne corrected him. 'We need him to talk.'

'But what I mean,' I said in French, 'is not his name, but why he is doing it. Why *she* is doing it. Are they the Mafia, political opposition, who?'

'The English, maybe?' the ex-lemon-seller said, but he was only teasing me.

'A jealous husband? There must be a few of those,' his twin suggested.

'Let's hope it's the unions,' Leather Jacket said. 'Then the killer will go on strike.'

Léanne held up a hand to restore discipline. 'The reason is not our problem. Our job is to make sure he fails. Now the President will arrive at eight this evening, and perform the ceremony at nine. He will stay for some of your dinner, Pol, so it had better be good.'

'If a bullet doesn't get him, the English food will, uh?' It was Leather Jacket, seriously tempting me to barbecue his face for him.

3

The morning flashed past, and the afternoon started to get worryingly old.

The marquee went up, fell down, and went up again.

Monsieur Yena almost got himself arrested when he appeared carrying a drum of petrol and a shotgun. The first, he explained, was to help light the barbecue – the wood he'd provided was a bit damp. And the second was to go and shoot some rabbits. He wasn't too keen on fish, and wanted to grill himself some meat on the side.

I saw Jake and Dadou together quite a lot, and remembered that Elodie had told her future father-in-law that Jake was gay. And Jake knew that Dadou was the man to talk to at the Ministry of Foreign Affairs. Their game of cat-and-mouse evolved during the day – first with Jake doing the pursuing, then Dadou, and finally Jake again, with Dadou looking as if he was being hunted by a crocodile. I guessed that Jake had decided to recite some of his swamp verse.

Around four, Jean-Marie called to tell me that the President wouldn't be coming, then stopped me in mid-leap of relief by chuckling and saying it was a joke. Jean-Marie was at Orly airport, with the presidential party no less, and they were expecting the man himself any minute.

Gilles and Benoit were mid-way through their tower of caramelized figs, both of them sweating in the hot kitchen, their fingers glued together with toffee, having to puff away the flies and children hovering around their bubbling cauldron. The hired cooking staff were gutting fish, chopping vegetables, splashing olive oil around like water.

I was having a short tea-time breather in the cool shade of the kitchen garden when Bonne Maman and Moo-Moo swanned up. The old lady put on an affronted scowl and Moo-Moo declared that they'd made a 'grave error' allowing me to do the catering.

'Why?' I wailed, and they beckoned me to follow them.

'Who did this?' Moo-Moo demanded, pointing down to one of the meticulously laid round tables that were evenly spread across the lawn like a formal garden of white lilies.

'Did what?' I asked.

'Look,' Moo-Moo hooted.

'Look,' Bonne Maman echoed.

I looked, but I didn't see. I'd made sure that the water glasses were bigger than the wine glasses, as you must. And that the place cards were exactly where they'd told me to put them. Everything looked perfect.

'The forks,' Moo-Moo gasped, as if it was a nasty word.

'What about them?'

'They are the wrong way up.' She bent forward and flipped one over, so that its points were touching the table rather than curving upwards.

'Ah, that is my fault,' I said. I had gone round earlier, turning them over. It had seemed wrong to me, to place the forks with their points downwards. They looked ungainly. 'I'll change them immediately.' I wondered how many valuable minutes of my life were going to be wasted turning over forks today.

'There's another thing.' Bonne Maman was shaking her head. 'There is no principal table. They are all round, and all together. It is too . . . democratic.' She shuddered.

There was no way we were moving the tables at this late stage. And there was no room to pull one of them out into a more prominent position.

'But surely, chère Madame,' I said, mustering all my French grammar and over-the-top manners, 'any table with both yourself and the President of France on it will automatically be the principal table?'

She stared at me for a few seconds. 'You are right,' she said at last. 'We must just make sure that he and I are sitting facing everyone else, so they can see us together.'

'Of course,' I agreed. If there were any stray bullets flying about, she was the perfect candidate.

Six o'clock came, seven. A cloud of Bonnepoires engulfed every square millimetre of the house and its immediate grounds.

In the kitchen, things were going crazy. Only the non-police waiting staff looked relaxed – most of them were enjoying a cigarette by the back door. I went to check on the wine cellar, which contained both the champagne and the pièce montée. It was on the floor in there, protected by a carefully balanced muslin shroud. I tried the door. It was securely locked.

Léanne came into the kitchen and gave me a final pep talk, or pep look. There were too many people around for her to come out of her waitress character. She stared me in the eyes and nodded encouragingly.

'M?' she whispered.

I shrugged. She'd been with Elodie for most of the day, but for all I knew, now she could have been out in the trees helping some guy to load his rifle. Weren't the police supposed to be watching her?

I looked at my watch. Almost eight. I checked my phone. Nothing. Wouldn't it be brilliant if Jean-Marie called and said that the President had got stuck in the aeroplane toilet? Anything to put a stop to the evening's violent agenda.

Thinking about the wedding ceremony reminded me that I hadn't seen Valéry for a worryingly long time. I hoped to God he wasn't too stoned or high to say 'I do.'

He was nowhere on the ground floor, so I went past the gun cabinet and up the stairs, asking every Bonnepoire I came across if they'd seen him. None of them had, and they all laughed. It was, they said, typical of him to go missing at a time like this.

I checked all the rooms on the first floor, including some darkly panelled bedrooms and a quaint old toilet with a polished wooden seat. I intruded on people changing, snogging, and in one case smearing a bed with Nutella – I shut the door quickly, pretending I hadn't witnessed this.

No sign of Valéry.

I went up another flight of stairs, still having to nudge past gossiping Bonnepoires at every step, and finally came across Moo-Moo standing outside a closed door.

'Is Valéry in there?' I asked her.

She was uncharacteristically silent. 'He is . . . not well,' she finally said.

'What's he doing?' I asked, fearing the reply.

'Bonne Maman is talking to him. He promised that he would not . . . He said he would refrain from . . .' Behind the blank wall of her self-righteousness and snobbery, she was a woman in considerable distress.

I took a risk and touched her arm.

'It is the emotion,' I said. 'The dealer tried to trick him, and now the President will marry him. C'est beaucoup.'

'He must change his ways,' she said. 'Or . . .' She raised her worried eyes to mine and I almost felt sorry for her.

The door opened and Bonne Maman came out, wringing her hands as if she'd just delivered a baby.

'Well, he is conscious, that is one consolation,' she said. 'Someone needs to put the young idiot right. A rich man with his habits is like a suicidal maniac at the helm of a yacht. He will sink himself and the boat.'

Wow, I thought, could it be that she actually had a humane reason for wanting to stop Valéry getting his hands on the inheritance – she thought he'd only stuff it all up his nostrils?

'Keep him in here until the ceremony,' Bonne Maman ordered Moo-Moo. 'If he's thirsty, he can have water. If he wants to piss, he can do it out of the window.'

I laughed. The bitch grand-mère may have been a snooty vache, but a vache with a sense of humour.

4

There was a murmur and then a collective intake of breath. The news flashed around the house as fast as a gunshot.

The President's car had entered the grounds.

Oh merde, I thought. This is it.

I looked out of the nearest window and saw a long, dark-blue limo, preceded by two motorbike riders and followed by one, slightly smaller, car.

Where was M? I hadn't seen her for at least an hour. Perhaps she'd received a tip-off that the target was in sight and had melted away. Her job was done.

No, there she was with Elodie, both of them dressed to

kill, dashing down the stairs to be present when the President got out of his car. M was carrying her make-up case, as though she wanted to put on a last-minute coat of lipstick or eyeliner. I followed, trying my best to catch up with them through the crowd that was heading downstairs.

There was a loud cheer from the front of the house. Out of a landing window I saw that the car had stopped, and was being mobbed by shoving, applauding Bonnepoires. I studied all the faces I could see, looking for someone who didn't belong, or any sign of a weapon. Nothing, just a crowd of well-wishers.

In the hallway, I caught sight of Léanne trying to push through the throng to the front door, and being told off for getting above her station. Waiting staff round the back entrance, they seemed to be saying. One of her replies made a woman blush. Léanne must have told her to stick her snobbery in her own back entrance.

I stayed on the stairs, watching. Elodie and M were also trying to push forward, but there were so many people that it was impossible.

Meanwhile, the cheering outside got louder – the President must have got out of the car – and then seemed to fade, as if the breeze was carrying the voices away.

The crush eased and people were able to get across the hall and outside. I came down and headed for the front door. Just before I got there, I saw Valéry coming downstairs.

'He's here,' I told him. In reply he gave a weak thumbs-up. He looked reasonably alert, though. Nothing that a glass of organic champagne wouldn't cure.

Outside, the crowd was flowing across the front of the house and round to the side. Léanne was dodging her way forward like a rugby player trying to break through a tight defence. I could see no sign of the President, although a group of bulky guys in suits had materialized, and uniformed police were taking up positions by the cars and the front door.

I looked out across the grounds, scanning the tree line. Now would be the perfect time for me to catch sight of a crouching silhouette. There was nothing out there, though, except impenetrable evening shadow.

Around the back of the house I found a scene of calm confusion. The President had gone in through the kitchen door, it seemed, and the welcoming party was over for the time being. A bodyguard was blocking the doorway. I saw Léanne try to push past and get told to stand back. She argued, but he wasn't going to change his mind. She came running towards me.

'The front door,' she said. 'We've got to get in the house.'

We both jogged back to the front door. The uniformed cop tried to stop Léanne, but she told him to 'get his ass out of the way, or she would eat it'. This had to be some kind of official French police jargon, because he stepped aside and let us in.

'He's gone – disappeared.' In the hallway, Leather Jacket was looking much less smug than usual.

'Who's in the house?' Léanne asked.

'Tons of people,' he said. 'We don't know.'

'Of *our* people, cretin,' she said.

'Oh, all of us.'

'OK, tell everyone to start searching the rooms. I'll go to the bell panel.'

'Oui, Madame.' In the heat of the action Leather Jacket had become almost passive.

'Why don't you just ask the President's bodyguards where he is?' I suggested.

'Huh.' Léanne didn't seem to think that would do much good.

In the serving room, we found Jake, his mouth full of tapenade. He was helping himself from one of the trays covering the long table.

'Hey, you're not supposed to be eating that,' I told him.

'Sorry, man. It was that Dadou. I was reciting my posy and he insisted I eat something. Like, practically stuffed it in my bouche. It's really bon. Hey.' He had finished ogling Léanne and decided he liked what he saw. 'Are you une Occitane?' he asked her.

'Jake . . .' I frowned at him. He'd obviously branched out from his policy of trying to shag one woman of every nationality, and was now going for ancient European ethnic group. Soon he'd be asking English girls if they were Picts.

Léanne ignored him, as the first bell rang to show that one of the rooms was clear. She marked the space on the glass with a smudge of tapenade.

'The Prayzidon is here, right?' Jake said. 'I'm gonna ask him about my fon.'

'Yeah, you do that, Jake,' I said, as other bells rang. 'In fact, you could go and look for him to ask him now.'

'Yeah? You lost him?' Jake gave a laugh that was shot out of the air by a murderous glance from Léanne.

Elodie and M came in from the hall, and looked at us as if they didn't understand what the tension was all about. Léanne stared at M for a second, before returning her gaze to the bell panel.

'They lost the Prayzidon,' Jake giggled. I motioned to the girls that it wasn't as big a joke as Jake seemed to think.

M was looking understandably nervous. Her guy would be searching for the President as well, and she had a million euros riding on the winner of the manhunt.

'Merde, where is he?' Léanne swore, marking off more and more bells. 'He's in the house, right? Did you see him pass?' she asked Jake. M looked at her in surprise, understanding for the first time that Léanne was more than a waitress.

'I have not seen him,' Jake said. 'I was with Dadou. He adores posy, and I was asking for his aid to ameliorate one of my posics. It's this one about some shrimps and a Cajun femme. You want to hear it, Paul?'

'Later, Jake, much later.'

'C'est pas possible!' Léanne stood back from the bell panel and gazed at it. All the bells were marked off.

'The kitchen,' I said. 'He must be in there.'

'No, he's not in there, we looked,' she said.

'You're wrong,' I said, in a sudden flash of realization. 'Come with me, *vite!*'

We ran into the kitchen, which was empty except for one bodyguard. Even the cooks had been chucked out, and their goat's cheese amuse-bouches were sitting around on trays, half-finished.

'He's in the wine cellar,' I said. 'It's the only place without a bell.'

'Stay away from that door.' The bodyguard moved a hand towards his armpit.

'I'm in command of the police contingent,' Léanne said. 'Is he in there alone? You have to tell me. Now.'

'Alone? Er, no,' the bodyguard admitted, suddenly looking extremely worried.

Léanne reached up and grabbed him by the lapels. 'Who's in there with him?' she shouted.

'A woman and a man.'

'Merde.' Léanne pointed to the door and the bodyguard

needed no more prompting. He pulled the door open, his gun already halfway out of its holster.

Silent now, we all peered into the small room, expecting to see a defunct President bludgeoned with a champagne bottle or impaled on the pièce montée.

But all that met our eyes was an abashed Valéry sitting on a stool, with a presidential hand clamped to his shoulder, and Bonne Maman's eyes drilling into his head.

The President held out a restraining palm to his bodyguard and murmured a few more words to Valéry, the last of which were 'OK, mon petit?'

Valéry nodded. It looked like a paternalistic pull-your-socks-up talk from the highest authority in the land.

'Bonsoir,' the President said to us all as he stepped out of the wine cellar, followed by a serenely smiling Bonne Maman and a shell-shocked Valéry.

Léanne breathed a sigh of relief and patted me on the back, but we both knew that the reprieve was only temporary. The evening, and the danger, was just beginning.

'Paul?' It was Elodie, nodding towards Léanne, asking for an explanation. She assumed, rightly, that I must have known some of my waiting staff were cops. M, too, looked interested in what I'd have to say.

But I had turned away from them. A man was coming into the kitchen. He was dressed as a waiter, and I hadn't seen him before. Not tonight, anyway. When I looked him in the eye, he grinned at me. And suddenly I remembered. He'd been in Bandol. He was the guy at the singalong restaurant who'd been ogling M.

Léanne had told me to watch out for guys that M might not actually approach, people she might just exchange glances with. And back in Bandol, this guy had not only been exchanging glances. He'd been trying to send semaphore messages with his trouser bulge. What was more, he was edging past Jake towards Léanne, towards the President. And if I wasn't mistaken, he had a bulge in his trouser pocket again. No doubt a gun this time.

'It's him!' I yelled. 'Stop him, Jake!'

Although Jake often gives the impression that he is living on another planet, on this occasion he reacted with the speed of an Arles bullfighter. He grabbed the nearest weapon to hand, a plate of round goat's cheese balls covered in olive oil, and rammed it in the new arrival's face. OK, not exactly a weapon of mass destruction, but it did the trick. The guy was stopped in his tracks long enough for the bodyguard to jump on him and flatten him to the ground.

The back door opened and a second guard dashed in to join the fray. Within seconds they had bundled the intruder across the floor and out of the kitchen into the serving room, putting a brick wall between the President and his assailant.

The intended victim froze for an instant, and then relaxed.

'Alors, là!' The President laughed, no doubt listening to the percentage points ticking upwards in the polls.

Léanne ran out into the serving room to help the guards. I stayed to stare at this man I'd seen so often on TV and in the papers, and who was now reaching out to shake Jake's hand.

'Merci, Monsieur . . . ?'

'Jake,' he answered. 'Aimez-vous la posy?'

The question was so sudden and so weird that the President blinked it away and turned to me.

'And you, Monsieur?'

'West,' I said. 'Paul West.'

He shook my hand. 'Ah, two Anglo-Saxons? It seems zat you av say-ved me,' he said in English, with an accent that could have been a joke. I didn't dare laugh.

I turned to share my moment of glory with Elodie, and was shocked to see M still there. She was standing by the sink, taking things out of her make-up bag.

Huh, women, I thought. She knows she'll be arrested, and she's putting on her face ready for the cameras.

She turned towards us, a fixed smile on her face.

'You must have a glass of champagne to celebrate, Monsieur le Président,' she said, walking towards him with a single tall flute in her hands.

She must have opened a bottle herself, I thought. The champagne wasn't supposed to be uncorked until after the President's speech. It's always the way in France – bla-bla first, drinks afterwards.

Sure enough, an open bottle was standing by the sink, next to M's make-up bag and – bizarrely – the bottle of edible sex oil.

'A votre santé,' she said. Your health. She held out the glass, and the President, obviously entranced by this beautiful girl bearing gifts, let go of my hand and reached for the champagne.

'No!' I punched it out of his hand.

Valéry, Elodie and Bonne Maman gasped. The Englishman had hit le Président. This meant war, at the very least.

'Paul! How could you?' For a split second, M looked at me as though she was about to cry, and then she ran out of the kitchen door.

There were Bonnepoires all around the house, including kids playing tag in the forest of family legs. I dodged through the crowd as I sprinted after M.

301

She had gone around the side of the house and was heading for the meadows. By now it was very dark. If she got out on to the marshes where she'd been on so many exploratory walks, it'd be impossible to find her before dawn.

As I ran, I tried to piece things together. Her little bottle hadn't contained edible sex oil after all – it was poison. Lucky I hadn't tasted it. It looked as though Léanne had got things badly wrong – M hadn't been just the cash-delivery girl, she was the back-up, on hand to have a second stab if the main hitman fluffed. Which he had, pathetically.

M was very fit, and was running fast. I had wondered why she'd chosen to wear low-heeled shoes to the wedding. Now I understood. She had already reached the first big drainage ditch. I was a good twenty yards behind, and not gaining. Not losing ground, though. If I kept up my pace, I'd manage to stay close and see where she went.

I heard a muddy splash. M obviously hadn't made it over the ditch. When I reached the edge, I saw that she was trying to climb up the slippery bank.

She stared up at me. It was so dark out here that I could only see her face as a pale shadow.

'You, Paul?' she said. 'Of all people, why did *you* have to stop me?'

'And of all people, why did *you* have to try and kill the President?'

In reply, she only shook her head.

'You knew that waitress was a cop, didn't you?' she demanded.

'Yes, I knew. They've been on to you for ages. I've known ever since that night in Bandol. That's when they told me who you really were.'

'What?' I could see M ticking boxes in her head. My

302

weird behaviour was all being explained away. 'What did they tell you?' she asked.

'That you were travelling around the coast, looking for a hitman.'

She laughed bitterly. 'Hiring a killer? Bollocks. I wanted to do it myself.'

'Then who was that twat who just tried to jump the President?'

'That guy? I don't know who he was or what he was doing. This was a solo job.'

We both heard a shout. I looked towards the house. People were running out into the grounds. Léanne and the other cops, I guessed, searching for us.

Something made me jump into the ditch out of sight. I landed with a cold squelch. So much for my best suit and leather shoes.

'Who hired you?' I asked.

'No one *hired* me, Paul.' She tutted in disbelief. 'This was purely personal.'

'But what about all your meetings, then? And those guys you were hanging out with last summer in Saint Tropez?'

'The cops told you about them?' She sounded astonished that she'd been so well researched. 'Those guys in Saint Tropez were just some dickheads I bumped into while I was working on the caviar investigation.'

'So all the stuff about sturgeon wasn't just a smoke screen?'

'No.' In the shadows, I saw her shake her head emphatically. 'I heard that some people had been boasting about selling illegal French caviar as Iranian, so I went along to listen, and played the bimbo on their yacht for a week. And ever since, I've been begging the scientists down here to help me nail the traffickers with hard evidence. I haven't been trying to hire a killer, Paul – I've been trying to save an endangered species.'

Which all sounded incredibly noble. But she was forgetting something.

'I don't get it, though,' I said, shifting uneasily in the cold slop. 'Why would you want to whack the President of France?'

'Because it's quicker than whacking the whole French government.' Suddenly she sounded capable of killing with her bare hands. 'You asked me about my dad's boat accident. Did you ever hear of the *Rainbow Warrior?*'

'Of course,' I said. The ecologists' boat that was blown up in New Zealand by French saboteurs after it had been protesting against nuclear testing in the Pacific.

'People think that only one guy was killed, a Portuguese photographer. But there were two. My dad was in a coma for six months before he died. The French government killed him.'

'Shit.'

'They've never revealed who actually planted the bombs,' M continued. 'Only two of the six saboteurs were convicted, and the French wangled their repatriation. Neither of them served more than two years. And who gave the order for the attack? President Mitterrand. Personally.'

She fell silent. In the distance, I could hear Léanne calling my name.

'But why try to kill the current President?' I asked. 'After all these years?'

'The French have just released documents about the bombing,' M replied. 'With all the important details taken out, of course. And it's sent Maman over the edge. She's started writing letters to Dad, posting them to New Zealand. She's got a whole team of therapists trying to persuade her that he's not going to come sailing home on the *Rainbow Warrior*. So I thought it was time for some real justice. I bought the poison, and planned to use it when the President came down to his chateau at Brégançon later in the month. But then you handed me the perfect opportunity. Sorry, Paul . . .'

There was nothing I could say.

'Are you going to try and take me back to meet your waitress friend?' M asked.

I squelched from one foot to the other. Decision time again. All these heavy moral choices I was being forced to make, when all I really wanted to do down here in the South of France was go snorkelling and organize a barbecue for Elodie.

'Are you planning to have another go at the President?' I asked.

M laughed. 'Huh, no. I think I've kind of blown my cover. And I'm really not cut out for this assassination lark.'

All I could see of her was a silhouette standing out against the faint moonglow from the water. It was much too dark to look her in the eye. Anyway, the days when I thought I could tell whether a woman was lying were long gone. She might be pointing some kind of weapon at me, planning to put me out of action if I tried to stop her escaping.

'I can't let you go,' I said, and took a heavy, wet step towards her.

M tensed.

'Not without a goodbye hug,' I added.

She sobbed once, loudly, and pressed herself hard to my chest.

I wanted to tell her how I would have loved to help her nail the caviar smugglers or organize a protest about the

Rainbow Warrior outside the President's chateau. It would have been fun just to be down here in the South of France with her, soaking up the sun and the rosé while campaigning for her good causes. If she hadn't screwed things up with her deception and this botched poisoning, things could have worked out spectacularly well between us.

But there was no time for speeches. The voices were getting closer. The cops were spreading out.

'You've got to go,' I whispered. 'I'll stay in the ditch until they find me.'

'Thanks,' she said.

'I can't move anyway, my feet are stuck.'

She kissed me hard on the lips, and turned away.

I had the brief pleasure of grasping her backside to give her a heave up the bank, and then she was gone, crouching low as she ran for the cover of the trees.

I peeped over the lip of the ditch, back towards the house. Most of the shadows were dashing in completely the wrong direction, along the drive to the main road. M would get away, I calculated, at least as far as the open marsh. I didn't know what she'd planned after that, but she seemed pretty good at subterfuge. I guessed she'd be OK.

I stood in the mud and wondered why I'd let her get away.

Perhaps all of us Mata Haris were destined to betray France, I thought. The country seemed to bring out the traitor in everyone.

Or maybe my old confusion about how to pronounce the French word for caterer had come home to roost – I really was a *traître*, and not a *traiteur*.

But I had to let M go, anyway, I told myself.

Call me an old-fashioned Englishman and a soft-hearted romantic, but you just don't sleep with a girl and then hand her over to the cops. Especially not for trying to kill a politician.

5

I was waltzing with Elodie. She'd had five lessons, she told me, but you wouldn't have known it. She was crushing my toes to a blue pulp. All the more so, because they were bare. I didn't have any dry shoes, and was dancing barefoot on the prickly lawn.

'I don't understand,' Elodie said. 'M was so friendly to me. Like, all day.'

'Guilt,' I said. 'She knew she was going to mess up your wedding.'

'Well, she was right.' Elodie amputated a couple more of my toes, and then leaned in close for a good weep. She'd been indulging wholeheartedly in this newfound crying habit of hers all evening. She had deposited most of her eye make-up on Valéry's chest, and he was sitting at the table looking as if someone had burnt two huge holes in his shirt with a poker.

I soaked up my share of Elodie's tears, feeling deeply sorry for her. It was after eleven thirty, and she still wasn't married.

Proceedings had, understandably, got a little behind schedule because of the assassination attempt. I'd had to wait the best part of an hour to be discovered in my muddy hiding place. Just before the cop shone his torch over the lip of the ditch, I'd slid forward into the mire and pretended to be semi-conscious.

After that, there had been the de-briefing. All I could remember, I told Léanne and Leather Jacket, was that I'd chased M as far as the ditch, stumbled, fallen in, and then been pulled out of the water by the kind gendarme with his torch.

How, they asked, had I managed to survive face-down in water for an hour without drowning? It had to be all the snorkelling practice I'd been getting, I told them.

But had they really been listening to M's phone calls, I asked. They seemed to have got things seriously wrong.

Léanne looked uncomfortable and replied that they thought she'd been talking in code.

'Did M tell you anything new?' she wanted to know.

I shook my head, doing my best to look innocent and ignorant. I felt a twinge of guilt holding out on Léanne, but then she'd withheld plenty of information from me, including some key stuff that might have made me feel sympathy for M. Her dad's identity, for example. It looked as though Léanne had known that all along. So in a way, we were even. An eye for an eye, an untruth for an untruth.

The cops were suspicious, of course, but they had no time to go into details. Leather Jacket took the poison bottle to Marseille to get it analysed. The two white-haired guys were checking through a letter that M had left in Elodie's room, listing the names of every caviar smuggler she'd met in Saint Tropez.

Léanne explained sheepishly that the guy Jake had assaulted with goat's cheese was a cop. That was why I'd noticed him in Bandol. He'd been keeping a (too) close eye on M and me. And I hadn't seen him earlier in the evening, because he'd only just arrived. He had come into the kitchen to report to Léanne for duty. The President's security guards had managed to dislocate one of the guy's arms and crack a couple of his ribs before they cleaned off the goat's cheese and Léanne recognized her man. By which time, I was already chasing M across the meadows.

The security people had wanted to get the President out of the chateau straight away, but he'd refused. He wanted to stay on and perform the ceremony for his young, reformed friend Valéry. But only after giving a full round of interviews and press conferences, of course. No time like the present for boosting his ratings.

Dinner had been served – the fish had crackled on the barbecue, the family rosé had been guzzled, my Muscat sorbet had been a tongue-frazzling knockout. Only the pièce montée survived, shrouded in the wine cellar like a bride in waiting.

The minutes, the hours, had ticked by, while the President held court to the journalists, and Elodie went from extreme impatience to semi-drunken fury, and then despair. Her chances of getting married before midnight, in time to collect Valéry's inheritance, were fading away like the bubbles in a long-opened bottle of champagne.

Her dad, Jean-Marie, was there, resplendent in one of his shimmering grey suits and a salmon-pink shirt. He'd been in the second car of the President's cortège with Elodie's mum and the spokeswoman, Ludivine. But he wasn't devoting much time to his daughter. He schmoozed, tried it on with Sixtine, hovered close to the President to get in the photos and TV shots, and appeared to forget about the wedding completely.

Elodie eventually gave up all hope at a quarter to midnight. The younger and more elderly family members had already dozed off, the curé had got drunk, and Elodie was still single.

So was Valéry, of course, and he was sitting there mutely, looking as pale as the clean parts of his white shirt. He had remained steadfastly sober all evening, having long seen the cold light of truth. He wasn't going to get married before his thirtieth birthday. He wasn't going to get his lifetime gift. Bonne Maman had won, like she always did.

Elodie was dripping tears into her sorbet at about ten to midnight when the old vache herself came over for a gloat. Or so it seemed.

'Don't cry, my child,' she said. 'It has been a lucky night, really. Just think, if the President had been . . .' She didn't even want to pronounce the deathly word. 'It wouldn't have been a happy wedding day, would it?'

'You seem happy enough,' Elodie retorted.

'Happy that disaster has been avoided, yes.'

'Huh.' Elodie seemed to assume that the old bitch was referring to the potential disaster of Valéry marrying before his thirtieth birthday and taking some of her fortune away. 'You know, Madame,' she said, 'I don't care about the money. I just want to get married to Valéry.' She started blubbing again, the tears streaming down into her sorbet bowl. I took it away and gave her a paper napkin. If someone else inadvertently tasted her ice cream, they were going to think I'd added way too much salt.

'My child,' Bonne Maman said, 'there's no need to cry. Listen to me.' She sat down beside Elodie, who kept her face jammed into the napkin. 'There is something I want to tell you. Valéry thinks he knows everything about his grandfather's will, but he doesn't. There is a clause whereby, even after Valéry's thirtieth birthday, if I give my consent, he can still benefit from a *donation*.'

Elodie stopped crying and looked up. This was news to her.

'Naturally,' Bonne Maman continued, 'that consent would depend on Valéry's behaviour. He has to grow up, stop taking those stupid drugs, and act like an adult. I would like to hope that the President's words have at last broken through that thick, bony skull of his, n'est-ce pas, Valéry?' She gave him a glare, and he flinched.

Bonne Maman turned back to Elodie. 'As I said at the bastide, getting married might be a healthy step towards that maturity.' She smiled. 'And now, perhaps, is the time to take that step. Let's go and ask Monsieur le Président if he is ready to marry you, shall we?'

Elodie wiped away a tear and looked suddenly tired, as if she was emerging from a troubled sleep. She took a long, deep breath.

'No,' she said. 'I don't think it is the right time.'

Bonne Maman and Valéry recoiled in shock. This girl was refusing to marry into their family? With the President performing the ceremony? It was an affront to history as big as the French Revolution.

'No,' Elodie repeated calmly. 'I thank you for this kind suggestion, Madame, but for Valéry's sake, I think we should wait until after midnight. You, Madame, must decide whether he is worthy of his grandfather's gift.'

Even I gasped in shock. Elodie, who had always seemed as money-oriented as a one-armed bandit, was willing to risk missing out on the inheritance?

Bonne Maman looked at Elodie as if she'd turned into the Virgin Mary. Her hands fluttered about in the air and a red flush coloured her pale cheeks.

'Well,' she finally said, still gazing in awe at Elodie, 'if we have a few minutes to spare, then I must go upstairs for a moment. I must fetch my veil from my bedroom. I would like you to wear it, if you will.'

'It would be an honour, Madame Bonnepoire,' Elodie said.

'You must call me Bonne Maman. And I would like to call you *tu*, if I may.'

'Bonne Maman,' Elodie replied, and the two women held hands in a ceremony of family bonding. Now Elodie was one of them.

A stern look suddenly flashed across Bonne Maman's face, and she turned to Valéry. 'Now *this* is the kind of girl you should have been looking for since you were eighteen,' she told him. 'Instead of trying to impregnate all your cousins.'

ALL THE PRESIDENT'S MERDE

Epilogue

IT WAS TWO MONTHS LATER. I was standing on the thickest carpet I'd ever felt beneath my feet, waiting nervously between Léanne and Jake in a reception room at the Elysée palace.

I'd cleaned all the mud off my best suit, Jake had actually got an almost-human haircut, and Léanne was in a ceremonial police outfit, with a knee-length skirt and a tight blue braided jacket. She was looking hot.

We were in a line facing the gilt-edged door through which the President was due to enter the room. Around us was a small crowd of guests, held back by a silk rope strung between heavy golden posts.

I knew that behind me, standing below a vast chandelier, were Elodie and Valéry, wedding rings on their fingers. Bonne Maman was with them, no doubt looking as though she owned the place. Jean-Marie, Benoit and Elodie's mother would be there too, Jean-Marie smiling with only mild irritation because he was relegated to the guest enclosure rather than being allowed to enter with the President.

'Monsieur le Président de la République!' An usher in a

long embroidered frock coat barked out the announcement, and everyone fell silent.

The man himself entered, looking exactly as he had last time I saw him. Same suit, same tie. You didn't have time to bother with petty dress details when you were President, it seemed. Only his smile had changed. It was bigger, more firmly fixed. His dare-devil antics had been widely reported in the press – especially the way he had tackled the suspected gunman and karate-chopped the poisoned chalice out of M's hand – and his ratings had never been higher.

He stood at a lectern in front of Léanne, Jake and me and bestowed us with a look of intense affection, as if he'd just learned that we'd all voted for him.

'Mes amis,' he said, 'my saviours. You did a great service for France. For one of you, it was a duty. For the others, a gesture of international friendship. The Republic thanks you.'

I wondered whether *he* thanked us too. After all, it wouldn't have been the Republic getting its stomach pumped if M had given him the champagne. Not that pumping would have done much good – tests had revealed that the poison was based on the venom of a stone-fish found only in the atolls where France had done its nuclear blasting. One droplet was capable of shutting down the brain almost instantly, for ever.

'I say that it was a duty for one of you, but of course not every one of our police officers acts with such courage and insight.' The President beamed at Léanne. 'And not every one of our officers has such a charming smile. It is a smile that honours the Republic.' I could feel the warmth of her blush from a foot away. 'Our police force is of course a fine body of men and women . . .' He paused for effect. 'But some parts of that body are finer than others.'

The sly bastard, I thought. He's meant to be making a public speech and he turns it into a blatant come-on. And we've all got to stand here and put up with it.

Despite myself, I felt jealous. Léanne and I were going out for dinner after the ceremony, and I had high hopes of – well – making our reunion a memorable one.

When he'd finished telling Léanne that she was a hottie, the President turned his attentions briefly to Jake and me, the two guys who'd intervened physically to stop him getting killed. He said we had proved 'that France can always count on its allies in the United Kingdom and the United States, even though we cannot always agree to accompany them if they stray along paths that we consider unwise'.

Christ, I thought, can't they ever drop the politics? All I did was knock poisoned wine out of his hand. I didn't ask him to invade Iraq with me.

The President wrapped things up by congratulating us all on meriting France's greatest award, the Légion d'Honneur, and walked towards us, almost bouncing on the inch-deep carpet. An usher with three red-ribbonned medals materialized beside him.

'Felicitations et merci,' the President said to Jake, pinning the medal to his chest and rubbing cheeks with him. 'I understand that your admirable attempt to forward the cause of the French language is to receive finance from my department of Francophonie?'

'Oui, Monsieur le Président,' Jake said, 'and I have brought a small example of our Cajun posy.' He handed a little booklet to the President, who passed it to the usher.

Please God don't let him read that, I prayed, or Jake will be deported tonight and lose any hope of getting a single euro of French subsidy.

'Felicitations et merci,' the President said, looking up at me from chest level. There was a pressure over my heart and then a double waft of eau de toilette as his smooth cheeks touched mine. 'I am told that, despite lengthy interrogation, you have still not revealed the truth.'

I blanched. Were they going to carry on hassling me about M? I thought they'd given her up for lost. Even I had received no sign of life from her, apart from an anonymous e-card of a grinning sturgeon.

'About your recipe for the fig pièce montée,' the President added. 'The secret belongs in France, you know.' Everyone in the room laughed politely at his banter.

'Well, in fact it was a Franco-British collaboration—' I began, but the President had already moved on to Léanne, and was taking his time pinning her medal on.

'It is a great pleasure,' he said, clearly referring to the way she was letting him brush her left boob with his knuckles. 'We had so little time to talk at the chateau, when you saved my life.' He leaned in even closer. 'Why don't you have dinner with me here at the Elysée this evening? The food is quite good, you know.' He gave a little chuckle at his own witticism.

'Merci, Monsieur le Président,' Léanne whispered, and the President grinned triumphantly.

'However . . .' Léanne paused. 'This evening I am going to be putting the spirit of your speech into action, and working on Anglo-French relations.' She turned to smile at me.

The President's face puffed with fury, and everyone in the room heard his reaction.

'Merde!'

FIN